Adolescent Literature as a Complement to the Classics

Adolescent Literature as a Complement to the Classics

Edited by
Joan F. Kaywell
University of South Florida

Christopher-Gordon Publishers, Inc.
Norwood, MA

Credits

Chapter 8: Poem "A Work of Artifice" by Marge Piercy from *To Be of Use*, copyright © 1973 by Doubleday reprinted by permission.

Chapter 14: Excerpts from *Back to Class*, copyright © 1988 by Mel Glenn and published by Clarion Books and *My Friend's Got This Problem*, Mr. Chandler, copyright © 1991 by Mel Glenn and also published by Clarion Books reprinted by permission of Clarion Books/Houghton Mifflin, Co.

Cover design by Carolyn Woodard, About Face Graphic Design Studio, Lakeland, Florida.

Every effort has been made to contact copyright holders for permission to reprint borrowed material where necessary. We apologize for any oversights and would be happy to rectify them in future printings.

Christopher-Gordon Publishers, Inc.
480 Washington Street
Norwood, MA 02062

Printed in the United States of America

10 9 8 7 6 5 4 3 2   98 97 96 95 94

ISBN 0-926842-23-4

Dedication

To my father
and
my right and left wings:
Ted Hipple and Robert Wright

Acknowledgments

My first thanks must go to my Department Chair, Howard Johnston, who gave me the confidence necessary to ask my colleagues to contribute chapters to this book. Next, I'd like to thank my colleagues who agreed to write chapters, met their deadlines, and extended their friendships: Kay and John Bushman, Sissi Carroll, Leila Christenbury, Ruth Cline, Bonnie Ericson, Joan Fowinkle, Jo Higgins, Ted Hipple, Pat Kelly, Diana Mitchell, Betty Poe, Charlie Reed, Bobbi Samuels, and Bob Small. A special thanks is extended to Sue Canavan, the Executive Vice President of Christopher-Gordon Publishers, who gave me a chance, "held my hand every step of the way," and offered her friendship. Thanks, Sue!

And finally, I'd like to thank my family, friends, and various faculty and staff at the University of South Florida for supporting me and giving me the time and encouragement necessary to complete this task, especially Stephen M. Kaywell, Susan S. Maida, Christopher S. Maida, Carol D. Kelly, Julie Lambert, Scott Seifreit, Carine Feyten, Susan Homan, Jim King, Connie Brinson, and Cheryl Henry.

A special thanks to Carolyn Woodard for doing the cover art.

Table of Contents

Preface

Adolescent Literature as a Complement to the Classics is based on two assumptions: 1) The classics comprise the canon of literature that is mostly taught in our schools; and 2) most teachers are familiar with adolescent literature, or young adult novels, but are unsure how to incorporate their use in classrooms. This book provides the necessary information so that teachers may confidently use young adult novels in conjunction with commonly taught classics.

Why should teachers try to get students to read more when it is already difficult getting them to read the required material? I'll tell you. Part of the problem, as most teachers are fully aware, is that the classics are often too distant from our students' experiences or the reading level is too difficult. Students often question why they have to study something, read the Cliff's notes, or watch the movie version of the required classic. As a result, not only are students not reading the classics, but they are also not reading much of anything!

By using young adult novels in conjunction with the classics, teachers can expose students to reading that becomes relevant and meaningful. Additionally, the reading levels of most young adult books are within a range of ease that most students can master. Reading, as with any type of human development, requires practice. The problem that occurs in our schools, however, is that we often place our students into reading practice that we require, a practice our students view as forced, meaningless, and too difficult. To make my point, let me draw an analogy to the developmental process of eating.

Just like a newborn baby has to be fed milk, a newborn reader needs to be read to. Babies begin with baby foods that are easily digested; something too solid will cause the baby to reject it—so too with reading. Young readers need to start with easy readers, ones that are easily consumed. Eventually, young children desire foods that have a little more substance—vegetables, eggs, and some palatable meats. Similarly, young readers might find delight in such books as Nancy Drew or Hardy Boys mysteries. Just as children regurgitate and learn to hate certain foods if forced too early to consume them, so will novice readers learn to hate certain books, or books in general, if forced to read books that are beyond their capabilities. As children reach adolescence, they will consume vast quantities of "hamburgers" in the form of adolescent literature— if we let them.

Like any concerned parent, we want our children to eat a proper diet, so we make them eat balanced meals much like the way we have our children read certain books. Ideally our children will learn to appreciate fine cuisine in the form of the classics. For some, they may find the experience too much for their stomachs to handle and will snub their noses at lobster newburg and *The Scarlet Letter* for something a bit lighter. For others, unfortunately, they may never get exposed to that level, but they still can survive, unaware of what they are missing. But some of our students, however, will learn to enjoy and appreciate the delicacies of fine literature. It's all in the presentation, and adolescent literature can help make our teaching of the classics more appealing.

Now you are probably saying, "I am sold on exposing my students to adolescent literature, but why **this** book?" First, the biggest names in the field of adolescent literature have contributed chapters: Kay Bushman, the current president of ALAN (the Assembly on Literature for Adolescents); Ted Hipple, Patricia Kelly, Betty Poe, Bobbie Samuels, former presidents of ALAN; Leila Christenbury and Bob Small, the current co-editors of *The ALAN Review*, Charlie Reed, the past editor of *The ALAN Review*; and the past president of NCTE, Ruth Cline, among others.

Second, all chapters stand alone, but an experienced teacher can easily adapt the strategies employed in one chapter to fit his or her particular situation. For example, a teacher may not be required to teach *A Diary of a Young Girl* but may choose to incorporate the multi-text strategy to whatever classic is required. Or, a teacher might be required to teach the aforementioned novel but could choose to approach its teaching under the theme of abusing power incorporating the strategies suggested for teaching *1984* and *Lord of the Flies*. In other words, several different approaches are suggested so that a teacher who likes a certain strategy could omit the suggested novels and insert the ones of choice. Because young adult novels are frequently out of print, there are enough suggestions and other resources listed to assist teachers and their students with their search for complementary novels. Single novels that are out of print are often found in used bookstores.

Third, this book is on the cutting edge, incorporating all of the latest research in reader response theory, student ownership, and collaborative learning. Each chapter is written so that each student from the least to the most talented can learn at his or her optimum level. Each student is a vital contributor to the class, and each student gets exposed to the classics in meaningful, relevant ways. As far as I know, this is the first and only text of its kind. The book is written for middle and high school English teachers; however, university professors who teach preservice teachers and graduate students may also find this text valuable.

J.K.
September 1992

Organization

The first three chapters focus on three classics, *To Kill a Mockingbird*, *The Diary of a Young Girl*, and *The Adventures of Huckleberry Finn*, that deal with the theme of prejudice. In Chapter One, all students read the core novel and one from among six young adult books. Students are grouped according to the young adult book chosen. In Chapter Two, all students read the core novel and each student reads a different young adult book and are grouped according to topic. Chapter Three has students reading one young adult novel on various topics related to prejudice in preparation to reading the core novel.

Chapters Four, Five, and Six focus on these classics, *Catcher in the Rye*, *Death of a Salesman*, and *Romeo and Juliet*, and deal with various adolescent concerns: growing up and the rights of passage, family relationships and communication breakdowns, and first loves. The strategies range from a multi-text approach to pairing the classic with one young adult novel.

The next two chapters focus on these classics, *Great Expectations* and *A Doll House* in terms of points of view: the masculine and the feminist perspectives. Chapters Nine and Ten focus on *The Great Gatsby* and the pursuit of the American Dream, and *Their Eyes Were Watching God* and the black Southern female perspective.

Chapters Eleven, Twelve, and Thirteen pair *The Scarlet Letter*, *Lord of the Flies*, and *1984* with *The Chocolate War*, a novel that is considered a classic in the field of young adult literature. It is interesting to note how the same young adult novel can be used in conjunction with three commonly taught classics.

The last chapter does not focus on a classic novel or play, but, rather, adds the final literary touch by pairing the poetry of Keats with the more contemporary poetry of Mel Glenn. In this chapter, as in all of the others, the poet is "given a chance to speak to [our students]—though almost two centuries stand between [them]—because" these classic authors have something to say to all of us.

Chapter 1

Introducing *To Kill a Mockingbird* with Collaborative Group Reading of Related Young Adult Novels

BONNIE O. ERICSON

Introduction

The Pulitzer Prize-winning *To Kill a Mockingbird* is a classic more accessible to students than many other standard high school works. It is a perennial favorite, largely because of characters like Scout and Jem and Dill but also because of themes compelling to adolescents: growing up and the resulting loss of innocence, the courage to do what is right, the acceptance of others who are different, the power of family love and community, and the dehumanizing effects of prejudice and hypocrisy.

Why, then, do I take the time to teach *To Kill a Mockingbird* with adolescent literature? Even though Harper Lee's novel has built-in appeal for high school students, there are still obstacles, especially for average ability readers. These include a sometimes bewildering array of characters, an unfamiliar setting, interwoven plots and subplots, and complex themes. Introducing *To Kill a Mockingbird* with the collaborative group reading of a variety of carefully selected young adult novels is an effective approach for addressing some of these obstacles.

By reading the young adult novels, some students will become familiar with the ambiance of small town Southern life; all will grapple with their book's depiction of family influences and relationships, coming of age issues, prejudice, and justice and injustice. For many students, the enjoyable and relatively easy experience with an adolescent novel will lead to an easier understanding of the core novel, as well as richer responses to it. At the same time, comparing and contrasting different authors' treatments of similar issues may result in a more genuine examination of the students' individual beliefs and ideas—certainly an outcome I want to encourage.

Beyond the reading of a companion young adult novel, my decision to use collaborative reading groups offers an alternative to the more common whole-class, guided reading of literature or independent, unguided reading by individuals. With collaborative reading, each group of four to six students reads and discusses a different young adult novel and then shares it with the rest of the class. Students select what they will read from a number of choices offered and assume full responsibility for that reading in their groups. As a result, student-centered responses to the novels are not only possible but central. But unlike independent reading, where students are more or less on their own, the group collaboration allows individuals to clarify, reexamine, verify, and extend their initial responses. By using collaborative reading groups, I hope to establish a habit of individual responses extended by group discussions, and I intend for this habit to transfer from the collaborative reading of young adult novels to the whole class reading of a classic in this unit and others.

In the pages that follow, I describe in detail how I organize this two-part unit: the group reading of adolescent literature selections followed by the whole class reading of *To Kill a Mockingbird*. While the time needed for this unit is flexible and will vary with different classes, the collaborative reading portion will require approximately three weeks and the core reading portion approximately four weeks.

Collaborative Group Reading of Young Adult Novels

The main facets of the collaborative reading include student selection of novels based on teacher presented previews, individual reading, writing of literature log entries, group discussions of the novel, and group presentations to the class.

Student Selection of Young Adult Novels

The first day, I preview each of the young adult novels available for group reading by showing students the cover and giving a summary of key characters, events, and conflicts. I may read a page or two from the beginning or an exciting or emotional portion of the novel to give students an idea of the book's style and difficulty. Or, I may ask several questions to pique their interest. For example, after describing *All Together Now*, I ask, "Will Dwayne find out that Casey is a girl, and if he does will this destroy their friendship? Do you think Casey should tell him? Do you think Casey should even be his friend, given that he is an adult with the mind of a twelve-year-old?" In the same way that a movie preview attempts to entice would-be viewers to see a new movie, a book preview should entice students to read a book. It should also give them an idea of a book's difficulty.

For introducing *To Kill a Mockingbird*, I recommend the following selections. The choices described are all compelling novels with themes related to those in *To Kill a Mockingbird*, and all are appropriate for high school students. I present them here in order of difficulty, from the easy to the more difficult.

1. *Words by Heart* by Ouida Sebestyen (162 pp.). Hoping to build a better life, Lena Sills' father moves his family from the South to the Southwest in the early 1900s. There Lena wins a scripture quoting competition, but she doesn't win the approval she'd hoped for, either from her family or the community. Her stepmother would rather she not prove herself better than the white children. And the threat of violence—a knife stuck through a loaf of bread and into the kitchen table—greets the family upon their return home from the competition. Violence continues to threaten the only "colored" family in this small town, and Lena and her stepmother Claudie, as well as others in the community, must decide how to respond to racial prejudice. This touching novel is narrated by a young girl, an interesting point of comparison with *To Kill a Mockingbird*. The book shares with *To Kill a Mockingbird* a similar setting and several themes. (Easy reading)

2. *More Than Meets the Eye* by Jeanne Betancourt (166 pp.). Ben Lee, a Chinese-American student attending a Vermont high school, is vying with Liz Gaynor for number one standing in the senior class. Liz likes Ben, but others, including her mother, seem to see only that Ben is Chinese. Meanwhile, when a Cambodian family and a Korean family move into the community, racial prejudice and stereotyping become apparent. This book works well with *To Kill a Mockingbird* because it points to present-day discrimination against a group other than African-Americans. While it does not help students by giving them insight into the setting of *To Kill a Mockingbird*, its treatment of similar issues and extention of those issues to another group and time are valuable. (Easy reading)

3. *The Day That Elvis Came to Town* by Jan Marino (204 pp.). Don't be put off by the title; this is a fine young adult novel. Wanda Dohr escapes the difficulties of dealing with her demanding mother and her alcoholic father as many teens escape their difficulties: She idolizes a rising singing star, in this case, Elvis Presley. She also admires Mercedes, a jazz singer who rooms with the Dohrs and who, coincidentally, attended high school with Elvis. When Wanda learns that Mercedes was an unpopular girl in high school because she is half Black, Wanda must confront her own prejudices. This book makes an interesting companion to *To Kill a Mockingbird* in light of this quotation from *To Kill a Mockingbird*: "Negro blood is sure powerful—because just one drop of black blood makes you a colored man." Reading this selection will also give some insight into small town, Southern living. (Moderate difficulty)

4. *All Together Now* by Sue Ellen Bridgers (184 pp.). Twelve-year-old Casey goes to spend the summer in a small Southern town with her grandparents and uncle while her father serves as a pilot in the Korean War and her mother works. Casey is hardly excited by the prospect of this summer, but she gradually comes

to care very much for a number of different people in the community, including Dwayne, a mentally retarded adult neighbor who endlessly plays baseball and baseball commentator. This novel beautifully depicts the complexity of human relationships as well as life in a small Southern town. It makes a marvelous companion book for *To Kill a Mockingbird* because of the treatment of themes about growing up, accepting others who are different, and the power of family and community. (Moderate difficulty)

5. *The Autobiography of Miss Jane Pittman* by Ernest Gaines (246 pp.). While "Autobiography" appears in the title, this is actually a work of fiction. By tracing the life of the 110-year-old Miss Jane Pittman in a series of tape-recorded interviews, a fascinating history of African-Americans from slavery to the Civil Rights Movement emerges. In the inspiring ending, the title character, a former slave, leads a freedom march. This book provides a valuable context for *To Kill a Mockingbird* by giving historical background both prior to and following the years of the classic. (Moderate difficulty and lengthy)

6. *Let the Circle Be Unbroken* by Mildred Taylor (394 pp.). This very powerful novel might be thought of as a *To Kill a Mockingbird* from the black perspective. Cassie Logan's family struggles to survive in the South during the Depression years. Prejudice is pervasive: In scenes reminiscent of *To Kill a Mockingbird*, an innocent young man is tried for the murder of a shopkeeper, and despite evidence to the contrary, he is found guilty by the all-white jury; Cassie's half-white cousin, Suzella, comes to live with the Logans and when she passes for white on one occasion, the consequences are devastating; when an old woman registers to vote, she and others are thrown out of their homes by the landowner. Despite these hardships, courage and family love see Cassie and the Logans through these years. This novel was preceded by Taylor's *Roll of Thunder, Hear My Cry* and is followed by *The Road to Memphis*. (Difficult due to length and dialect)

You will want to read and evaluate these works with your students in mind making modifications in the choices as needed. With larger numbers of at-risk students in a class, for example, you may opt to select shorter books or those that are easy or relatively easy to read. Judy Blume's *Iggie's House* is another title to consider for such a class. Helpful sources for other possible titles are the *ALAN Review* and NCTE's *Books for You, High Interest—Easy Reading*, and *Your Reading*.

For a class of 30 students, six copies of five to six different titles will be needed. For a class of 40 students, you could either arrange for six copies of seven to eight different novels, or you may wish to have ten copies of five titles (so that two different groups could be reading the same work). Many English departments are willing to purchase paperback novels, but in some cases students can purchase the books or borrow them from a public or school library.

Once the books have been previewed, I display them at different desks in the room and let students browse through them. Students then form the collaborative reading groups with a maximum of five or six allowed in a group. Alternatively, students could list first, second, and third choice books, and teachers could establish groups based on these choices.

After groups have been established, each group meets to develop a calendar for the next three weeks. The group decides to have completed a certain number of pages or chapters by mid-week and the end of the week, and the book is to be completed by the end of the second week. A fair amount of class time should be allotted for reading and for writing response log entries, but at least twice during each of the two weeks, groups should schedule discussion days. Time at the beginning of the third week will be spent developing presentations to be given the latter part of the week.

Literature Logs for Exploring Individual Responses

Individuals write daily entries in their literature logs, spiral or three-ring notebooks, which are shared with me and their peers in the group. The literature log entries may be open; that is, students simply respond with their thoughts and feelings about the book, or they may react in writing to any of the topics or questions that I provide:

1. Describe one character's problem or a choice to be made. What advice do you have for the character?

2. Explain why you think a character is acting as he or she is.

3. Copy a provocative/interesting/important/enjoyable passage and comment on it.

4. From what you have read so far, make predictions about what could happen next, explaining the reasons for your predictions.

5. Explain why you would or would not like to have a particular character as a friend.

6. Explain why you would or would not like to have lived in the time and place of this novel.

7. Write questions about a part you had difficulty understanding. Choose one question and explore possible answers.

8. Examine the values of a character you like/dislike.

9. What real-life persons or events are you reminded of by characters or events in the story?

10. Reread your entries to date and discuss what your main reactions to this book seem to be so far.

I skim students' literature log entries once or twice a week and write comments intended to encourage thoughtful reading and responding. I may agree with the content of one student's entry or write a question that probes another's vague or more superficial response. If a student has a question I may respond to it, or, more likely, ask the student to bring it up in the group discussion. I do not correct mechanical or grammatical errors that appear, but a completion grade is given.

Group Discussions to Clarify, Verify, and Extend Responses

Each group meets at least four times during the two-week period to discuss the novel. The conversation usually begins with a quick review of characters and events and moves to addressing any questions group members have. Individuals also select a literature log entry or entries to share so that others may react. During this discussion, students inevitably articulate their judgments about the book and begin to make connections with their own experiences.

I like to sit in on the discussions for brief periods, mostly because I am curious about the students' responses. Occasionally I can encourage students to expand their own responses in light of what others have to say. With gentle questioning, students will explain the reasons for their comments and will begin to make connections between themselves and the book. Modeling this sort of questioning is helpful; I've found that other students readily adopt these sorts of questions. Also, teachers can join small group discussions to assist them in their assignation of participation grades.

Group Activities for Sharing and Comparing Responses to Novels

During the third week, groups meet to plan 10-15 minute presentations about their novel to the rest of the class. One group might opt to give a readers' theatre presentation of a key scene. Another group might script and present an interview of characters, perhaps in the style of Oprah Winfrey or Phil Donahue. Yet another group might focus on a central character's development, with different students reading passages from various points in the novel which depict the character's growth. As a highlight of the entire unit, I've videotaped such presentations to share with parents and administrators—and visiting credentialing teams.

The presentations serve a number of purposes. Perhaps most obviously, in this way students can learn about the books read by other groups. A strong presentation may even encourage students from other groups to read the novel independently. But this activity also takes students back into the novel they've just completed and lets them reread and re-experience it.

Following presentations, and as a transition to beginning *To Kill a Mocking-bird*, I have students form new groups so that each new group has a representative from each of the collaborative reading groups. In other words, the new groups consist of students who have all read different young adult novels. These new groups will function throughout the reading of *To Kill a Mockingbird*. Groups discuss the following:

1. Do any of the characters in these novels grow up over the course of the book? What changes do they make? What kinds of challenges do they encounter? What do these authors seem to be saying about the process of growing up or becoming mature? Do you agree?

2. How are families and the community depicted in these novels? What influences do the family and community have? What do these authors seem to be saying about the family and the community? Do you agree? In other words, do their views mesh with your experiences?

3. What forms of prejudice appear in these novels? What are the effects of prejudice, for both those displaying prejudice and those who are victims of prejudice? What answers to prejudice are offered? What do these authors seem to be saying about prejudice? Do you agree?

4. Is courage displayed by any of the characters? Describe that courage and your responses to it. What do these authors seem to be saying about courage? Do their views agree with your experiences?

5. Is tolerance or acceptance displayed toward those with emotional or mental handicaps by any of the charac-ters? Describe that tolerance and your responses to it. What do these authors seem to be saying about accepting others who are different? Do you agree?

Groups share their conclusions about these issues in a whole class discussion, and students are then well prepared to begin their study of the core novel.

Whole Class Reading of *To Kill a Mockingbird*

The main facets of this portion of the unit include individual and class reading, individual literature log entries, and group and whole class discussions and activities. I will also describe two unit closure activities. To accomplish this progression, I divide the novel into 10 chapter groupings: Chapters 1, 2-3, 4-6, 7-8, 9-11, 12-15, 16-18, 19-22, 23-27, and 28-31. The pace at which I proceed depends on a number of factors, including the time available and the ability of the class.

Reading *To Kill a Mockingbird*

I use a variety of approaches with the reading. I read aloud or play a tape recording of Chapter 1 to bring students into the novel, and I organize a readers' theatre approach for key portions of Chapters 16-22 to bring the trial to life. Students occasionally read aloud, voluntarily, in their small groups; and, of course, I assign independent reading for homework to make timely progress.

During the reading of the novel, the class develops a character chart, updating it as new characters are introduced. The chart is kept on paper on a bulletin board and includes names, brief descriptions, character traits, and important incidents involving each character. The chart is not a central activity, but it does help students keep track of the large number of characters and distinguish major from minor characters. Similarly, at appropriate points, the class develops a map of Maycomb, plotting the school; the town square; and the homes of the Finches, Mrs. Dubose, Miss Rachel, Mr. Avery, Miss Maudie, Miss Stephanie Crawford, and the Radleys. The map helps students more vividly picture a number of scenes, including Bob Ewell's attack on the children near the end of the novel.

Literature Logs and Group Discussions

Literature log entries are written for each of the 10 chapter groupings. Students may again write free responses, or they may refer to the topics and questions used for the young adult novels. One literature log entry is assigned and written in class: After Atticus' closing argument at the trial, I ask students to comment on Tom Robinson's guilt or innocence, predict the jury's decision, and explain the reasons for their predictions. Interestingly, although well prepared for the jury's verdict, some, like Dill, believe that justice will prevail.

Again, I read and comment on the response entries, encouraging students to make connections among *To Kill a Mockingbird*, the young adult novel read earlier, and their own experiences. The entries serve as a check to be certain that students are keeping up with the reading, and they provide ideas for the small group and whole class discussions. While key issues for discussion arise in the log entries, I may pose questions to prod students to think about other relevant points during small group and whole class conversations.

After Chapter 8, attention will shift from the Radleys to the trial of Tom Robinson. At this juncture, I ask students in their small groups to discuss the following five issues, which relate *To Kill a Mockingbird* with the young adult novels read previously and the students' experiences.

1   Why do you think Harper Lee chose Scout to narrate this story? What effect does this choice have? Did any of your novels have first person narrators? Compare and contrast these narrators and Scout.

2.   What are the attitudes of Scout and Atticus toward school? How do these compare with the attitudes of characters from the young adult novels toward school and education? How do these attitudes compare to those held by you and your parents?

3.   How would you describe the relationship between Atticus Finch and his children? How does this compare to parent-child relationships in the young adult novels? Which relationships do you think are positive? Why?

4.   Contrast the different ways that Jem, Scout, Dill, Atticus, and Miss Maudie view the Radleys. How do characters from the young adult novels view those who are different? What are your ideas about this issue?

5.   Why should you never kill a mockingbird? What characters from *To Kill a Mockingbird* and the young adult novels might be thought of as mockingbirds? Who are the mockingbirds in society today?

Additional Activities for Extending Responses

After students finish reading the novel, writing their individual responses, and discussing the ending, I've found that the activities described below will further enhance students' understanding, enjoyment, and appreciation of *To Kill a Mockingbird*. Time is always an issue so there are occasions when I am able to arrange for all of these; more commonly, I must select from them.

*   Students bring in current newspaper stories about justice and injustice, hypocrisy, prejudice, courage, and so forth. These are posted on a bulletin board for students to read in order to make the point that the issues of *To Kill a Mockingbird* aren't limited to the South during the Depression years but are current and pervasive issues.

*   Students view the videotape or laserdisk of *To Kill a Mockingbird* that stars Gregory Peck. They compare and contrast the film and the novel and discuss the effectiveness of both.

*   Most readers have forgotten the frame of the first chapter so they reread Chapter 1 and then attempt to answer Scout's question about when "it" all began. They also discuss what "it" is and speculate about what kind of adult Jean Louise became.

*   Literature has long been a source of inspiration for writing assignments, and *To Kill a Mockingbird* is no exception. I encourage the class to generate ideas for writing, keeping in mind literature log entries and discussions. Alternatively, students could select from these quite varied topics:

1. Reflect on the meaning of courage, prejudice, justice, hypocrisy, or another issue from *To Kill a Mockingbird*. Use examples from the novels read and from your own experiences to come to some conclusions about your topic. (Reflective essay)

2. Compare and contrast related characters from *To Kill a Mockingbird*, or from *To Kill a Mockingbird* and the adolescent novel you read. (Analysis)

3. Scout describes very vividly a number of her school experiences. Describe a pleasant or an unpleasant school experience of yours and explain either directly or indirectly the significance of this experience. (Autobiographical incident)

4. The prejudice manifested at the trial of Tom Robinson had very strong impacts on Dill and Jem. Describe a situation you witnessed in which prejudice or discrimination was evident. Explain what happened and what impact this incident had on you. (Eyewitness account)

5. Aunt Alexandra is often critical of Atticus' parenting decisions. Yet most readers consider Atticus a very able parent. What is your definition of a good parent? After writing and explaining your definition, evaluate whether or not Atticus and one of the young adult novel parents were good parents according to the criteria you have developed. (Evaluation)

Unit Closure

To provide closure for the unit, I ask individuals to complete a Response Guide (See Figure 1.1). Such guides are used more commonly to introduce units, but here the Response Guide very effectively challenges students to address and connect the complex issues of their young adult novels and *To Kill a Mockingbird*. An animated discussion invariably ensues when individuals share their answers and their reasons for those answers.

Figure 1.1

Response Guide

Directions: In Column 1, indicate your personal reaction to each of the statements; in Column 2, respond to the statement as if you were Harper Lee; in Column 3, respond to the statement as if you were the author of the young adult novel you read. A = I agree; D = I disagree. Be prepared to discuss your answers, as well as the reasons for them.

1	2	3		
___	___	___	1.	Discrimination is inevitable because everyone has prejudices.
___	___	___	2.	Values and attitudes are developed during childhood, and they are learned from parents.
___	___	___	3.	All people are created equal and should be treated equally.
___	___	___	4.	In America, the legal system ensures that justice will be served.
___	___	___	5.	An important part of growing up is learning to accept life's unfairnesses.
___	___	___	6.	The time and place where you live have minimal influence on your attitudes and values.
___	___	___	7.	Real courage is rarely displayed.
___	___	___	8.	All people who are emotionally or mentally disabled should be treated with tolerance.
___	___	___	9.	Fear is the main reason for the existence of prejudice.
___	___	___	10.	A good education is necessary for doing well in life.

A second activity for providing closure to the unit begins when I ask students to reread their literature logs. They then write a final entry describing their reactions to the entire unit. In particular, I ask them to comment on the collaborative reading of novels for introducing *To Kill a Mockingbird*. I also ask them how their responses to the whole-class novel developed during their reading, and I ask which activities they most enjoyed or found helpful. I've learned a great deal from the final log entries, as have the students, who only occasionally are asked to reflect on their own learning.

Requesting student evaluations is an extension of an approach that recognizes the importance of student responses, both for the literary experience and the classroom experience. Introducing *To Kill a Mockingbird* with the collaborative reading of a variety of young adult novels is my attempt to provide students with satisfying literary and classroom experiences. My hope is that such positive and rewarding experiences will translate to a life-long love of reading literature.

References

Betancourt, J. (1990). *More than meets the eye*. New York: Bantam Books.

Bridgers, S.E. (1979). *All together now*. New York: Bantam Books.

Gaines, E.J. (1971). *The autobiography of Miss Jane Pittman*. New York: Bantam Books.

Gallo, D.R., (Chair) and the Committee on the Senior High School Booklist. (1985). *Books for you: A booklist for senior high students*. Urbana, Illinois: National Council of Teachers of English.

Lee, H. (1960). *To kill a mockingbird*. New York: Warner Books.

Marino, J. (1990). *The day that Elvis came to town*. Boston: Little, Brown, & Company.

Matthews, D., (Chair) and the Committee to Revise *High Interest—Easy Reading*. (1988). *High interest—easy reading for junior and senior high school students*. 5th ed. Urbana, Illinois: National Council of Teachers of English.

Nilsen, A.P. (Ed.), and the Committee on the Junior High and Middle School Booklist. (1991). *Your reading: A booklist for junior high and middle school students*. 8th ed. Urbana, Illinois: National Council of Teachers of English.

Sebestyen, O. (1968). *Words by heart*. Boston: Little, Brown, & Company.

Taylor, M. (1981). *Let the circle be unbroken*. New York: Puffin Books.

Chapter 2

Anne Frank's *The Diary of a Young Girl:* World War II and Young Adult Literature

JOAN F. KAYWELL

Introduction

When I first taught this novel to a group of tenth graders, I presented it in a very traditional fashion. We read the book, discussed certain sections, and saw the movie. No doubt I did the most work since I was the one leading the discussions while several students simply dismissed the topic as being irrelevant to modern times. Now that young adult literature is readily available, my classes have a depth and breadth about them that I always wanted but didn't know how to achieve. Through young adult literature, students are exposed to a myriad of perspectives concerning World War II. In this unit, students will be able to acquire enough background knowledge about the Holocaust to participate in several meaningful class discussions and produce several unique group projects. This is different from the teacher telling students what to think since each student is responsible for reading and sharing something about World War II. In essence, the students are responsible for their learning and the teacher learns too. Through young adult literature, all students (even the least motivated) may become engaged with the material.

There are several different ways to set up the classroom to achieve the same goals. Ideally, you will present the accompanying list of young adult novel annotations and let each student choose a different book of choice. For less skilled readers, you can suggest some shorter or less difficult novels such as Abells' *The Children We Remember* (a picture essay) or Volakova's *I Never Saw Another Butterfly* (a collection of drawings and poems produced by children in the camps). The books are within their skill level and yet can yield powerful contributions to the class projects. Many students, however, will be able to read beyond reading level since this unit is extremely motivational.

Already I am anticipating that many of you are saying, "Yea, right! I have a hard enough time getting my students to read the required book let alone read another one!" The group projects require participation from each group member to be successful; the projects are meaningful, relevant, and fun. Additionally, this unit has built-in peer pressure. If one student chooses to read Siegal's U*pon the Head of a Goat* and another chooses Siegal's *Grace in the Wilderness,* you can be sure that the class will not be satisfied knowing the life of Piri at nine when another classmate was supposed to read about her life at seventeen.

After the students select the book they want to read outside of class, I would group them according to topic with no more than five students in one group. For the sake of convenience, I have included the annotations of the books that I would use in clusters depending upon their topic. Group project suggestions will follow each cluster, but students know they are encouraged to develop their own group project if they are interested in a specific topic.

The annotations that are included are not exhaustive. Other good sources for annotations include the *ALAN Review, The English Journal,* and several NCTE publications such as *Books for You: A Booklist for Senior High Students* and *Your Reading: A Booklist for Junior High and Middle School Students.* Teachers are encouraged to borrow their librarian's *Booklist* of May 1988 that contains an excellent annotated bibliography of 55 books dealing with "Growing Up Jewish." Also, Marsha Rudman and Susan P. Rosenberg's article "Confronting History: Holocaust Books for Children" discusses some two dozen books and lists another 50 titles. And finally, in the September 1982 issue of the *English Journal,* there is an excellent description of films and literature available.

Group One:
Other Jewish Children's Experiences During World War II

1. *Gideon.* by Chester Aaron (181 pp.). The author tells the story as if he is Gideon, recounting the events of his teenage years to his wife and children. Based on historical fact, *Gideon* is a fictional account of a 15-year-old boy's struggle to survive in the Warsaw ghetto during World War II. Although Gideon is Jewish, he uses his Aryan looks and bribery to sneak out of the ghetto to obtain food and other necessities for the other Jews living there. The reader shares in Gideon's many losses of family and friends, his escape from the ghetto, and his horrific experiences at the Treblinka Work Camp.

2. *Alicia: My Story* by Alicia Appleman-Jurman (433 pp.). Alicia was only 13 years old when she began saving Jewish lives in war-ravaged Poland. In this nonfiction account of the Holocaust, Alicia recalls how she stood on her brother's grave and vowed she would tell his story.(8th) (1989 Christopher Award Winner.)

3. *Memories of My Life in a Polish Village: 1930-1949* by Toby Knobel Fluek (110 pp.). Toby Fluek was a small Jewish girl growing up in Czernica, Poland, when World War II started. She and her family moved to a Jewish ghetto and

went into hiding several times to save their lives. By the war's end, only she and her mother had survived. Now an artist in New York City, the author presents her story through her paintings and their descriptions.

4. *The Endless Steppe* by Esther Hautzig (243 pp.). When the Russians took over Poland in June of 1941, Esther Rudomin and her family are arrested for being "capitalists." Esther, her parents, and her grandmother are sent to Siberia in crowded cattle cars where they struggle to live for five years. The adults are required to work in gypsum mines that provide the material for casts for the soldiers while Esther, a child, is required to work in the potato fields. When the Nazis invade Russia, her father is forced to join the military to defend Russia, which makes it even more difficult for the women to survive.

5. *The Painted Bird* by Jerzhy Kosinsky (213 pp.). This brilliant but horrifying novel is the story of an abandoned boy, who looks like a Jew or a gypsy, and his aimless meanderings throughout Eastern Europe during World War II. The novel unsparingly and graphically paints a picture of human evil, ignorance, and cruelty. Due to some extremely brutal rape scenes depicted, you should require students to obtain parental permission to read it.

6. *Shadow of the Wall* by Christa Laird (144 pp.). Although 13-year-old Mischa is a fictional character, the novel is based on historical documents and records. Mischa shares what it was like for him and his sisters growing up in the Warsaw ghetto from 1939 to 1942 at Dr. Janusz Korzcak's orphanage.

7. *Journey to America* by Sonia Levitin (150 pp.). Lisa Platt was a young Jewish girl living in Germany in 1938, a time when life was changing drastically for the Jews. The restrictions were becoming increasingly more severe: First, it was the yellow stars that must be worn, then there were schools they could not attend, and then there were things they were forbidden to do. Lisa's father goes to America in the hopes of establishing himself and bringing his family over. Meanwhile, Lisa, her mother, and two sisters find it necessary to flee Germany and settle elsewhere. Most of the story is about the hardships they suffer while being separated from their father.

8. *Friedrich* by Hans Peter Richter (149 pp.). The tragedy and terror suffered by German Jews are made more vivid by the simplicity and candor of a child's viewpoint and by the focus on one small, obscure family. The story of Friedrich Schneider, a young German Jewish boy, is told by a German friend who lived in the same apartment house. After Hitler took over, Friedrich is expelled from school, his father is deported, and his mother dies. Although the boys remain friends, Friedrich is left to rely on his own resources for food, shelter, and protection from the Nazis.(6th)

9. *Touch Wood: A Girlhood in Occupied France* by Renee Roth-Hano (304 pp.). The author grew up as a Jewish girl in France during World War II. Written in the form of a diary, Renee tells how her family was separated and how she and her sisters were cared for by Catholic nuns until her family was reunited.

10. *The Cage* by Ruth Minsky Sender (224 pp.). This is the memoir of a Nazi Holocaust survivor. This grandmother speaks from her experiences in the Lodz ghetto in Poland and Auschwitz when she was a teenager. Riva Minska vividly shares how the Nazis destroyed her family, her community, and her way of life and tells how she managed to survive the death camps of World War II.(5th) (NCSS-CBC Notable Children's Book in the Field of Social Studies.)

11. *The Cigarette Sellers of Three Crosses Square* by Joseph Zieman (162 pp.). This is the story about a group of children who help each other survive in the Nazi ghettos of Poland.

Group Two: The Concentration Camps

1. *The Children We Remember* by Chana Abells (48 pp.). This nonfiction photo essay focuses on the children in the concentration camps during World War II.

2. *Fragments of Isabella* by Isabella Leitner and Irving A. Leitner (128 pp.). This is the true, heart-wrenching, and unforgettable story of the author's experiences at Auschwitz during the Holocaust. The reader will be shocked by the atrocities and the horror that she faced but will be moved by her courage and willpower to survive.(American Library Association Best Book for Young Adults.)

3. *I Am Rosemarie* by Marietta D. Moskin (256 pp.). Drawn from the author's own experiences, this is the moving story of a young Jewish girl, Rosemarie Brenner, and her experiences in a concentration camp during World War II.(7th)

4. *Upon the Head of the Goat: A Childhood in Hungary 1939-1944* by Aranka Siegal (192 pp.). Piri is nine years old at the onset of World War II, and her life becomes a nightmare when the Nazis invade Hungary. Her Jewish family is placed into a ghetto to await the trains that will take them to the concentration camps. Although the Nazis have little to no regard for them as people, Piri's mother courageously attempts to instill the values of human dignity and respect in her family.

This sensitive fictionalized autobiography depicts the value of life in direct contrast to others' total disregard for humanity. In the end, Piri survives the horrors of Auschwitz.(6th) (1981 Newbery Honor Book and SLJ Best Young Adult Book.)

5. *I Never Saw Another Butterfly* by Hana Volavkova, (Editor) (80 pp.). This nonfiction book is a collection of drawings and poems that were done by children who grew up in the Terezin Concentration Camp in Czechoslovakia between 1942 and 1944. The terror, the pleas for rescue, and the reflections of beliefs and values of these children who lived during World War II are vividly captured.

6. *Night* by Elie Wiesel (translated by Stella Rodway) (112 pp.). This short autobiographical novel is Wiesel's rendering of his terrifying experiences as a teenager at Auschwitz and Buchenwald, Nazi death camps. Wiesel graphically describes his witnessing the death of his father, his innocence, and his God. Wiesel analyzes himself as incisively as he does others.(7th)

Group Three: Those who Risked Their Lives

1. *The Traitors* by James Forman (238 pp.). Pastor Eichhorn, though German, is against the Nazis. His adopted son, Paul, joins him in trying to thwart the progress of the Nazi march while hiding a Jewish friend. Eichhorn's biological son, Kurt, is pro-Hitler and sees the relationship between Paul and his father threatening. Although the story is fiction, it is powerful because it could have happened. Readers realize that not all Germans supported Hitler and the Nazis.

2. *War Without Friends* by Evert Hartman (translated by Patricia Crampton) (218 pp.). Arnold was taught by his family to believe that the Dutch National Socialist Party (NSB) was the patriotic way to support Hitler's Germany in 1942. Arnold questions this position when he reads, in an underground newspaper, about the treatment of the Jews in concentration camps and witnesses ruthless attacks on Dutch citizens who did not support Hitler's Germany.
This coming-of-age story depicts a young man who has the courage to select his values intellectually rather than blindly accept the values prescripted by others. Although his values are contrary to the values of his family, his choice is consistent with the majority of the Dutch people who lived during World War II.

3. *My Hundred Children* by Lena Kuchler-Silberman (256 pp.). This is the true story about the author, a survivor of the Holocaust, and her courageous struggle to lead 100 Jewish war orphans out of Poland to refuge in Israel during World War II.(7th)

4. *Tug of War* by Joan Lingard (194 pp.). Hugo and Astra, 14-year-old Latvian twins, are separated when the Russians invade their country in 1944. Hugo ends up in Hamburg, Germany, where a family takes care of him until the end of the war. Meanwhile, his family waits out the war in a refugee camp. When they are

finally reunited, his family is disgruntled by Hugo's German girlfriend and places him in a choice situation.

5. *Number the Stars* by Lois Lowry (160 pp.). One day in 1943 Annemarie and Ellen are playing in German-occupied Copenhagen, and the next day Ellen and her family face the possibility of relocation since they are Jewish. Annemarie decides that she must help her best friend escape from Norway and go to Sweden where they will be safe. Before she knows it, ten-year-old Annemarie finds herself involved in a dangerous mission.

6. *Good Night, Mr. Tom* by Michelle Magorian (336 pp.). This historical novel portrays the beginning of World War II as it was felt in a small town in England. Although this village is only indirectly affected by the war, its citizens rally to protect their values whenever the need arises. The story focuses on the relationship that develops between William, an abused child who flees from London, and Tom Oakley, a villager who takes him in support of the war effort.

7. *Rescue: The Story of How Gentiles Saved Jews in the Holocaust* by Milton Meltzer (167 pp.). This author looks at the Christians who risked their lives to hide and protect the Jews during the Holocaust. The horrific experiences of the Jews and those who were caught trying to save them are vividly presented.

8. *One Man's Valor: Leo Baeck and the Holocaust* by Anne E. Neimark (113 pp.). This easy-to-read biography vividly portrays the horror of the Holocaust and the courage of one man, Leo Baeck, and his fight to save his Jewish brethren. After helping thousands of Jews escape Germany and refusing to flee himself, Baeck realizes that cooperation with the Nazis would not save the Jewish people from destruction. He was arrested and sent to the Theresienstadt Concentration Camp and later eventually freed and came to be a respected Jewish leader.

9. *Star Without a Sky* by Leonie Ossowski (translated by Ruth Crowley) (204 pp.). In April 1945, four adolescent East German boys and a girl find a young Jewish boy hiding in a cellar. They are faced with an awful dilemma: Should they protect him or turn him over to the authorities? Crowley comments that it is necessary "to explain to young people today what it was like to experience Hitler's Germany and the war's end—and to warn against the dangers of blind obedience." (7th)

10. *The Upstairs Room* by Johanna Reiss (182 pp.). During the occupation of the German forces in Holland, Annie and her sister, Sini, find themselves separated from the rest of their Jewish family. The Hannicks allow them to stay upstairs in an attic until Mr. Hannick begins to fear for his own family's safety. He takes them to another family and says he will be back in a week but never

returns. The Oosterveld family keeps them in hiding in a small room for nearly three years until the war ends.

11. *The Courage to Care* by Carol Rittner (Ed.). (176 pp.). Rittner captures the stories of a few non-Jews who risked their lives to rescue and protect Jews during the Holocaust.

12. *The Hiding Place* by Corrie ten Boom, John Sherrill, and Elizabeth Sherrill (256 pp.). This nonfiction novel is the description of how this heroine of the anti-Nazi underground in Holland and her family hid persecuted Jews in their home. Eventually they were betrayed, and they, too, spent some time in concentration camps.(6th)

13. *Have You Forgotten: A Memoir of Poland 1939-1945* by Christine Zamoyska-Panek and Fred Benton Holmberg (256 pp.). A former Polish countess describes the German's occupation of her father's estate, her efforts as a Resistance worker, and her eventual escape to freedom.

Group Four:
The Japanese, Japanese-American,
and American Perspectives

1. *The War at Home* by Connie Jordan Green (136 pp.). Set during World War II, this novel is primarily about family togetherness. Twelve-year-old Maggie McDowell ponders on several kinds of death: a rabbit senselessly shot by her cousin, her Aunt Opal's accidental death, and the thousands who died from the atomic bombings of Hiroshima and Nagasaki.

2. *Hiroshima* by John Hersey (196 pp.). Pulitzer Prize-winner John Hersey interviewed survivors of Hiroshima's bomb while the ashes were still warm. Hersey describes the lives of six people—a clerk, a widowed seamstress, a physician, a Methodist minister, a surgeon, and a German Catholic priest— shortly before and for about a year after the bombing. While describing the ordeals of these individuals, Hersey manages to convey the devastation and the suffering experienced by the people of Hiroshima on August 6, 1945. The final chapter was added in 1985 and continues with the lives of these six people.(7th)

3. *Farewell to Manzanar* by Jeanne Wakatsuki Houston and James D. Houston (160 pp.). This is the true story of one spirited Japanese-American family's attempt to survive the indignities of forced detention as seen through the eyes of a child. The family was detained for four years at the Manzanar Internment Camp during World War II.(6th)

4. *Alan and Naomi* by Myron Levoy (192 pp.). During World War II, many Americans were safe at home and listened to the atrocities on the radio—such was the case for Alan Silverman and his family. The war becomes real for Alan when he befriends Naomi, a girl who witnessed the brutal murder of her father for being a member of the Underground French Resistance. After her father was tortured and killed by the Nazis, Naomi withdraws into herself and stops speaking. Her family escaped to the United States in hopes of leaving the memories behind.

It is quite an accomplishment when Naomi learns to trust Alan enough to tell him about her life, but she suffers a major setback when some anti-Semitic bullies taunt and chase her. Alan experiences the bitterness of war through this incident.

5. *Hiroshima No Pika* by Toshi Maruki (48 pp.). This picture book presents the devastation of Hiroshima after the atomic bomb on August 6, 1945. Maruki graphically shows piles of dead bodies, the injured with no available medical treatment, destroyed buildings, and the mass confusion and fear. She points out that many people are still dying of radiation sickness and tells of the commemoration day honoring those who died as a result of the Holocaust.

The author admits that this bomb stopped the war, but she questions whether it was worth the price. In the afterword, Maruki states, "It is very difficult to tell young people about something very bad that happened in the hope that their knowing will help keep this from happening again."

6. *Journey to Topaz* by Yoshiko Uchida (160 pp.). This historical novel is based on the experiences of the author's family and those of other Japanese-Americans who were sent to relocation concentration camps after the Japanese bombed Pearl Harbor during World War II. Eleven-year-old Yuki and her family feel as American as anyone else but are denied their Constitutional Rights because they are visibly from another heritage. They are forced to live at a racetrack, the horse stalls serving as apartments until they are transferred to the holding camp where they are to await their fate. The feelings of abandonment and betrayal felt by Japanese-Americans during this extreme period of confusion in the United States are poignantly portrayed.

Group Five: The Soldiers' Stories

1. *Forever Nineteen* by Grigory Baklanov (translated from Russian by Antonina W. Bouis) (166 pp.). Nineteen-year-old Volodya Tretyakov dreams of becoming a hero when he proudly leaves his family and his small Russian village to serve in World War II. His dreams turn into nightmares as he learns firsthand about the harsh realities of war.

2. *Stand Up and Fight: The Story of Emil Brigg* by Emil Brigg (175 pp.). This nonfiction book deals with the author's only reason for surviving the Holocaust: to seek revenge on those who killed his family. When he was 14 years old, he and his father were forced to join the military shortly after Germany invaded Poland on September 7, 1939. When he and 3,000 armed men of the Polish Militia surrender to a small group of Russians, Emil's fight for survival begins. He eventually joins the Partisans and, after the war is over, participates in the execution of Nazi war criminals.

Pages 1-118 are outstanding, but the rest of the book should be read only by extremely mature students. Emil's actions after the war are questionable when he admittedly takes matters into his own hands.

3. *Summer of My German Soldier* by Bette Greene (199 pp.). Patty, an abused girl, befriends an escaped German prisoner of war. In spite of what her parents and others say about the Germans, Patty gets to know Anton and falls in love with his gentle spirit.(American Library Association Notable Book.)

4. *The Last Mission* by Harry Mazer (192 pp.). Jack Raab, a too-young American-Jewish boy, uses an older brother's identification and lies his way into military service during World War II. This 16-year-old vividly shares his experiences, including his harsh imprisonment and release from a German camp. The horrors of a war that he never should have fought in make him an adult before his time.(6th) (American Library Association Best of the Best Books for Young Adults and *New York Times* Outstanding Book of the Year.)

5. *And No Birds Sang* by Farley Mowat (208 pp.). Mowat retells his own experiences as a young soldier during World War II. At first he was very idealistic and romanticized the war effort but after exposure to many atrocities, he grows and learns painfully to see war as it is.

6. *I was There* by Hans Peter Richter (translated by Edite Kroll) (204 pp.). In this nonfiction book, Richter tells what it was like for him and two of his friends when they were members of the Hitler Youth Movement in Nazi Germany during the Third Reich. Richter recounts the daily events and attitudes of young German people under Hitler.(6th)

7. *Dawn* by Elie Wiesel (112 pp.). A young Jew is faced with the duty of executing a British hostage in occupied Palestine.

Group Six: Contemporary Prejudice

1. *Anti-Semitism: A Modern Perspective.* by Caroline Arnold and Herma Silverstein (includes black and white photos and drawings) (223 pp.). Many

people assume that anti-Semitism ended with World War II but that is not true. The Anti-Defamation League, an organization that monitors anti-Semitic incidents, reported 377 anti-Semitic episodes in the United States in 1980, and the number is on the rise. These episodes include firebombings, desecrations of synagogues, hate mail, death threats, and other violations of human rights.

2. *Chernowitz* by Fran Arrick (192 pp.). Bobby Cherno, a freshman at Middleboro High School, is disliked by Emmet Sundback, a known bully. Bobby is unjustly discriminated against by Emmet and his friends because he is Jewish. This dramatic and intense story graphically depicts how hatred quickly spreads and how it can be painful to innocent people. Arrick draws the familiar and contemporary topic of prejudice out into the open as she poignantly describes the torment and anguish that Bobby feels.(6th)

3. *Kim/Kimi* by Hadley Irwin (200 pp.). When Kim Andrews looks in the mirror, Kimi Yogushi looks back. Even though Kim feels American she looks Japanese. At 16, Kim feels unsure of her true heritage since she has never met any of her Japanese relatives; her Japanese father died before she was born. Her search-for-self takes her to Tule Lake in California, one of the Japanese-American concentration camps of World War II, where her father was once held. Kim grows up when she stops running, confronts truth, and learns that "life is cause and effect—that what you do has consequences."
Irwin successfully reminds us that it is important to remember the painful incidents of the past, such as the incarceration of loyal Japanese-Americans during World War II, so we won't make the same mistakes and can get on with our future.

4. *Gentlehands* by M. E. Kerr (144 pp.). This is the story of a traumatic summer in Buddy Boyle's life. While trying to impress Skye Pennington and adjust to her well-to-do lifestyle, Buddy must deal with his feelings of alienation and identity as the press brings out his family's mysterious past. Buddy's special relationship with his refined and cultured grandfather is severed when Buddy finds out that this sensitive old man has been accused of being a Nazi murderer, Gentlehands, in a World War II concentration camp.(6th)

5. *The War Between the Classes* by Gloria D. Miklowitz (176 pp.). Amy Sumoto, the daughter of traditionalist Japanese parents, and Adam Tarcher, the son of a snobby upper-class mother, are determined to have a relationship with one another. At the same time, their school is participating in an experiment, the Color Game, where students are put into social classes according to specific rules in order to teach them about prejudice. Not only is Amy upset by the humiliation of it all, but she fears that the game is threatening her relationship with Adam. Amy plans to sabotage the game but not without consequences.(6th)

Group Seven: After the War—

The Effects on Families and What We've Learned

1. *We Remember the Holocaust* by David A. Adler (147 pp.). This nonfiction text deals with the events leading up to and throughout the Nazi occupation of Europe. Personal accounts from survivors, who were children during the Holocaust, are included with corresponding childhood pictures. Their recollections provide information about Kristallnacht; the roundups; those who risked their lives to help the Jews; and the transportation to, the life in, and the liberation of the concentration camps. A time line and glossary of terms are included.

2. *The Other Victims: First Person Stories of Non-Jews Persecuted by the Nazis* by Ina R. Friedman (214 pp.). The Jews were not the only people persecuted under Hitler's orders. This nonfiction book is organized into these categories: "Those 'Unworthy of Life,'" "The War Against the Church," "Racial Purification: Breeding the Master Race," "Mind Control," and "Slaves for the Nazi Empire."

3. *The Journey Back* by Johanna Reiss (224 pp.). Annie and her sister spent three years hiding from the Nazis, trying to save their lives. Now that the war is over, Annie must try to make a normal life for herself.(5th)

4. *The Cunning of History: The Holocaust and the American Future* by Richard Rubenstein (113 pp.). Rubenstein explores the inner workings of the Germans before and during the Holocaust. The methods used by Hitler to carry out his plans are also discussed.

5. *Escape from Warsaw* by Ian Serraillier (218 pp.). Originally titled *The Silver Sword*, this story is about the separation of the Balicki family during World War II. Joseph is arrested for turning Hitler's picture to face the wall during a religion lesson. After he escapes from prison and returns home, he finds his house destroyed and his wife and three children missing. He befriends Jan, a boy who listens to his laments about his own children. Joseph asks Jan to go with him to Switzerland where his family was to meet in the event of a separation. When Jan refuses, Joseph gives him a family trinket—a small silver sword—as a gift. When Joseph's children meet Jan, they recognize the silver sword and learn of their father's whereabouts.

6. *Grace in the Wilderness: After the Liberation 1945-1948* by Aranka Siegal (199 pp.). Piri, now 17, resides with a Swedish family while she searches for news of family and friends who also might have survived the Nazi concentration

camps. Although the Swedes accept her as their own daughter, she strives to hold on to her own identity and dreams of finding her blood relatives. The novel is dedicated to the many people who assisted the Jews in their efforts to find their families after the war.(7th)

7. *Roll of Thunder, Hear my Cry* by Mildred D. Taylor (210 pp.). Cassie Logan is being raised in a strong, determined family who constantly fights against the odds. The Logans are the only family who owns their own land; their friends are sharecroppers to the rich, white folks. Her family refuses to surrender to the prejudice and discrimination they are forced to face everyday due to their being black. Cassie learns firsthand what pride and courage mean as she faces the injustices, the indignities, and the frustrations her family is forced to confront.(6th) (Newbery Award Winner, an American Library Association Notable Children's Book and Best of the Best Books for Young Adults, and a National Book Award Nominee.)

World War II and Young Adult Novel Possibilities

Activities to Enhance Learning

There are several possible projects that students may construct as part of their collaborative group assignments. Allow students to choose the ones that work best for their respective novels and topics. I have included examples when possible.

1. Single-entry Literature/Composition Activities

Have students select a poignant passage from the book they have read. Have them copy the passage verbatim, including all bibliographic information. Then have them create three to five possible composition prompts that can be responded to without their having to read the entire book. The following example was created by Jerri Norris (See Example 2.1):

Example 2.1

Richter, Hans Peter.(1987). *Friedrich*. Translated by Edite Kroll. New York: Viking Penguin/Puffin Books.149 pp.(ISBN: 0-14-032205-1)

Jews are accused of being crafty and sly. How could they be anything else? Someone who must always live in fear of being tormented and hunted must be very strong in his soul to remain an upright human being.

Directions: Select one of the following writing assignments to complete. Peer response groups will meet tomorrow, and your first draft is due the following day. Be sure to provide examples whenever possible.

1) What minority groups can you think of whose title could be substituted for "Jews" in the above paragraph? In what ways have they been tormented or hunted to your knowledge?

2) Define an upright human being. Do most people fit into this category? What happens to the ones who don't? What are the rewards, if any, for the ones who do?

3) Teacher Neudorf speaks of being strong in the soul. What does he mean, specifically? Give your opinion of what "strong in the soul" is, and include examples of people that you feel best illustrate this description and explain why.

Besides learning how to cite material accurately, students get exposed to lots of reading material. Some students might choose to read some additional works beyond the class requirements. By having students spend five minutes doing free-writes, meaningful discussions can ensue.

2. Double-entry Literature/Composition Activities

Have each student select a poignant passage from his or her book and team up with another class member. By juxtaposing the passages, students are able to generate some provocative writing prompts (See Example 2.2).

Example 2.2

In *Roll of Thunder, Hear My Cry,* Cassie is treated as an inferior because she is black:

I started past her again, and again she got in my way.
"Ah, let her pass Lillian Jean," said Jeremy."She ain't done nothin' to you."
"She done something to me just standing in front of me."
With that, she reached for my arm and attempted to push me off the sidewalk. I braced myself and swept my arm backward, out of Lillian Jean's reach. But someone caught it from behind, painfully twisting it, and shoved me off the sidewalk into the road. I landed bottom first on the ground.(p. 86)

In *Summer of My German Soldier,* Anton, an escaped prisoner of war, gives Patty, an abused girl, a gift:

"The greater the value, the greater the pleasure in giving it. The ring is yours, P. B."
Then in the darkened silence, I heard him breathe in deeply."Am I still your teacher?" Without pausing for an answer, he continued, "Then I want you to learn this, our last, lesson. Even if you forget everything else I want you to remember that you are a person of value, and you have a friend who loved you enough to give you his most valued possession." (pp. 134-135)

1) Hitler believed that the Germans were the Master Race, better than any other human beings; Lillian Jean, a white girl, thinks she is better than Cassie who is black; and Patty, who was verbally and physically abused by her parents, thinks she is a worthless human being. What makes people believe that they are better or worse than somebody else? Is there such a thing as a person who is better or worse than another? For someone who thinks that way, how do they treat others or how are they treated?

2) We have all been told to "love one another as ourselves." Why is that so hard to do? What makes people be so hateful and hurtful to other human beings?

3. Lines to Create a Feeling

Have each student choose five passages of one to three lines. Working in groups, they should discard two lines apiece and organize the remaining passages to evoke some kind of mood. Encourage them to add a visual or auditory touch to enhance the effect. The following poem entitled "Never Forget" was created by Wendy S. Brown, Darin Dillard, Odalys Gordillo, and Lynn Miles (See Example 2.3).

Example 2.3

Never Forget

"Numbly I began to walk. Everyone's head was turned toward us. We were the only ones in the car who had to leave. With every step I took the aisle seemed to stretch out longer, but I put one foot in front of the other and kept my eyes straight ahead." (Levitin, p. 49)

NEVER FORGET

"Whenever I dreamed of a better world, I could only imagine a universe with no bells." (Wiesel, p. 84)

NEVER FORGET

"A mother knows. Don't you think I could see that you weren't getting enough to eat? No routine, no care at all—like little lost souls, all those children looking out of the windows!" (Levitin, p. 95)

NEVER FORGET

"Herr Schneider, the rabbi, and Friedrich all looked at me. I didn't know what to do. The rabbi was a stranger to me. And what about my mother and father? Didn't they stand closer to me than this Jew? Might I endanger myself and them for the sake of a stranger? (Richter, p. 126)

NEVER FORGET

"Even the most innocent victim is part of the process of his own undoing by virtue of the fact that he did not or could not take protective measures." (Rubenstein)

NEVER FORGET

"His luck he died THIS way." (Richter, p. 147)

NEVER FORGET

"From the depths of the mirror a corpse gazed back at me. The look in his eyes, as they stared into mine, has never left me.(Wiesel, p. 109)

NEVER FORGET

"'I'll never forget the sight,' Mother whispered. Beside us an old woman wept, her head pressed against her husband's shoulder.'America! God be praised!'" (Levitin, p. 148)

NEVER FORGET

"'What does he mean? What is Pearl Harbor?'" (Houston, p. 5)

NEVER FORGET

"That night Papa burned the flag he had brought with him from Hiroshima 35 years earlier. He burned a lot of papers too, documents, anything that might suggest he still had some connection with Japan. These precautions didn't do him much good." (Houston, p. 5)

NEVER FORGET

"Never shall I forget those frames which consumed my faith forever." (Wiesel, p. 32)

NEVER FORGET

"Never shall I forget these things, even if I am condemned to live as long as God Himself. Never!" ((Wiesel, p. 32)

NEVER FORGET

"The reasoning: wartime necessity." (Houston, p. 91)

NEVER FORGET

4. Dioramas

Have students create a visual representation of a memorable scene in their books using a shoe box as the stage. After reading *Alicia, My Story*, one of my students created a diorama of one of the bunkers (a small space dug underneath a room) Alicia hid in during one of the Nazi actions. Because Nazis would shout and fire their guns to try to make babies cry, babies were hidden elsewhere since their crying could give away their hideout. In Chapter Eight, Alicia goes up to give baby Shmuel more camomile tea to make him sleep and faints when she finds him shot to death by a German soldier. Her family and friends are beneath her unaware of the tragedy they'll discover when they reemerge.

5. Memorabilia Bags

While reading their novels, students gather a minimum of 15 objects representative of their stories. I have students number their objects and provide a brief explanation for each. After reading *Summer of My German Soldier*, Laurie A. Van Zant created the following bag with these items (See Example 2.4).

Example 2.4

1) a female doll - represents Patty
2) a bag of sand - from Sharon's sandbox
3) a dictionary - Patty read in one every day
4) small red comb - the one Patty's mother made her use to comb her hair
5) a shoe - from the shoe department in Patty's parents' store
6) a belt - Patty's father beat her with one
7) cotton balls - the prisoners were made to pick them
8) a train - the train brought the prisoners to town and Anton escaped on the 10:15
9) post card from Tennessee - represents Patty's trip to her grandmother's
10) two hard cover books - Patty bought them using the money given to her by her grandmother
11) a monogrammed, blue shirt with a blood stain on it - the one Patty gave to her father for Father's Day, which he never wore and subsequently gave to Anton to help him escape
12) $4.67 - the amount of money Patty gave to Anton
13) a gold ring - Anton's prized possession which he gave to Patty
14) a black Bible - the sheriff gave one to Patty
15) yellow shoe box tied with a red ribbon - Ruth brought Patty chicken breasts in one to eat while she was in the reformatory

---

6. Collages

Very similar to memorabilia bags, students create a collage of their novels using magazine pictures. Each student is required to explain how each picture relates to the story in an oral presentation. As an added bonus, students often are exposed to different magazines and read many additional articles not required in your class as they browse.

7. A Dictionary of Terms

Have each student select a minimum of five vocabulary words from their individual books. Students are to find others who have identified the same word and derive a common definition for a class vocabulary book. Definitions must be paraphrased (See Example 2.5).

Example 2.5

1) Allies: The anti-German nations during World War II: Russia, England, and the United States.

2) Anti-Semitism: Being hostile to or discriminatory against Jews.

3) Aryans: Hitler's master race—tall, blonde, and fair-skinned.

4) Auschwitz, Treblinka, Maidanek, Kulmhof, Lublin: death camps in Poland that had gas chambers.

5) Boche: an uncomplimentary nickname given to Germans, from the German word meaning "hard skull."

6) Dachau: an infamous concentration camp near Munich.

7) D-Day: On June 6, 1944, the combined Allied Forces crossed the English Channel to France to begin retaking occupied Europe.

8) Deport: to expel from a country.

9) Einsatz gruppen (special duty groups): When Germany invaded Russia in 1941, these groups rounded up the Jews, tortured them, made them dig their own graves, and shot them. Their estimated murders are 1.5 million.

10) Emigrate: to leave a county in order to reside elsewhere.

11) Fuhrer: Hitler's political title.

12) Ge(heime) Sta(ats)po(lizei): Germany's state police, better known as the Gestapo; led by Heydrich.

13) Judenrate: Jewish councils in Germany ordered to carry out Nazi orders.

14) Kristallnacht: The Night of the Broken Glass, November 9, 1938, when SS members broke windows of Jewish shops and homes in response to the murder of the German ambassador to France by a young Jew whose family had been sent to a concentration camp.

15) Liberation: release from oppression such as the freeing of Holland from German control.

8. Additional Annotations of Nonfiction Articles

Each student is to find and write an annotation for at least one outside newspaper, journal, or magazine article that relates in some way to their reading. For someone who read a book in "Group Three: Those Who Risked Their Lives," a possible example might be the following:

Gies, Miep and Allison Gold.(1987, May 5)."The Woman Who Hid Anne Frank." *Family Circle,* 88-96.

> This excerpt from the book includes a detailed account of how Miep hid the Franks and how Anne's diary was preserved and returned to Mr. Frank.

For someone who read a book in "Group Seven: After the War—The Effects on Families and What We've Learned," a possible example might be the following:

Camper, John.(1978, April 16)."The Holocaust: Hitler's Final Solution." *Gainesville Sun.*

> This information-packed article is a journalist's analysis of how and why the Holocaust happened.

9. A Timeline

Take some butcher paper and tape it on two walls or halfway around the classroom at eye level. Segment the paper by year starting with 1938 and ending with 1945, but allow students to extend the timeline in either direction if necessary. Draw a line, horizontally, about one third of the way down the entire length of the paper. While students are reading their respective books, have them jot down on scrap paper all dates and information, paraphrased, about the material they are reading. On the top third of the butcher paper, have students record historic dates with their corresponding events in black ink. On the bottom two thirds, have students write the corresponding vignettes about the people they are reading about. It is helpful to keep the vignettes color-coded by books, and by having students include their initials, those who want to discuss a specific occurrence can consult "the expert." As material accumulates, the interest level is heightened and students gain a sense of chronology about the war (Example 2.6).

Example 2.6

November 9, 1938 - Kristallnacht

The first act of anti-Semitism hit the Appleman family when
Alicia's oldest brother, Zachary, is attacked by five Polish university students on his way to school in May of 1938. They kicked him in the ribs, treated him like a punching bag, and smashed his violin, all because of his religious beliefs.

In 1938, there were 18,000 Jews in the Polish city of Buczacz, which was about one-third of the total population.

December 7, 1941 - the bombing of Pearl Harbor
America's entry into the war

In 1941, Alicia survives a jump from a moving train en route to a labor camp and learns that her brother, Bunio, has been murdered by the Nazis.

---

10. A Map Display

A lot of these books refer to specific locations and become confusing after a while. By having students keep records of the locations of the people in their books by charting their progress on maps, students gain a better sense of the story and acquire memorable, geographical information. Maps should be displayed on one or more of the walls in the classroom.

11. A Classroom Museum

Each student brings in an artifact representative of World War II for display. For example, when a student brings in some "zlotys," Polish currency, for others to see, it really makes the time period come alive for others.

Additionally, each student is to bring in at least three pictures depicting the time period. Have students form teams through the creation of logical groupings of the pictures, not exceeding five people per team. Have each team arrange the pictures for display on some room dividers. If room dividers are unavailable, makeshift displays can be made with two-by-fours, sheets of plywood, and wallpaper. Have students research, write, and record information about their pictures on cassette recorders. By attaching headphones, visitors and other students can listen to the recorded information while looking at the photos.

12. A Documentary

Students prepare a documentary incorporating information from each of the books that were read. Visuals, such as time lines and maps, should be used whenever possible.

13. Compare and Contrast Then and Now

Not long ago, we experienced the 50th anniversary of the bombing of Pearl Harbor. There were television documentaries and newspapers' accounts of what happened. Students find it interesting to read actual articles from newspapers dated December 7, 1941, and to view news footage from that time period and compare and contrast that information with what we know today.

The United States Holocaust Memorial Council was established in 1980, with Elie Wiesel now serving as its chairman. Additional information about the organization can be obtained by writing to the following address: 2000 L Street, N. W., Suite 588, Washington, DC, 20036.

After students interview various World War II veterans about their impressions of the war, have them then ask the same questions of students in another grade level. The difference in attitudes is often frightening and lends itself to discussions on why *Anne Frank: Diary of a Young Girl* is required reading in most schools.

14. Examples of Prejudice Today

Each student is to find a newspaper or magazine account of some act of discrimination today. Students are often shocked by the many forms of prejudice and become painfully aware of the relevancy of World War II to us today, especially when they read about political candidates like David Duke. There are often extreme examples in their own communities: In Jacksonville, Florida, a judge with more than 30 years' experience made unbelievable racial slurs that brought Jesse Jackson to the scene; in Tampa, "Skinheads" or Neo-Nazis go around beating up blacks and homosexuals; and in Orlando, churches are being burned by arson. It is, unfortunately, easy for students to find current reports about the ill-treatment of people based on various differences such as race, religion, age, gender, sexual preference, handicaps, and diseases, to name a few.

15. Their Own Ideas

By always having this as an option, I have built up my repertoire of useful ideas through the suggestions made by my students. Students in my last class came up with these possibilities:

* Prepare a book talk.
* Create a dinner party inviting a key character from each book.
* Identify key scenes in each book and rewrite them in play form. Sequence the scenes and perform a readers' theatre.
* Like Anne in A *Diary of a Young Girl*, write a week's worth of diary entries for one of the characters in each book.
* Contact one of the authors and invite him or her to speak to the class. One of my students contacted Alicia Appleman-Jurman and orchestrated a project to raise money to bring her to our school. By contacting your author's publisher, you may be able to arrange him or her to speak for the price of a plane ticket and lodging.

Conclusion

In previous years, I have been bombarded by students asking, "Why do we have to read this?" while studying *Anne Frank: Diary of a Young Girl*. Never have I had that question asked since I began incorporating the use of adolescent literature with this classic. My students become painfully aware of hierarchies, manipulation, and prejudice. In this world of cultural diversity, it is imperative that we teach our students to celebrate—not condemn—our differences.

References

Aaron, C.(1982). *Gideon*. Philadelphia: J. B. Lippincott Company.

Abells, C.(1986). *The children we remember*. New York: Greenwillow Books.

Adler, D. A.(1989). *We remember the Holocaust*. New York: Henry Holt & Company.

Appleman-Jurman, A.(1990). *Alicia: My story*. New York: Bantam Books.

Arnold, C. & Silverstein, H.(1985). *Anti-Semitism: A modern perspective*. New York: Julian Messner.

Arrick, F.(1981). *Chernowitz*. New York: Bradbury Press.

Baklanov, G.(1989). *Forever nineteen*. Translated from Russian by Antonina W. Bouis. Philadelphia: J. B. Lippincott Company.

Brigg, E.(1972). *Stand up and fight: The story of Emil Brigg*. London: George G. Harrap & Company.

Fluek, T. K.(1990). *Memories of my life in a Polish village: 1930-1949*. New York: Alfred A. Knopf.

Forman, J.(1968). *The traitors*. New York: Farrar, Straus, & Giroux.

Frank, A.(1972). *Anne Frank: The diary of a young girl*. New York: Pocket Books.

Friedman, I. R.(1990). *The other victims: First person stories of non-Jews persecuted by the Nazis*. Boston: Houghton Mifflin.

Gallo, D. R., Chair and the Committee on the Senior High School Booklist.(1985). *Books for you: A booklist for senior high students*. Urbana, Illinois: National Council of Teachers of English.

Green, C. J.(1989). *The war at home*. New York: Macmillan/McElderry.

Greene, B.(1973). *Summer of my German soldier*. New York: Dial Press.

Hartman, E.(1982). *War without friends*. Translated by Patricia Crampton. New York: Crown.

Hautzig, E.(1987). *The endless steppe*. New York: Harper Keypoint.

Hersey, J.(1946). *Hiroshima*. New York: Alfred A. Knopf, Inc.

Houston, J. W. & Houston, J. D.(1990). *Farewell to Manzanar*. New York: Bantam Books.

Irwin, Hadley.(1987). *Kim / Kimi* New York: Macmillan.

Kerr, M. E.(1978). *Gentlehands*. New York: Bantam Books.

Kosinsky, J.(1972). *The painted bird*. New York: Bantam Books.

Kuchler-Silberman, L.(1990). *My hundred children*. New York: Dell Laurel-Leaf.

Laird, C.(1990). *Shadow of the wall*. New York: Greenwillow Books.

Leitner, I. & Leitner, I. A.(1990). *Fragments of Isabella*. New York: Dell Laurel Paperback.

Levitin, S.(1970). *Journey to America*. New York: Macmillan.

Levoy, M.(1977). *Alan and Naomi*. New York: Harper & Row.

Lingard, J.(1990). *Tug of war*. New York: Lodestar Books.

Lowry, L.(1989). *Number the stars*. New York: Dell Yearling.

Magorian, M.(1981). *Good night, Mr. Tom*. New York: Harper & Row.

Maruki, T.(1980). *Hiroshima no pika*. New York: Lothrop, Lee & Shepard.

Mazer, H.(1990). *The last mission*. New York: Dell Laurel-Leaf.

Meltzer, M.(1988). *Rescue: The story of how Gentiles saved Jews in the Holocaust*. New York: Harper & Row.

Miklowitz, G. D.(1990). *The war between the classes*. New York: Dell Laurel-Leaf.

Moskin, M. D.(1990). *I am Rosemarie*. New York: Dell Laurel-Leaf.

Mowat, F.(1990). *And no birds sang*. New York: Bantam Seal Paperback.

Neimark, A. E.(1986). *One man's valor: Leo Baeck and the Holocaust*. New York: Lodestar.

Nilsen, A. P. (Ed.), and the Committee on the Junior High and Middle School Booklist.(1991). *Your reading: A booklist for junior high and middle school students*.8th ed. Urbana, Illinois: National Council of Teachers of English.

Ossowski, L.(1985). *Star without a sky*. Translated by Ruth Crowley. Minneapolis: Lerner.

Reiss, J.(1972). *The upstairs room*. New York: Harper & Row.

Reiss, J.(1987). *The journey back*. New York: Harper & Row.

Richter, H. P.(1987). *Friedrich*. Translated by Edite Kroll. New York: Viking Penguin/Puffin Books.

Richter, H. P.(1987). *I was there*. Translated by Edite Kroll. New York: Viking Penguin/Puffin Books.

Rittner, C.(Ed.).(1986). *The courage to care*. New York: University Press.

Roth-Hano, R.(1988). *Touch wood: A girlhood in occupied France*. New York: Four Winds Press.

Rubenstein, R.(1975). *The cunning of history: The Holocaust and the American future*. New York: Harper & Row.

Rudman, M. & Rosenberg's, S. P.(summer, 1991). Confronting history: Holocaust books for children. *The New Advocate, 4* (3).

Sender, R. M.(1990). *The cage*. New York: Bantam Books.

Serraillier, I.(1974). *Escape from Warsaw*. New York: Scholastic.

Siegal, A.(1985). *Grace in the wilderness: After the liberation 1945-1948*. New York: Farrar, Straus, & Giroux.

Siegal, A.(1981). U*pon the head of the goat: A childhood in Hungary 1939-1944.* New York: Farrar Straus & Giroux.

Taylor, M. D.(1976). R*oll of thunder, hear my cry.* New York: Bantam Books.

ten Boom, C., Sherrill, J. & Sherrill, E.(1990). Th*e hiding place.* New York: Bantam Books.

Uchida, Y.(1977). *Journey to Topaz.* New York: Charles Scribner's Sons.

Volavkova, H.(Ed.).(1971). I *never saw another butterfly.*2nd ed. New York: McGraw Hill.

Wiesel, E.(1990). N*ight.* Translated by Stella Rodway. New York: Bantam Books.

Wiesel, E.(1982). Da*wn.* New York: Bantam Books.

Zamoyska-Panek, C. & Holmberg, F. B.(1990). Ha*ve you forgotten: A memoir of Poland 1939-1945.* New York: Doubleday Books.

Zieman, J.(1977). Th*e cigarette sellers of Three Crosses Square.* New York: Avon.

Chapter 3

The Adventures of Huckleberry Finn, Prejudice, and Adolescent Literature

JO HIGGINS AND JOAN FOWINKLE

Introduction

When given a novel such as *The Adventures of Huckleberry Finn*, students often respond with statements like, "Why do we have to read this? Slavery was a long time ago," or "I don't see what this has to do with me." They raise a good point. Through the use of adolescent literature, we can modernize an otherwise seemingly outdated theme. This chapter is designed to enable students to experience vicariously some situations in which prejudice occurs. Having these vicarious experiences and responding to them may help students develop more empathy and help them clarify some of their own attitudes and values.

The young adult literature used in this chapter was chosen for several reasons: It reflects the diversity of prejudice, promotes thoughtful exploration of the human dilemma, and is relevant to the lives of our students; and the use of this literature provides a means of creating a bridge to the often required reading of the classic The *Adventures of Huckleberry Finn*.

This chapter provides the opportunity for students to work cooperatively as well as individually. Activities have been planned to meet the needs and desires of students' various learning styles. Our goal is to offer students a variety of activities while still providing a structural base.

Preparation

The activities described in this chapter are designed to take place approximately one week before actually teaching The *Adventures of Huckleberry Finn*; however, some additional preparation is necessary before beginning these activities.

Three to Four Weeks Before Teaching *The Adventures of Huckleberry Finn*

Several weeks before teaching *The Adventures of Huckleberry Finn*, the teacher should select a day to brainstorm some ideas concerning prejudice, divide the class into groups, and assign novels to read outside of class. We suggest that the teacher and students brainstorm all the possible kinds of prejudice that exist, list them on the board, and then see if the list can be broken down into categories. We came up with five major categories of prejudice: racial, age, class/status, religion/lifestyle, and handicap. Any categories may be used as long as corresponding young adult novels are found.

Figure 3.1

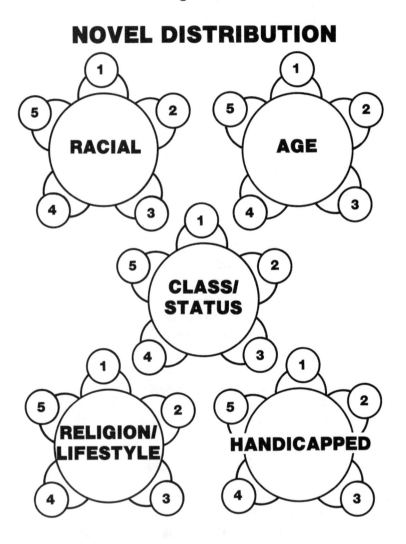

NOVEL DISTRIBUTION

The next step is to put the students into five groups, each of which will read young adult novels on a particular kind of prejudice. One group would read novels about racial prejudice, another about age prejudice, and so on. (See figure

3.1) While the teacher may assign the groups, more interest may be generated if students are allowed to pick the topic of prejudice most interesting to them.

After the groups are selected, young adult novels about prejudice should be introduced to the students. This can be done in a variety of ways. The teacher can give an oral summary of each book, books can be given to each group for the students to peruse, or a book pass can be conducted (Tchudi & Mitchell, 139-140).

The purpose of the book pass is to expose each student to as many books as possible in a limited amount of time. There should be enough young adult novels for each student to have one. Have each student get out a sheet of paper, a pen or a pencil, and then give each one a book. Instruct the students to find out as much about the book as they can before time is called. They may do this by reading the cover, the introduction, or by simply starting to read the book. After two minutes, call time. If students feel the book is one that they might like to read then the author, title, and one descriptive line are jotted down on the paper. At this point, students then pass the book onto the next person, and this continues until each student has had a chance to peruse about 15 books. Have students rank order their preferences and allow students to negotiate who will read which book.

By the end of the class period, each student should have selected a young adult novel within his or her area of prejudice to read outside of class. The length of time given to read the novel will depend on the class size, concurrent activities, and the ability level of the class.

We have compiled a suggested reading list of young adult novels that address the various forms of prejudice mentioned above. This is by no means an exhaustive list but rather a place to start. (See Figure 3.2) Complete bibliographic information can be found at the end of the chapter.

Figure 3.2
Suggested Reading List

Racial Prejudice
1. *I Know Why the Caged Bird Sings* by Maya Angelou
2. *Sounder* by William H. Armstrong
3. *Iggie's House* by Judy Blume
4. *When the Legends Die* by H. Borland
5. *Cornbread, Earl, and Me* by R.L. Fair
6. *Julie of the Wolves* by Jean Craighead George
7. *Farewell to Manzanar* by J.W. & J.D. Houston
8. *Their Eyes were Watching God* by Zora Neale Hurston
9. *In a Bluebird's Eye* by A. Kornfeld
10. *Carlota* by Scott O'Dell
11. *Roll of Thunder, Hear My Cry* by Mildred D. Taylor
12. *It's Crazy to Stay Chinese in Minnesota* by E. Telemaque
13. *Come a Stranger* by Cynthia Voigt

Age

1. *Better than Laughter* by C. Aaron
2. *Nobody's Baby Now* by C.L. Benjamin
3. *Toby, Granny and George* by R. Branscum
4. *Marvin and Tige* by F. Glass
5. *What About Grandma?* by Hadley and Irwin
6. *Gentlehands* by M.E. Kerr
7. *Going Backwards* by Norma Klein
8. *Anastasia Again* by Lois Lowry.
9. *The Summer of the Great Grandfather* by Madeleine L'Engle
10. *After the Rain* by Norma Fox Mazer
11. *Won't Know Till I Get There* by Walter Dean Myers
12. *The Adrian Mole Diaries* by Sue Townsend

Class/Status

1. *Yes is Better than No* by B. Baylor
2. *Viva Chicano* by Frank Bonham
3. *Home Before Dark* by Sue Ellen Bridgers
4. *Outside Looking In* by James Lincoln Collier
5. *When the Stars Begin to Fall* by James Lincoln Collier
6. *The Chocolate War* by Robert Cormier
7. *Thursday's Children* by Rumer Godden
8. *The Outsiders* by S.E. Hinton
9. *In With the Out Crowd* by Norma Howe
10. *Go Up the Road* by E.S. Lampman
11. *One Fat Summer* by Robert Lipsyte
12. *The Meantime* by Bernie MacKinnon
13. *The War Between the Classes* by Gloria D. Miklowitz
14. *Hoops* by Walter Dean Myers
15. *The Crossing* by Gary Paulsen
16. *Famous All Over Town* by Danny Santiago

Religion/Lifestyle

1. *Chernowitz* by Fran Arrick
2. *Are You There, God? It's Me, Margaret* by Judy Blume
3. *People Like Us* by Barbara Cohen
4. *Anne Frank: The Diary of a Young Girl* by Anne Frank
5. *Man Without a Face* by Isabelle Holland
6. *Nite Kites* by M.E. Kerr
7. *Now That I Know* by Norma Klein
8. *Pageant* by Kathryn Lasky
9. *No Way Home* by M. Levy
10. *My Name is Asher Lev* by Chaim Potok
11. *The Chosen* by Chaim Potok
12. *The Upstairs Room* by J. Reiss
13. *Happy Endings are All Alike* by Sandra Scoppettone
14. *Trying Hard to Hear You* by Sandra Scoppettone

Handicap

1. *Deenie* by Judy Blume
2. *Winning* by Robin Brancato
3. *The Crazy Horse Electric Game* by Chris Crutcher
4. *Running Loose* by Chris Crutcher
5. *Joni* by J. Erickson

6. *I Never Promised You a Rose Garden* by Joanne Greenberg
7. *It's Too Late for Sorry* by E. Hanlon
8. *The Story of Stevie Wonder* by J. Haskins
9. *Tell Me that You Love Me, Junie Moon* by M. Kellogg
10. *Little Little* by M.E. Kerr
11. *A Boy Called Hopeless* by D. Melton
12. *Wheels for Walking* by Sandra Richmond
13. *Only Love* by S. Sallis
14. *Izzy, Willy-Nilly* by Cynthia Voigt

Application

This part of the chapter is divided into three primary sections in relation to teaching *The Adventures of Huckleberry Finn*. First, Introductory Activities, includes an overview of prejudice and organizes the students' collaborative group activities. Next, Concurrent Activities, involves teaching the novel while allowing students time to work in their groups on various projects. Finally, Concluding Activities, is designed to synthesize both the themes of the *Adventures of Huckleberry Finn* and prejudice in general. (See Figure 3.3)

Figure 3.3

STRUCTURE OF APPLICATION

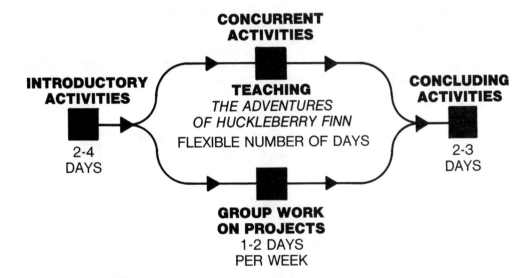

Introductory Activities

This part of the unit was designed to take approximately four days but may be expanded or reduced to fit individual schedules and interests. For the sake of clarity, we are going to organize and refer to each section as a "day," that is understood to be one or more actual teaching days depending on the needs and interests of the teacher and class.

Day One

The first day of Introductory Activities should begin with some kind of hook to capture the students' interest in the topic of prejudice. In our case, we use a slide presentation on racism that Jo created that involves a series of black and white slides set to the music of Paul McCartney's "Ebony and Ivory.". There are any number of things that could be used although we feel that something with a strong visual or auditory impact is most effective—perhaps a clip from the evening news, a feature article from the local paper, a video of the Civil Rights Movement during the 60s, or a poignant scene from a young adult novel.

After your introduction, have the students freewrite a response to the presentation for five to seven minutes. Then ask for volunteers to share their freewrites and discuss them. At this point the teacher can segue into a discussion of key terms, noting their definitions and making distinctions between them. We suggest the following terms:

1. *prejudice* - prejudgment of people on the basis of their membership in a particular group;

2. *discrimination* - acting differently toward people on the basis of their membership in a particular group;

3. *racism* - holding negative attitudes toward and discriminating against people on the basis of a belief that one race is inherently superior to another.

At this point, the teacher may wish to distribute a list to each student of the kinds of prejudice and categories that were developed earlier and may also, at this time, give an overview of the week's activities.

Day Two (By this time all students should be finished reading their young adult novels.)

This day begins with an opening activity called "Picture Categorizing." A group of approximately ten pictures, clearly numbered, should be displayed around the room. These pictures should be of all kinds of people: black, white, young, old, men, women, and so forth. Three or four of the pictures should be of people who are considered successful but may not look as if they are. Ask each student to categorize the pictures by giving each one a rating between one and ten (one being the most likely, ten the least) in response to the following questions:

1. Which person is the most intelligent?

2. Which person is the nicest?

3. Which person is the most successful?

After the students have rated the pictures, the teacher reveals the known identities of the photographs. This should be followed by a discussion of why the students chose different people over others. The teacher may also want to discuss the idea that it is normal and often necessary to make discriminations.

The students should then assemble into their groups according to the young adult novels they read, and list the ways that prejudice manifests itself in their respective young adult books. They should make a second list of the specific solutions to the prejudicial conflicts presented. Both lists may be written on large pieces of paper and shared with the other groups, thus exposing the whole class to a wide range of prejudices and possible solutions.

Day Three

While some teachers may be comfortable with group work, other may not be. We have found that our groups work more efficiently when they have some basic structure. We operate groups on the basic premise that each and every person is an integral part of the group and that in order for the group to function each person has specific tasks for which she or he is responsible. A group folder containing organizational material is essential to the success of the group. To help build group unity, the teacher may allow students two to five minutes to come up with a group name, which can then be used to decorate the group folder. At this point, we distribute the "Group Projects Responsibility Sheet." (See Figure 3.4)

Figure 3.4

Group Name _____Period _____

Group Projects Responsibility Sheet

Record Keeper _____
The Record Keeper will be responsible for the writing and record keeping for the group. S/he will update, and maintain this sheet. This person will also write and submit a detailed, daily progress report. The report will contain an account of all the activities the group completed that day.

Time/Task Coordinator _____
The Time/Task Coordinator will be responsible for developing a schedule to ensure that the group will be able to complete the project on time. The schedule should be written and submitted to the teacher at the beginning of the second class period. This person is also responsible for keeping the group focused and on task.

Supplies/Equipment Manager _____
The Supplies/Equipment Manager will be responsible for gathering the supplies needed to complete the project. S/he may submit a written list to the Record Keeper to attach to the daily progress report so the teacher will be aware of the group's needs and can offer assistance.

Extra _____
The extra will fill in for anyone who is absent. S/he will also help in any capacity that is needed in order for the project to be completed.

Ambassador _____
The ambassador will monitor and assess the group's functioning. S/he will be responsible for designating tasks. If the group has any questions or problems, he or she will be responsible for asking the teacher for help.

Group Project(s):

We then go over each responsibility in detail with the entire class. After we have answered all questions, the students in each group decide which responsibility they prefer and fill out the top part of the sheet. The sheet can then be glued to the inside of the group folder. The next decision for the group to make is the project they are going to work on that will reflect the type of prejudice identified in their individual young adult novels.

There are three basic approaches to the group projects. All projects should revolve around the kind of prejudice depicted in the adolescent literature read by the students. The group can choose to concentrate on one member's novel if they feel that it is the best representation of the type of prejudice they are addressing. In this case, the group member who read the book will need to share in detail what his or her book was about and may even want to come up with an outline or plot summary. The group's second option is to do a group project that incorporates ideas or events from all of the young adult novels they have read. The third option available is for the group members to do individual projects on their young adult novels but to present them in some cohesive fashion as a group. This option allows group members to work more independently but requires more creativity on their part in presenting the projects. (See Figure 3.5)

Figure 3.5

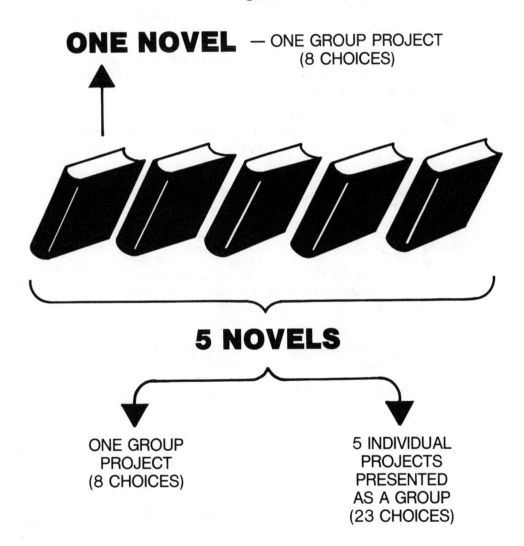

ONE NOVEL — ONE GROUP PROJECT (8 CHOICES)

5 NOVELS

ONE GROUP PROJECT (8 CHOICES)

5 INDIVIDUAL PROJECTS PRESENTED AS A GROUP (23 CHOICES)

When explaining these three options to the class, the teacher may distribute the "Group Projects" handout. (See Figure 3.6).

Figure 3.6
Group Projects

Each group must choose either a group project or five individual projects that can be presented in a cohesive fashion. Some group projects require the group to concentrate on one particular book while others can bring together a theme or idea presented in a number of books. If your group chooses to do individual projects, it is recommended that one person be a spokesperson who introduces the theme the group is working on and the individual projects the group members have done.

If you come up with an idea that is not on this list, you can present it to the teacher. If it is accepted, it will be included as a permanent idea for future group projects. Each group should decide upon a project or projects fairly quickly.

After your group chooses an idea (or ideas) that you wish to work on, look up the specific details in the idea file box at the back of the room. The ideas are filed alphabetically. Once a project is selected, begin working on a plan of action with each of you doing your part.

Your group's presentation to the class should be five to ten minutes long. Presentations will be graded according to appropriate content, creativity, evidence of time spent, thoroughness, neatness, and cohesiveness/flow.

Group Projects—One Novel	Group Projects—Several Novels
Group Debate	Group Debate
Newspaper	Group Role-play
Panel Discussion	Newspaper
Rewrite as a Play	Panel Discussion
Slide/photo Presentation	Play
Time Period Presentation	Slide/photo Presentation

Individual Projects—To Be Presented As a Group

Alternate Ending	Design a Game
Background Music	Design a Symbol
Book Jacket	Diorama or Model
Bulletin Board Character Sketch	Dramatic/mood Lighting
Bulletin Board Display	Newspaper Articles
Cartoon Strips	Oral Presentation
Character Sketch	Personality Folder
Character Sketchbook	Story Sales-pitch
Create a Book	TV Commercial
Create a Collage	Take on the Author
Create a Diary	Vocabulary
Current Events	

This list of projects is by no means exclusive. There may be some projects that a teacher would like to add or delete. Detailed descriptions of the projects can be listed on paper and a complete set given to each group. Another option is to place the project descriptions on index cards and keep them in a file box somewhere in the room. The specific projects that we have listed on the "Group Projects" handout are detailed and set up so that you may copy them and paste them on index cards for students' use. (See Figure 3.7).

Figure 3.7
Group Projects (One Novel)

Group Debate

Knowing that a debate is the intelligent, constructive exchange of ideas and opinions, have each person in your group choose a character in the story he or she wants to represent and set up a debate between characters. The debate may center around one particular conflict or an entire theme. If there are not enough characters in the story for each person to have a part, one person can act as the mediator. The debate should be written up and submitted at the time of the presentation.

Group Role-Play

Role-playing is the taking on of another's position and psychological perspective to gain greater insight into a person's psyche. Have each person in your group choose a character in a novel and play out a scene (or several scenes). Each person should try to assume the character's position and perspective as much as possible. A written script must accompany the presentation.

Mock Trial

Set up a mock trial to determine the guilt or innocence of a character in your novel. You can have one person be the judge, one the accused, one the prosecutor, one the defense attorney, and the class will be jurors. Be sure to have the attorneys ask questions that effectively reveal the crime so that the rest of the class will know what happened. Another alternative is to put the author of the book on trial. This is particularly effective if you feel the author was unjust or biased in his/her writing. A written script must be submitted at the time of the presentation.

Newspaper

Design a newspaper (a minimum of two pages) that includes articles reporting different conflicts from the story. Be sure to include catchy headlines, a few pictures, and one or two advertisements. You can divide your group according to specific tasks: one person is the editor, one or two reporters, one layout person, and so forth, or all members can work together on each aspect of the paper.

Panel Discussion

Each person is responsible for presenting the views of one person in the novel. If there are not enough main characters, one person can be the moderator and ask key questions. Questions should be made up ahead of time and should reveal the details of the book's main conflicts so the rest of the class can follow. Some questions can be given to members of the class ahead of time, and, if time permits, classmates can ask questions that are not preselected. Another alternative to this activity is to create a panel of experts (e.g., doctor, lawyer, clergy, etc.) to answer questions about the events of the novel from their perspective.

Rewrite as a Play

Rewrite the novel as an abridged play. Be sure to include as many of the main events as possible. Your group can work on the script together, or you can divide the story up and have each person write a scene. If you divide it up, however, you will need to make your writing styles match. If you are having difficulty writing a scene, have some of your group-mates act out the conflict to give you a better idea of how it actually happened.

Slide/photo Presentation

Create a photo or slide story of scenes from the novel, or create a presentation that represents the theme from the novel. Scenes can be staged using a few props and some costumes. Either write a script or find some dramatic music to accompany your presen-tation. It will probably be best to record the music/narration on a tape to play along with the pictures/slides so that the timing will be accurate.

Time Period Presentation

Authors are often strongly influenced by the times in which they lived. Present a skit that depicts the time period in which your story took place or the time period in which your author wrote/grew up. Be sure to study and include costumes, lingo, mannerisms, and so forth as much as possible. A written script must accompany the presentation.

Chronological Scenes

This project can only be done if the topic you are discussing has changed over a period of time. If it has, your group can write and act out a series of short scenes that depict the various stages in the development of your topic. For example, if your topic is the Civil Rights Movement, you could act out a scene from before the Civil War, just before the turn of the century, the Depression, the '60s, and the present. Each scene does not have to contain every group member, but be sure to include all group members at least once. Or, one or two members can write the scripts and the rest act them out. Or, one or two people can narrate the scenes while two or three others act them out. A written script must accompany the presentation.

Group Projects (Several Novels)

Create a Book

Create a book that reflects the main theme or idea of the novels your group has read. Your book can include poetry, illustrations, interviews, comic strips, and so forth. Each person can contribute one page for each section of the book (poetry, illustrations, etc.), or one person can be in charge of creating an entire section. Your presentation to the class will consist of reading the book aloud and explaining how the illustrations relate to the theme.

Group Debate

Pick one person as the mediator and divide the rest of your group into two. Knowing that a debate is the intelligent constructive exchange of ideas and opinions, have each group take a side concerning your topic and debate the pros and cons of the issue. It is helpful if you have questions and arguments written before you present the debate. You can also involve your classmates by letting them ask questions.

Group Role-Play

Role-playing is the taking on of another's position and psychological perspective to gain greater insight into a person's psyche. Have each person in your group write a short skit depicting a conflict from her or his novel. Assign the roles and act out the scenes. Make sure the topic you are representing is clearly shown in each skit.

Newspaper

Design a newspaper (two or three pages is sufficient) that includes articles reporting different conflicts from the novels your group members have read. Be sure to include catchy headlines, a few pictures, and one or two advertisements. You can divide your group according to specific tasks (one person is the editor, one or two reporters, one layout person, etc.) or all members can work together on each aspect of the paper.

Panel Discussion

Each person is responsible for his or her own book. Generate a list of questions that you could answer about your book that would reveal the major events in the story (group members can help by asking you questions that they have about your book). Pick several of your classmates and give each of them one question to ask your panel. If time permits, classmates may also be permitted to ask questions of their own.

Play

Write a play that incorporates conflicts from all of the novels your group members have read. Choose parts and perform them. Your group can work on the script together or can divide it up according to scenes. If you divide it up, however, you will need to make your writing styles match. If you are having difficulty writing a scene, have some of your group members act out the conflict to give you a better idea of how it actually happened.

Slide/photo Presentation

Create a photo or slide show depicting various conflicts concerning your topic as presented in your novels. Scenes can be staged using a few props and some costumes. Either write a script or find some dramatic music to accompany your presentation. It will probably be best to record the music/narration on a tape to play along with the pictures/slides so that the timing will be accurate.

Individual Projects

Alternate Ending

This is a good project to do if you are not pleased with the way your novel ended. Pretend that you are the author and write an alternate ending to the story. Be sure to include information that tells the reader where your ending begins. Try to imitate the author's style as much as possible. When you present your ending to the class, you will also need to give a brief explanation of the story and how the author ended it.

Background Music

While your group is giving their presentation, provide a background of appropriate sound effects, whether live or on tape. Some record distributors have sound effects albums that you might be able to use.

Book Jacket

Create a book jacket for your novel. Along with the title, create an illustration of an important incident, character, or object in the book. You can use any medium (chalk, crayons, paints, magazine cut-outs, etc.). Inside the book cover, on the two flaps, fasten a brief book report including a summary that alludes to the significance of the cover illustration. Also include a brief statement about the author if possible.

Bulletin Board Character Sketch

Create cutout sketches of each character in your novel, and mount the sketches on the bulletin board. Write a short script depicting the characters' development throughout the novel. Read the script aloud to the class and move the sketches on the bulletin board accordingly. If it is too much to do the entire novel, pick several important scenes and portray them.

Bulletin Board Display

Fill the bulletin board with pictures, quotes, and original art. Number each item. Make a tape (or script) that identifies each item and its significance in reference to your novel and your group's topic. Play the tape or read the script to the class.

Cartoon Strips

Create a series (at least five) of cartoon strips that reflect the main theme of your novel. Be sure to include some of the major conflicts presented in the book or create similar modern-day conflicts between your cartoon characters.

Character Sketches

Create a character sketchbook of the characters in your novel by having each page contain an accurate, easily recognized representation of each character. You can cut out pictures from magazines or draw your own. Below each illustration, write a caption (perhaps a quotation from the book) or a brief explanation as to why the picture or drawing is appropriate for the character.

Create a Book

Create a book that reflects the main theme or idea of your novel. Your book can include poetry, illustrations, comic strips, interviews, and so forth. Your presentation to the class will consist of reading the book aloud and explaining how the illustrations relate to the theme. A variation of this is to create a book for elementary-age students based on your novel.

Create a Collage

Draw or locate pictures for a collage to illustrate the main theme of your novel, and glue them to a large piece of poster paper. Add some appropriate quotations to the illustrations and write a detailed explanation of the significance of each picture.

Create a Diary

Create a diary that might have been kept by the most or least likable character in your novel. You can include entries that reflect the main events in the story or you can write entries concerning things you think will happen to the character in the future. Your entries should be consistent with the character's actions and personality. If the character speaks with an accent or uses a particular lingo, it would be good to write the diary using the same form.

Current Events

Gather a large collection of current events (newspaper clippings, advertisements, magazine articles, cartoons, etc.) that reflect incidents that closely parallel those in your novel. You can place the clippings in a scrapbook, make a collage, and so forth. Include a few sentences with each item that tell how it relates to your book.

Design a Game

Create a game (crossword puzzle, find-a-word, scrambled words, and the like.) that involves key characters and/or words from the novels your group has read. Present your game to the class by explaining the words or character used. The game can later be distributed to the class and used as a review.

Design a Symbol

Design a symbol (coat of arms, a flag, or another motif) for your novel or a character in your novel. You can draw the symbol or make it. Write about the symbol detailing what each part represents.

Diorama or Model

Create a diorama or a model of a climactic scene in your novel. A diorama is a three-dimensional miniature scene with painted models, wax figures, or stuffed animals against a background. It can also be a scene reproduced on cloth transparencies with various lights shining through the cloths to produce changes in effect and viewed through a small opening. For more information you might want to talk to the art teacher or consult an art book.

Dramatic/Mood Lighting

The purpose of this project is to create a dramatic mood or atmosphere while the rest of your group is giving their presentation. Use different colored spot lights to add emphasis to a dramatic conflict, or project slides of appropriate scenes on the wall (or a sheet) as a background. Include a written explanation as to why you did what you did.

Newspaper Articles

Write two newspaper articles that report a couple of major events from your novel. If your novel is set in a particular time period, you can write the articles as they might have been written at that time. Be sure to include catchy headlines and one or two pictures. It would be good to create a layout of the top half of a front page using your articles.

Oral Presentation

Memorize a poignant scene from your novel and present it orally to the class. You should act it out using accents, props, etc., to make your audience empathize with the character(s) presented. Be sure to pick a piece that represents the theme your group is working on.

Personality Folder

Choose a colorful character, one with a lot of personality, from your novel. Take a file folder and create a montage of pictures portraying the character's personality (appearance, likes, dislikes, interests, occupation, and so forth.) on one side. On the other side, write a detailed explanation of the illustrations.

Story Sales-pitch

Create a sales-pitch designed to persuade your classmates to read the book you have read. Try to incorporate advertisers' lingo and be as persuasive as possible. Make posters or collages to accompany your pitch. You may also persuade one of your group members to dress up as one of the characters in your novel (or the author) and use him or her in your presentation.

Take on the Author

Write a letter to the author detailing how you feel about the book. Don't be afraid to challenge the author concerning something in the book you found questionable. Or, pretend you are a character in the novel and write a letter to the author about your treatment in the story. Or, write up a staged interview between you and the author. You might even be able to persuade another member of the group to play the part of the author and you could interview her or him for the class.

TV Commercial

Write a TV commercial that promotes your novel. Be sure to include some quotations from the book. The commercial can either be written, detailing the script, actor/actress, scene, lighting, music, and so forth, or you can actually perform it for the class using music, props, and the like.

Vocabulary

If the author of your novel or a particular character in the novel uses unusual vocabulary, present the vocabulary in a creative fashion to the class. You can design a book by putting each word on a separate page and illustrating it with pictures from magazines or original drawings. On the bottom of the page, write a sentence using the word or copy a sentence from the novel that contains the word.

Day Four

If the students have not had enough time to look over the various project options, or if the teacher feels the groups need more time to get organized another day can be taken to address this. We have found that it is good to give the groups time in the beginning to get their ideas firmly established. Allowing extra time also gives those students who might not have finished reading their young adult novels a chance to finish them.

Concurrent Activities

During the instruction of *The Adventures of Huckleberry Finn*, regular times need to be provided for the groups to work on their projects—usually one or two days a week. Since most teachers are familiar with the novel, we do not include a specific approach but rather a few suggestions or ideas that might be helpful.

Since *The Adventures of Huckleberry Finn* has been banned in many areas due to the language used, we feel that it is wise to address this issue head-on. In his tape, *The Genius of Mark Twain*, Dr. Elliot Engel engages in a sensitive discussion of this issue that is beneficial to students who are going to read the book. Dr. Engel also quotes Mark Twain concerning his feelings about the character, Jim, and black people in general.

A map of the Mississippi River is always a helpful tool to have while teaching *The Adventures of Huckleberry Finn*. One of the most difficult things about this classic is trying to keep track of all the characters and events that Huck and Jim encounter. We have found that laminating a map of the Mississippi and using different color dry-erase markers is an excellent way to track the characters' progress. The teacher, from students' input, can mark characters in one color, places in another, significant events in a third, and so on.

An interesting other comparison can be made between the novel and the popular fairy tale, "The Emperor's New Clothes." In both stories, society believes one thing—that all black people are subhuman or that the emperor's "clothes" are wonderful—and there is a considerable amount of pressure on everyone to uphold these beliefs. However, when the beliefs come face to face with someone who has not been influenced by the dictates of society (Huck and the boy in the crowd), they take on fresh meaning. Both boys ignore what society has told them and follow their own instincts. Huck decides that no matter what everyone has told him about black people, Jim is a pretty swell guy. The boy in the crowd who views the royal procession and hears those around him exclaim about the emperor's new clothes, simply says, "He doesn't have any clothes on!"

Toward the end of instruction, an activity that joins the novel and the group work together might be beneficial. Students can be asked to come up with ideas concerning the relevance of their young adult novels and *The Adventures of Huckleberry Finn*. They can also make educated assumptions about how they think Huckleberry would have dealt with the prejudice that they are addressing within their groups.

Concluding Activities

After concluding instruction of the novel, students should be able to present their group projects. This generally takes one or two days depending on the class size and the length of the presentations. There are a number of approaches for evaluating group projects of this type. The project itself may be the subject of evaluation, or the project may be evaluated in conjunction with the presentation. A third possibility is to evaluate the project, presentation, and the group work involved. For example, in addition to assigning a grade to the project and presentation, the teacher may wish to give a grade that reflects the overall functioning of the group. This grade would reflect cooperation, punctuality, attitudes, usage of time, and so on. Any number of strategies can be used. One form that we have used to evaluate group projects is given in Figure 3.8.

Figure 3.8

Group Project Evaluation

Group Name _____

Group Members' Names & Responsibilities

_____ - _____
_____ - _____
_____ - _____
_____ - _____
_____ - _____

Presentation   _____
Creativity   _____
Appropriateness   _____
Timeliness   _____
Cooperation   _____
Comments _____

_____
_____
_____
_____
_____

Total Grade _____

The teacher may also wish to consider some sort of peer evaluation to aid in assessing the group projects.

In addition to the teacher's evaluation of the group work, we feel that the students need to be given the opportunity to synthesize their own group experience. This forces them to look at their individual roles in relation to the success or failure of their group and will aid them when choosing groups in the future. It also gives the teacher valuable insights that can be used to better structure group activities. A form that we use to solicit student response is shown in Figure 3.9.

Figure 3.9

Group Process Evaluation

Cooperative learning is a very popular movement in education today, and many people believe it is the key to our future. More and more research is being conducted concerning groups and their functions. Because of this, I am very interested in your opinions and observations of your team. Please help me in conducting my own research by taking a few minutes to fill out the following information. All answers will be kept confidential.

Team Name: _____

Your Name: _____

Your Group Responsibility: _____

1) How many times were you absent during the time your group has been working on their projects?

2) Was each group member responsible? Did they do their job as listed on the group task sheet? Why or why not?

3) How did your group make decisions? Was it a democracy, dictatorship, or something else? Explain.

4) Did the group, as a whole have a positive or negative attitude? Did attitudes change,? Explain.

5) Overall, did your group work well together? Why or why not? Explain.

6) Are you personally satisfied with how your group project turned out? Why or why not?

7) What did you learn from this experience?

8) Did you have fun?

Conceivably, a unit on *The Adventures of Huckleberry Finn* could end at this point. However, we have found that an additional day is helpful to ensure closure of ideas, activities, and the topic of prejudice in general.

Day Five

We begin the last day by reading selected pieces of poetry. We particularly like to use poems generated by students that deal with prejudice. However, any poems that discuss prejudice from a personal point of view could be used.

After reading and discussing the poetry, we define four additional terms:

1. *acceptance* - the act or process of taking or receiving willingly; regarding with favor or approval
2. *tolerance* - a disposition toward or capacity for allowing or respecting the beliefs or behavior of others when these differ from one's own
3. *individuality* - the quality of existing as a distinct entity; single; separate
4. *diversity* - variety in form; multiformity

We discuss these terms with our students to offset the terms given at the beginning of the unit. We feel that it is important to point out the positive aspects of diversity and individuality rather than always dwelling on the negative results of such differences. In addition to the terms mentioned above, we also discuss some key questions:

1. What is the difference between tolerance and acceptance?
2. Is it enough for us to be tolerant of people who are different, or do we need to also accept them?
3. Are there times that we need to discriminate? Alert the students to situations where discrimination is necessary for the safety of those involved (i.e., in the presence of a hitchhiker, a stranger off the street, etc.).
4. Would the world be a better place if everyone were the same?
5. What is the value of diversity?

The discussion of these questions can be conducted in groups or with the class as a whole.

The final activity we include in our discussion of prejudice in conjunction with the novel *The Adventures of Huckleberry Finn* is a challenge to our students to be like Huck and make a difference. We present this challenge to our students in the form of an informal discussion and brainstorming session concerning practical ways of creating change in our own community.

After the discussion, students engage in an activity called "Have a Better Day." Students make a list of ten people that they could be nice to and one thing they could do to make each person on their list have a better day. Give the students a couple of days to complete the items on their list and then have them turn in a summary about what they learned from this experience. Discuss the results and have individuals share their experiences with the class. In the words of Toni Morrison (1989), author of Pulitzer Prize winning novel, *Beloved*, ". . . racism is a scholarly pursuit . . . Human beings can change things."

References

Aaron, C. (1972). *Better than laughter.* New York: Harcourt, Brace, & Jovanovich.

Angelou, M. (1990). *I know why the caged bird sings.* New York: Bantam Books.

Armstrong, W.H. (1969). *Sounder.* New York: Scholastic.

Arrick, F. (1981). *Chernowitz.* New York: The New American Library.

Baylor, B. (1991). *Yes is better than no.* Treasure Chest.

Benjamin, C.L. (1984). *Nobody's baby now.* New York: Macmillan.

Blume, J. (1973). *Deenie.* New York: Dell Laurel-Leaf.

Blume, J. (1970). *Iggie's house.* New York: Bradbury Press.

Blume, J. (1970). *Are you there, God? It's me Margaret.* New York: Dell.

Bonham, F. (1970). *Viva Chicano.* New York: E.P. Dutton.

Borland, H. (1984). *When the legends die.* New York: Bantam Books.

Brancato, R. (1978). *Winning.* New York: Bantam Books.

Branscum, R. (1976). *Toby, Granny and George.* New York: Doubleday.

Bridgers, S.E. (1977). *Home before dark.* New York: Bantam Books.

Cohen, B. (1987). *People like us.* New York: Bantam Books.

Collier, J.L. (1987). *Outside looking in.* New York: Macmillan.

Collier, J.L. (1986). *When the stars begin to fall.* New York: Dell Laurel-Leaf.

Cormier, R. (1974). *The chocolate war.* New York: Pantheon (Dell).

Crutcher, C. (1990). *Running loose.* New York: Dell Laurel-Leaf.

Crutcher, C. (1987). *The crazy horse electric game.* New York: Greenwillow Books.

Engel, E. (1986). *The genius of Mark Twain.* Raleigh, North Carolina: Dickens Fellowship, Box 99008, 27624.

Erickson, J. (1984). *Joni.* New York: Bantam Books.

Fair, R.L. (1966). *Cornbread, Earl, and me.* New York: Bantam Books.

Frank, A. (1972). *Anne Frank: The diary of a young girl.* New York: Simon & Schuster, Inc.

George, J.C. (1972). *Julie of the wolves.* New York: Harper & Row.

Glass, F. (1977). *Marvin and Tige.* New York: St. Martin's Press.

Godden, R. (1990). *Thursday's children.* New York: Dell Laurel Leaf.

Greenberg, J. (1964). *I never promised you a rose garden.* New York: The New American Library.

Irwin, Hadley. (1982). *What about Grandma?* New York: Atheneum.

Hanlon, E. (1981). *It's too late for sorry.* New York: Dell Laurel-Leaf.

Haskins, J. (1976). *The story of Stevie Wonder.* New York: Lothrop, Lee, & Shepard.

Hinton, S.E. (1967). *The outsiders.* New York: Dell Laurel-Leaf.

Holland, I. (1972). *The man without a face.* Philadelphia: J.B. Lippincott Company.

Houston, J.W. & Houston, J.D. (1990). *Farewell to Manzanar.* New York: Bantam Books.

Howe, Norma. (1986). *In with the out crowd*. Boston: Houghton Mifflin.

Hurston, Z.N. (1990). *Their eyes were watching God*. New York: Harper & Row.

Kellogg, M. (1984). *Tell me that you love me, Junie Moon*. New York: Farrar, Straus, & Giroux.

Kerr, M.E. (1987). *Night kites*. New York: Harper & Row.

Kerr, M.E. (1982). *Little Little*. New York: Harper & Row.

Kerr, M.E. (1978). *Gentlehands*. New York: Bantam Books.

Klein, N. (1989). *Now that I know*. New York: Bantam Books.

Klein, N. (1986). *Going backwards*. New York: Scholastic.

Kornfeld, A. (1975). *In a bluebird's eye*. New York: Holt, Rinehart, & Winston.

Lampman, E.S. (1972). *Go up the road*. New York: Atheneum.

Lasky, K. (1986). *Pageant*. New York: Four Winds Press.

L'Engle, M. (1974). *The summer of the great grandfather*. New York: Farrar, Straus, & Giroux.

Levy, M. (1990). *No way home*. New York: Dell Laurel-Leaf.

Lipsyte, R. (1977). *One fat summer*. New York: Harper & Row.

Lowry, L. (1981). *Anastasia again*. Boston: Houghton Mifflin.

MacKinnon, B. (1984). *The meantime*. Boston: Houghton Mifflin.

Mazer, N.F. (1988). *After the rain*. New York: William Morrow.

McCartney, P. (1990). Ebony and ivory. *Tripping the Live Fantastic*. Hollywood: Capitol Records.

Melton, D. (1986). *A boy called hopeless*. Kansas, MO: Landmark.

Miklowitz, G.D. (1990). *The war between the classes*. New York: Dell Laurel-Leaf.

Morrison, T. (1989, May 22). The pain of being black. *Time*.

Myers, W.D. (1990). *Hoops*. New York: Dell Laurel-Leaf.

Myers, W.D. (1982). *Won't know till I get there*. New York: Viking Press.

O'Dell, S. (1977). *Carlota*. Boston: Houghton Mifflin.

Paulsen, G. (1990). *The crossing*. New York: Dell Laurel-Leaf.

Potok, C. (1991). *My name is Asher Lev*. New York: Fawcett Crest.

Potok, C. (1967). *The chosen*. New York: Fawcett Crest.

Reiss, J. (1972). *The upstairs room*. New York: Harper & Row.

Richmond, S. (1985). *Wheels for walking*. Boston: Atlantic Monthly Press.

Sallis, S. (1980). *Only love*. New York: Harper & Row.

Santiago, D. (1984). *Famous all over town*. New York: E.P. Dutton.

Scoppettone, S. (1991). *Happy endings are all alike*. Boston: Alyson Publications.

Scoppettone, S. (1981). *Trying hard to hear you*. New York: Bantam Books.

Taylor, M.D. (1976). *Roll of thunder, hear my cry*. New York: Bantam Books.

Telemaque, E. (1978). *It's crazy to stay Chinese in Minnesota*. Nashville: T. Nelson.

Tchudi, S. & Mitchell, D. (1989). *Explorations in the teaching of English*. New York: Harper & Row.

Townsend, S. (1986). *The Adrian Mole diaries*. Grove Press.

Twain, M. (1940). *The adventures of Huckleberry Finn*. New York: Heritage Press.

Voigt, C. (1986). *Come a stranger*. New York: Atheneum.

Voigt, C. (1986). *Izzy, willy-nilly*. New York: Atheneum.

Chapter 4

Catcher as Core and Catalyst

TED HIPPLE

Introduction

The Catcher in the Rye by J. D. Salinger: There it is. Surely no other novel of the 20th century has so aroused such extreme emotions among secondary school English language arts teachers. On the one hand *Catcher* is praised as the one novel of this century certain to be read several generations from now, certain to meet one of the common criteria for designation as a classic: It will stand the test of time. But other people are less flattering. "Trash," they call it—"literate pornography."

I remember an incident from the 60s when I taught in suburban Chicago and tried to convince a colleague to join my effort to make *Catcher* a required novel in our eleventh grade American literature sections. An intelligent woman and gifted teacher, she conscientiously began the novel but reported to me later, "About halfway through it, I felt I needed to take a bath." End of requirement decision.

Even today, well over two decades later, *Catcher* still raises serious problems in many school districts: Some teach it on a damn-the-torpedoes-full-steam-ahead basis, some have carefully crafted policies about who can be required to read the novel, some have rejected it outright, and some have lost teachers who were fired for their attempts to teach this novel.

What, then, of *Catcher*? Ought it to be a part of the high school English curriculum? Required? For all students? Suggested for only a few? In the school library? In the classroom library? Answers to these questions will vary, often even within an English department. It may be useful here to remind us all of the truth of the Latin expression "de gustibus non disputandum est," which translates loosely as "there's no arguing about taste." Different strokes for different folks, and all that.

But not entirely. One can't simply rely overmuch on this postulate and suggest that his or her opinion is as good as any other; to make curricular decisions and library selection judgments on such a basis becomes choice by personal belief. We teachers are, or ought to be, better than that. We ought at least to be able to articulate some reasons why we believe as we do; why, in this specific instance, we believe *Catcher* does or does not merit a place in the school literature program.

That's what I intend to try to do in the remainder of this chapter—to illustrate, persuasively I hope, that *Catcher* ought to be a required part of every secondary school student's literature study. I want teachers to **want** to teach this important novel. But I also want you to go beyond *Catcher* to other novels it relates to. This a part of my conviction that good literature not only can be studied on its own but has catalytic possibilities to enlarge the study of other literature as well.

A brief description of the literature program I'm recommending may be helpful. All students in the class will read *Catcher*, the core novel. But multiple copies of other novels, say five or so of each, will be around and students will be expected to read at least two of them. Classroom activities will focus on *Catcher* singularly some of the time, and, at other times, on how it and some of the other novels are related. For example, a student who has read *Catcher* and also Zindel's *The Amazing and Death-Defying Diary of Eugene Dingman* can write a paper or give a talk on how the first-person narration in each novel contributes to the story. Another student whose extra readings included Bridger's *Permanent Connections* and Paulsen's *The Monument* can examine the maturity of the protagonists in each novel. Some of the time, too, four or five students who all happen to have read Hoffman's *At Risk* can get together for a small group discussion of that work, relating it or not relating it to *Catcher*, as they choose.

In keeping with the general focus of this book I'm going to limit my discussion of other novels to young adult literature, though certainly with *Catcher* I could go well beyond adolescent literature. The Salinger classic has been widely linked in critical articles with works and characters as disparate as *Hamlet* and Huck Finn, *A Separate Peace* and Henry Fleming. But Shakespeare, Twain, Knowles, and Crane don't need any support for inclusion in the English class; young adult novels sometimes do. Thus, it makes sense to explore how *Catcher* can be taught on its own and can, at the same time, provide an entree to significant novels by such eminent writers of adolescent literature as Cormier, Zindel, Peck, Crutcher, Lipsyte, and others whose works I'll suggest in the pages that follow. But do keep in mind that the young adult novels I'm discussing are but suggestions; you can substitute others as you wish, with your own teaching favorites or those your students recommend.

I'm going to be occasionally prescriptive, but not with canned lesson plans that stipulate the establishment of set early in the class and the use of closure at the end. I am going to arrange my ideas in ways that I believe are teachable to, say, high school juniors. In each sub-section—theme, character, language— we'll look first at *Catcher*, and then at how this novel relates to other novels useful for these same kinds of students.

The Study of Theme

Those who comment on literature and say that some novels are better than others often choose the former on the basis of the novel's rich exploration of themes worth examining. By this kind of criterion *The Catcher in the Rye* is a major novel indeed. Not only does it examine significant themes, but it does so with significant insight as well.

The End of Innocence

The most compelling theme in *Catcher* is the coming of age of Holden Caulfied. Kicked out of prep school again (it's his third), with acquaintances but no real friends, at odds with all in his family except for his sister Phoebe, Holden represents the troubled adolescent emerging from the innocence of childhood into the experience of adulthood, to use the terms of romantic poet William Blake. But Holden can't go easily, without some metaphoric kicking and screaming and without considerable acting out of his ambivalence about the journey.

Take, as one threadlike example that runs throughout the novel, Holden's sexual experiences. He alternately envies, but deplores, the successful adventures of his roommate Stradlater, particularly early in the novel when he learns that Stradlater's date is Holden's former friend, Jane Gallagher. Holden had spent much of a summer playing checkers with her. It was she who kept her kings in the back row, exemplifying by that action a kind of resistance to adult responsibilities, a clinging to innocence, that mirrored Holden's own, and now she is going out on a blind date with the sexually active Stradlater. The mere thought of sex between Stradlater and Jane is almost more than Holden can handle on what turns out to be his final evening at Pencey Prep.

Yet Holden would also like some sexual experiences of his own. He laments his virginity often in the novel, and, in one pivotal incident, tries to do something about it by hiring the prostitute in the New York City hotel but fails to go beyond talking to her and then is depressed by his reluctance to do more. In a twist, injury is added to this self-imposed insult when the pimpish bellhop Maurice hits Holden for his refusal to pay the full amount for Sunny's time, if not for her services. Earlier Holden had failed to arrange a rendezvous with a woman he had never met, the friend of Eddie Birdsell, whom he had met once but from whom he had gotten a telephone number of Faith Cavendish "that wasn't exactly a whore or anything" (p. 63). After the incident with the prostitute, he and matinee date Sally Hayes "horsed around a little bit" (p. 125) in the back of a taxi as they go to the theater, yet even here Holden is ambivalent about sex for himself.

But not for others, particularly his younger sister Phoebe. In a passage regularly cited in the many censorship cases *Catcher* has inspired, Holden sees "fuck you" written on the walls of Phoebe's school. Suddenly a moralist, Holden is worried that "some dirty kid would tell them [Phoebe and her little innocent friends]—all cockeyed naturally—what it meant" (p. 201) and he wants to erase it.(Ironically, the censors who object to *Catcher* because of its coarse language and cite this particular passage are, in fact, much akin to Holden in their abhorrence, albeit perhaps for different reasons.)

Another example of Holden's uncertain and inconsistent clinging to innocence comes from the passages in the novel that provide its title. He is aimlessly walking the New York City streets and watches a family, a mother, father, and their six year old whom, according to Holden's standards, they are ignoring as the child walks along the busy street. Holden overhears the child misquoting the Robert Burns' poem by singing "If a boy catch a body coming through the rye" (p. 115). The walk both charms and annoys Holden, the unfeigned innocence of the little child and the dangerous inattention of his parents. The child needs saving from the busy street (which symbolizes adult and malevolent experience, just like the banks of the Mississippi in *The Adventures of Huckleberry Finn*) and Holden incorrectly fancies himself the person able to do it. Later, he tells Phoebe about his occupational preferences:

> And I'm standing on the edge of some crazy cliff. What I have to do, I have to catch everybody if they start to go over the cliff—I mean if they're running and they don't look where they're going I have to come out from somewhere and *catch* them. That's all I'd do all day, I'd just be the catcher in the rye and all.(p. 172)

Numerous other examples could be cited about Holden's ambiguous relationships with those whom he perceives as the enviable innocents in need of help and those adult phonies whom he too often encounters. Like the little children in the rye field, the nuns he meets are innocent (pp. 108-113); even the winter whereabouts of the ducks in Central Park concern him (p. 81-83). But the three Seattle women who ignore Holden in their search for celebrities even as they drink his liquor (pp. 70-75) are among the adult phonies, like bellhop Maurice the pimp, and, later and disturbingly, Antolini (pp. 180-193). But these few will suffice to suggest the potential richness of any classroom conversation that gets at Holden's rites of passage.

Adding more than a little fillip of interest to your classroom discussion will be your questioning students about their beliefs about Holden's self-knowledge. Urge them to find passages that indicate that Holden does know something about himself and others, where what he does clearly does not square with what he thinks he is doing, and where what he is differs from what he thinks he is. You can also go through the book in an orderly beginning-to-end way (recalling, however, that it is all flashback after Holden has gone to the sanitarium), and see if Holden increases any in his efforts to understand himself.

Family Relationships

A second theme (and I'm deliberately choosing themes from *Catcher* that have counterparts, or counterpoints, in other young adult novels that could be used in conjunction with *Catcher*) is the exploration of family life. Holden has an older brother, D. B., a writer who has, in Holden's judgment, sold out to Hollywood. His younger sister, Phoebe, lives with their parents in the New York City apartment house. And there's Allie, a younger brother whom Holden had worshipped and who had died of leukemia. Holden is, at best, ambivalent about his family, save for Phoebe, whom he wants to protect; witness his worries about the schoolhouse graffiti.

It's well worth classroom time to discuss with adolescents Holden's relationships with his family members, in part, at least, because of the potentially bibliotherapeutic effects for your students, almost all of whom, it goes without saying, are having some kinds of more or less difficult relationships with their own families. How is what Holden experiences the result of who he is? The result of who his family members are? Note the very opening sentences of the novel when Holden announces that his "parents would have about two hemorrhages apiece if I told anything pretty personal about them" (p. 1). Is Holden at fault? Is anyone? How does his experience relate to that of teenagers today?

There are numerous additional themes in *Catcher*—the notion of quest, man's inhumanity to man, the role of schooling, among others—but space limitations and the need to get onto other pedagogical possibilities force us onward to a look at three young adult novels that might be read by some students even as the entire class reads *Catcher*: *The Chocolate War*, *Permanent Connections*, and *Chinese Handcuffs*.

1. *The Chocolate War* by Robert Cormier (191 pp.). *The Chocolate War* is rapidly becoming one of the classics in the field of young adult literature. Almost from its publication in 1974, it has led virtually every survey that attempted to get at popularity and quality of young adult novels. It is widely read in the schools and in college adolescent literature courses. And, to our present purpose, it would richly complement the study of the themes in *Catcher*. Like Holden, Jerry Renault is something of a loner, eager to belong but uncertain just how to go about it. At first he believes that friendship, at his private day school, can result from his becoming a member of the Vigils, a secret fraternity that requires pledges to undertake "assignments" created by the malevolent Archie. Jerry begins to do his assignment—refusing to sell the chocolates in the school fund raiser—then reneges, with, one could argue, potentially disastrous results. In asking himself the question poet T. S. Eliot gives his sad creation J. Alfred Prufrock ("Do I dare disturb the universe?"), Jerry goes a bit beyond Holden in self-analysis. The answer Jerry gets, however, muddies the waters of self-understanding and he ends up, like Holden, as troubled as he began.

Like Holden, too, Jerry worries about his own sexuality. He masturbates, falls immediately in love (he thinks) with a girl he casually meets at a bus stop, is unable to discuss this most personal of topics with a friend at his school, and has no family with whom to explore the issue. He must, like all adolescents, go through his sexual/mental/emotional wars.

Holden Caulfield has a family but, save for Phoebe, little relationship with them. Jerry Renault is an only child. Just prior to the opening of the novel his mother has died of cancer. His pharmacist father is, for all intents and purposes, a cipher. He pads around their house like a man old beyond his years, crushed by his wife's tragedy, becoming one of Thoreau's masses of men "who live lives of quiet desperation." In sum, he is of almost no consequence in Jerry's life, just as Holden's parents have little impact on what he is or does.

2. *Permanent Connections* by Sue Ellen Bridgers (288 pp.). Another novel, a more recent one than *The Chocolate War*, that has significant thematic relationships with *Catcher*, and, thus would make a good small-group choice while the entire class is studying the Salinger work, is Bridger's *Permanent Connections*. Here, too, is the exploration of the loner coming through his rites of passage to adulthood and finding the route hard. Rob Dickson, nearly flunking out of school, alternately indifferent to and at war with his parents, is sent by his father from their New Jersey home to the backwoods of North Carolina to care for his aged grandfather, his agoraphobic aunt, and his newly crippled uncle until such time as Rob's father can find permanent help for these members of his family. Rob hates rural Tyler Mills, his responsibilities, his school, his life, and himself. He is utterly miserable at least until he meets Ellery, a girl his own age and, like him, a new move-in from the urban and sophisticated world.

Rob is a bit different from Holden, or at least would think that he is. In New Jersey he would have labeled himself the experienced adolescent Holden hopes to become, even if not one entirely worthy of emulation. Rob drinks, smokes (echoes of Holden), and probably has had sex, though Bridgers is discreet about that. But it is, to all but Rob, a patently false adulthood, a phony experience. And he must return to innocence in the North Carolina countryside to move to a newer and more mature adulthood. Rob discovers he has love for this rural family whom he earlier despised for their rural ways.

Rob shares Holden's ambivalence about who he is and what he is to do—not initially, when he knows that he does not want to go south, but later, when he begins to have feelings for his family and especially for Ellery, who, because of her uncertainty about their relationship, adds to his own uncertainty. Unlike Holden, Rob is sexually sophisticated and actually has sex with Ellery, but with an unsatisfactory aftermath: Rob thinks that now he owns Ellery, but she is very much her own person and is not about to be owned.

Students who examine the themes of *Catcher* and *Permanent Connections* will soon see the dissimilar and similar ways in which the two protagonists relate to themselves and to their families. To get away from it all, Holden drinks and fantasizes; Rob jogs in the woods. Later, he accidentally finds a mentoring minister in a country church. Your students may recognize that Holden, too, had a mentor, the psychiatrist at the hospital. Though Salinger chooses not to tell us what effect the psychiatrist has had on Holden, readers can assume it was at least a little; he is telling his story, after all. Both Holden and Rob are very distant from their immediate families; unlike Holden, Rob ultimately finds some identity and affection for the extended family he is forced to live with.

3. *Chinese Handcuffs* by Chris Crutcher (192 pp.). *Chinese Handcuffs* shares with *Catcher* more than the thematic connections described below. It is also widely praised or damned and for much the same reasons—coarse language and sexual situations. But for those teachers who choose to use it the dividends are many: a complex but compelling story well-told, a series of multifaceted characters, fine writing, and a turn-the-page intensity. Youthful readers will not forget either book.

But here our focus is on the themes of the two novels, and, again, there are many points that can be studied in a classroom examination of both works. In the Chris Crutcher novel, protagonist Dillon Hemingway is slowly emerging from the devastating effects of his brother's suicide.(Note the parallels with Holden's brother Allie and Jerry's mother in *The Chocolate War*.) Crutcher has Dillon write letters to the dead Preston, a novel and novelistic way to tell part of the story. Dillon's mother has left the family, and he lives with his father, with whom he has a reasonably mature but a bit distant relationship. There is, additionally, an interesting family twist: Preston's girlfriend Stacy, has recently adopted a baby, who, it not surprisingly turns out, is revealed to be her own and Preston's child.

Like Holden, Dillon often has sex on his mind and without significant success. As it turns out, the object of his desire, Jennifer Lawless, has a secret— sexual abuse by her stepfather—that blocks Dillon's attempts at intimacy. Dillon differs from Holden, however, in a number of ways that merit classroom exploration. He tries to take charge of what is going on: freeing Jennifer from her abusive step-father, for example; coming to the aid of Stacy; and even confronting the motorcycle gang that had been part of the cause of Preston's suicide. Unlike Holden, too, he is introspective. He knows himself better than Holden knows himself. And because self-knowledge is so important a part of the education of the young, these different perspectives on that theme can spark considerable classroom involvement.

In sum, then, the themes of *Catcher* are found in *The Chocolate War*, *Permanent Connections*, and *Chinese Handcuffs*, not in precisely the same way but in sufficient similarity to be useful means of learning about all four novels.

The Study of Character

For most secondary school readers the central appeal of a novel, young adult or adult, is probably its story, its what-happens-next dimensions. Themes or generalizations about life extracted from the plot are important. Also, the characters in that plot are significant—not only the major characters, the protagonists, but also some of the minor characters.

Major Characters

Holden Caulfield is the compelling center of *Catcher*, the person whose life— or a three day portion of it—we value reading about. It is he whom we alternately like or dislike, admire or reject but, in the end, we feel great empathy for and with. It is well to remember and to remind students, however, that Holden is telling his own story which thus, might be unreliable, given to bias or lies. What we see is what we get: Holden's story about himself. Happily, that is enough for some exciting classroom exchanges, some fascinating activities.

Suppose you asked your students to keep Holden's diary for an experience he did not record in the book but might have: an encounter with his mother, for example, when he visits Phoebe; being spotted by a teacher as he stares at the "fuck you" on Phoebe's schoolhouse wall; one of his interviews with the "psychoanalyst guy" (p. 213) he talks with at the sanitarium. What would they say? How would they reveal Holden and their understanding of him? Would they use his exaggeration? His disgust? His ambivalence? His inconsistencies? Would they play him off, even if through his own words, against other characters? (This kind of assignment, by the way, can be enriched if you ask students to try to capture Salinger's language—a topic we'll turn to in the next section of this chapter.)

Typically, readers learn about characters by looking at what they say and do and at what others say and do in reference to them. You might try to get at who Holden is by asking your students what others think of him—Ackley, Stradlater, Phoebe, Antolini, Sally Hayes. How do they treat him? How does he respond to them? You should also, of course, try to help your students sort out Holden's own feelings and actions. What makes him tick? What bothers him? Excites him? Causes him to be happy? Sad?

You may want to explore with your students Holden as the archetypal teenager. Is he? How is he like other teenagers? Different from them? What personal traits does he share with them, like his interest in alcohol, in sex, in using profanity? What of their traits does he not share, like his lack of interest in sports or in school-related activities of any kind?

It's but an easy remove from a consideration of Holden's typicality or atypicality to an examination of characters in other novels, including young adult novels. Here I've again suggested three young adult novels, all of which have first-person narrators who tell their own stories, and, thus, are subject to accusations of unreliability: *The Amazing and Death-Defying Diary of Eugene Dingman, The Brave,* and *The Monument.*

1. *The Amazing and Death-Defying Diary of Eugene Dingman* by Paul Zindel (224 pp.). Eugene Dingman is, according to the prolific Zindel, the boy Zindel

himself was a generation ago, when he, too, spent a summer as a waiter in a Catskill resort hotel. Like Zindel, Eugene went to this residential summer job from the house he shared with his divorced mother; both the real and the fictional fathers had left their wives when their sons were very young and had almost no further contact with them. His father's unwillingness to even see him weighs heavily on Eugene, possibly more than he really knows.

Yet Eugene's commitment to himself that summer is to learn more about who he is, an effort he believes can be helped if he keeps a diary.(That diary makes a useful rhetorical device for Zindel to use to tell the story of Eugene.) He also uses a fellow resort worker, an "old Indian, one of the Bombay ones," named Mahatma. Eugene falls in love, "lust" using Mahatma's wise term, with Della, who as it turns out, plays Eugene false, telling him that she is visiting with her Aunt Claire when, in fact, she is dating virtually every boy in the neighborhood. Eugene has further problems with one of the fellow waiters, Bunker, who treats him in ways reminiscent of the misery "old Maurice," the bellhop, dishes out to Holden in *Catcher*.

The very bitter subplot involving Eugene's frequent and pleading letters to his father for a visit or even a phone call contributes to the climax of the novel. The father and his new girlfriend do come to the resort but only to leave a present for Eugene. He sees them as they are driving away, knows that they see him, and suffers when they speed up.

His father's maltreatment aside, Eugene does come to terms with himself. At the end, he understands Della's refusal to be true to him; he turns the tables on Bunker; and, in a strong gesture that ultimately gets him fired, he refuses to serve bad food to a customer. Eugene can end his diary with a truthful final assertion: "Monday, September 2.... Eugene Dingman born."

Those of your students who read *Eugene Dingman* and compare the protagonist with Holden can explore a number of interesting similarities and differences. Both tell their story in the first person, suggesting, of course, that they might be biased in their own favor—this despite Eugene's assertions that he is going to tell the truth and Holden's certainly appearing to do so. Both are lonely. Both have spiritual guides of a sort, each with his own problems: Eugene with Mahatma, Holden with Antolini. Both are often victimized.

Your students can also explore the method of storytelling used by Salinger and Zindel. Is a diary more effective than the means Salinger employed, simply having Holden tell his story with the hint that maybe some of it was told to the California psychiatrist? You may want to ask your students to keep their own diaries for a while, perhaps echoing Eungene's habit of always beginning with important world events that occurred on the date he is writing.

Your students should focus, too, on how the central characters are revealed through the plot. Both *Catcher* and *Eugene Dingman* are episodic; rather than being built around one pivotal incident in the lives of Holden and Eugene, they move from event to event. Holden chooses to tell about "this madman stuff that happened last Christmas," and Eugene chooses to write about his adventures during his Catskill summer as a waiter. True, there are threads that hold these events in place, but, essentially, the characters are revealed in what might be termed an incremental pattern: They grow as they move through the episodes. The question for your students becomes, then, how are Holden and Eugene different at the end from the way they were at the beginning? Why?

2. *The Brave* by Robert Lipsyte (208 pp.). Commonly, sequels begin soon after the time at which the earlier book ends; they are virtually continuous. Not so Lipsyte's sequel of sorts to his 1967 classic novel, *The Contender*. In that novel we meet Alfred Brooks, a Black inner city youth, a dropout, one step away from joining a gang intent on burglary and well into drugs. Alfred rescues himself by becoming a boxer, a contender, and by refusing to participate in a robbery of the store where he works, even though his lifelong friend, James, will be one of the thieves. By the end of the novel, Alfred has grown considerably and has decided, with his trainer's help, that he really isn't cut out for boxing but does want something better than the wasted life of the ghetto. He plans a return to school and a middle-class life, even taking the drug-crazed James along.

In the sequel, 24 years later and Alfred has indeed made it, as we soon learn in *The Brave*. He is a New York City policeman, working the tough neighborhood around the Port Authority in Manhattan. Although this novel features the adult Alfred in significant ways, it is primarily about Sonny Bear, a half-white, half-Indian who lives on an upstate New York reservation. He boxes in what are called "Friday night smokers," bouts in which anyone who wants to fight can and, if successful, can pick up a little money. Sonny Bear is good enough to win these, but because of his half-breed status, he often has to flee with his Uncle Jake (a full-blooded Indian) away from the fight before he has collected what purse there is in order to escape the anger of the racist white crowd distressed that he won the fight. Sonny Bear's father is dead, his mother remarried and, for much of the novel, indifferent to Sonny Bear.

When she does emerge to take him away from the reservation, he decides he does not want to live with her and her current paramour and goes to the Big Apple, New York City instead. Once there at the Port Authority, he is "fresh meat," easy prey for Doll and Stick, part of a juvenile delinquent crowd who steal his money and set him up as a decoy while they make a crack delivery. Sonny Bear is arrested, but the officer is Alfred Brooks, who recognizes in the youngster something of himself a generation earlier. He also wants to use Sonny Bear to help him catch the elusive Doll and her main man, Stick.

But first Alfred indulges in Sonny Bear's determination to become a big-time boxer and takes him to the gym that once welcomed him and at which he maintains contacts. Sonny Bear is a success as a boxer, and, at the end of the novel when he is betrayed by Stick and Doll, he also succeeds in getting them arrested.

Sonny Bear is an arresting character. He possesses great loyalty, not only to Uncle Jake and Alfred Brooks but even to Doll and Stick. Despite their treating him badly, he refuses early in the novel to tell Brooks where they can be found. Sonny is diligent in his pursuit of a boxing career, working hard at it. He possesses some beliefs in the Indian ways that Uncle Jake uses to guide him (much as Antolini advises Holden and Mahatma helps Eugene Dingman), and yet he is a part of the city environment.

Your students may profitably read both *The Contender* and *The Brave*, examining the Alfred in each novel and also the way the earlier Alfred is seen in the later Sonny Bear. There are also valid comparisons with Holden Caulfield. Holden and Sonny Bear are nearly defeated by New York city—its indifference, its ugliness, its immorality—(this in spite of its being Holden's home city), and yet at the end, readers are likely to believe that they will survive. Further, Sonny Bear and Holden share views about family commitments, particularly to parents, that merit study. Students who read *Catcher* and then *The Brave* will doubtless find other aspects that make these very different novels more alike than it at first appears.

3. *The Monument* by Gary Paulsen (151 pp.). Gary Paulsen has burst on the young adult novel scene in a firestorm of highly praised books, and both his output and the popularity of that productivity seem to increase yearly. His 1991 *The Monument* may be his best book to date; certainly it affords a marvelous examination of character in novels. Like *Catcher, Eugene Dingman*, and *The Brave, The Monument* features a young person, somewhat crippled by circumstance, who is redeemed by the thoughtful and careful wisdom of an unlikely older person—in Rocky's case, the artist Mick Strum. Rocky has a bad leg and imagines a long teenage life as the orphan she is when she is adopted by the loving and kind Fred and Emma and taken to live in Bolton.

In more than one sense Bolton is itself almost a character in the novel. The city fathers, some of whom have actually seen the Vietnam War Memorial in Washington, D.C., decide that their little Kansas town should have a monument, too. They commission Mick Strum, a highly unusual artist, to come to Bolton and create that monument. Mick's credo comes from Katherine Anne Porter's statement that "Art is what we find when the ruins are cleared away" and the monument he creates (I won't tell you what it is; read this significant work to find out what it is) at first frustrates, then enchants Bolton and, with it, Rocky. She is herself a budding artist, and when Mick leaves Bolton there is, she thinks, a chance for her.

Rocky, Sonny Bear, Eugene Dingman, and Holden all tell their stories in the first person. You may want to ask your students what advantages this method of telling about oneself has. What disadvantages? How, for example, can the usual method of learning about a character by what others say about him or her be accommodated in a first-person novel? What if the story teller is, like Holden, a confessed liar? Can a reader believe what he says about himself?

You can add to this study of these characters by asking your students to write a bit about themselves in a first-person way. Are they instructed by someone older, not a parent or another relative, but someone who is interested in them for what they are, not who? And can they write about that relationship? Or can they write about a particular event in their lives and, by retelling it, reveal themselves to their readers? (These essays may be too personal for wide dissemination in your classroom.)

Minor Characters

No study of character is complete without some attention to the minor characters an author creates, and all four of these books are rich in minor characters—particularly *Catcher*. In some novels written for adolescent readers minor characters are cardboard cutouts, seeming almost to stand for one trait— honesty, friendliness, stupidity—but not so in Salinger's masterpiece. Ask your students what they think of Stradlater or Ackley at Pencey Prep, of Sunny and Maurice in the hotel, of Antolini and Phoebe. So rich is Salinger's ability at characterization that your students may also say they know two characters they meet only through Holden's memory—Jane and Allie.

Don't overlook the minor characters in the extra novels. Mahatma, Della, and Bunker add much to Eugene Dingman as person and as novel. Lipsyte has peopled the gym where Sonny Bear trains with an assortment of characters who are well drawn, just as he did in the earlier *Contender*. His creation of a sports milieu suggests why he is such a successful sports reporter as well as novelist. And Paulsen makes Bolton come alive: Your students will meet Fred and Emma, Rocky's dog Python, and the people of this small town who want a monument to their sons and daughters lost in the war. Their sadness, their initial annoyance at what artist Mick Strum does, and their later understanding reveal much about them.

A Study of Language

A third feature well worth classroom attention in any examination of literature, but probably short-changed in most such study, is language. Many literature lessons so focus on elements like plot or symbolism or irony or, yes, theme and character that the words the author uses, his or her language, gets set aside.

To use a very different example from our topic, take Shakespeare. One or more of his plays is featured in almost every year of the secondary school English program. *Romeo and Juliet* and *Julius Caesar* come perhaps as near as any literature ever to being universally read works. Yet such study often neglects any mention of Shakespeare's language. Teachers explore the feud between the

Montagues and the Capulets, the ways in which Cassius manipulates Brutus to join their conspiracy against Caesar and then loses control of that conspiracy to Brutus. Students write about ironies that abound in *Romeo and Juliet*, do character analyses of Antony, and yet ignore one of the signal elements that make Shakespeare Shakespeare: his use of language. Think of the words he coined and gave to the English language: "assassination," "bedroom," "dwindle," "impartial," "obscene," "useless," a few among the many that could be listed. Shakespeare also bequeathed to us many now common compounds: "barefaced," "heartsick," "leapfrog," "sea change," and "tongue-tied."

Need a title for your novel? Go to Shakespeare, as did Faulkner (*The Sound and the Fury*), Christie (*By the Pricking of My Thumbs*), Wilder (*The Ides of March*), Huxley (*Brave New World*), Maugham (*Cakes and Ale*), Steinbeck (*The Winter of Our Discontent*), again a few among many. Need a useful phrase to give an intellectual flavor to your speech? Just go to *Hamlet,* itself almost a chapter in the quotation books: "brevity is the soul of wit;" "to thine own self be true;" "every dog will have his day;" "there's the rub;" "to the manner born." And so on.

Neither Salinger nor the other novelists whose works are included in this essay will ever rival Shakespeare in their contributions to our language, but their language ought to be studied nonetheless. With Shakespeare, by the way, you can help students appreciate his genius by teaching them something about iambic pentameter, then asking them to write just four lines of it that make sense. Piece of cake, they'll think. But when they discover just how hard that task is, they'll have a different kind of respect for the Bard, who, after all, wrote thousands of such lines that made sense.

But what of the language of *Catcher*? How can you help your students study Salinger's language? Ask your students what they'd like to say about the language. Chances are their first response will be about Holden's profanity. And that's a good place to begin. At this point, too, you might remind them that Salinger was reputed to have spent hours in teenage hangouts of the late 40s, to try to capture the ways in which students talked, the words they used, the common phrases. Ask your students how accurate they think Salinger might be. What are some of Holden's common profanities? Does he differ from today's youth in the degree to which he uses profanity or in its repetition?

The "fuck you" episode will surely come up, albeit a bit obliquely at first. Students who use "fuck" every fifth word in their out-of-class conversations are still hesitant to voice it within the hallowed halls of English class. It is important that your students understand Holden's revulsion here, a feeling he would probably experience today if he were around. The schoolhouse graffiti Holden deplores and later sees at the Metropolitan Museum seems even more ubiquitous at the present time. And surely the word graces or disgraces the lips of more speakers today than in Holden's time. What do such shifts suggest about language in general, profanity in particular?

Another way of looking at language in *Catcher* or in any piece of literature for that matter is to ask students to find exemplars of linguistic use that they like, for whatever reasons. Be prepared for a denial—"I didn't like none of it"—but once you get started, even if your have to prime the pump with some suggestions of your own, you'll soon have most class members contributing something. Think of the passage where Holden is watching Phoebe on the merry-go-round:

> I felt so damn happy, if you want to know the truth. I don't know why. It was just that she looked so damn nice, the way she kept going around and around, in her blue coat and all. God, I wish you could've been there.(pp. 212-213)

And surely some of your students will wish they had indeed been there.

Another instance when Holden is "sort of crying" occurs the evening he leaves Pencey Prep, and it is another instance of Holden's courageous act being diminished by subsequent events (foreshadowing, perhaps, his refusal to pay Maurice the bellhop/pimp only to get hit in the stomach and have Maurice take the money anyway). The language Salinger uses to reveal Holden's final moments at Pencey are as poignant as the action:

> I was sort of crying. I don't know why. I put my red hunting cap on, and turned the peak around to the back the way I liked it, and then I yelled at the top of my goddam voice, *"Sleep tight, ya morons!"* I'll bet I woke up every bastard on the floor. Then I got the hell out.

Passages like these suggest Holden's vulnerability but do so by *showing,* not telling. Salinger uses language to convey meaning through the actions he depicts and the emotions he describes. He does not have to say that Holden seems to be one of life's losers at this time in his life; he lets words do the work.

Suppose you set your students a similar task, to use language to depict a state of mind, a characteristic, a condition. Ask them to describe someone who is poor yet proud but to do so without mentioning money (once fashionable clothes now badly out of date, with frayed sleeves and worn elbows, yet cleaned and pressed to the nines). Can they convey emotion—sadness, anger, fear—without resorting to those words or their synonyms? Let them find instances in *Catcher* where they learn about Holden, even through his own words about himself, without being specifically told what they are to know. Such is the power of language.

Ask your students about first impressions. When a new student comes to your school, what do they notice—clothes, carriage, manner of speaking? With a novel the first impression is the language of the opening page. Cormier begins *The Chocolate War* with "They murdered him," a line that has religious overtones revealed later in the opening pages and also foreshadows what happens to Jerry Renault. Sue Ellen Bridgers opens *All Together Now* with "Casey came unwillingly," words that set a stage for Casey's annoyance at being uprooted from her usual home and being sent to spend a summer with her grandparents. Openings invite readers, ask them to join. Note Susan Beth Pfeffer's beginning sentences in *Most Precious Blood*: "Of course, there was background. Words as angry as the ones pouring out of Michelle's mouth didn't emerge without some sort of history behind them." Or Gary Paulsen's *The Monument*: "Sometimes it's funny how we can't know things." Sometimes the beginning is intended mainly to grab, even to shock. Judy Blume's first sentence in *Forever* is "Sybil Davisson has a genius I. Q. and has been laid by at least six different guys." Blume writes of teenaged heterosexual love. In *Happy Endings Are All Alike* Sandra Scoppettone writes of lesbian love between two very able high school seniors and begins with this paragraph:

> Even though Jaret Taylor had no guilt or shame about her love affair with Peggy Danziger, she knew there were plenty of people in this world who would put it down. Especially in a small town like Gardener's Point, a hundred miles from New York City. She and Peggy didn't go around wearing banners, but there were some people who knew.(p. 1)

Salinger's introduction to *Catcher* and to Holden is similarly an invitation, though we readers are told that the party may be limited:

> If you really want to hear about it, the first thing you'll probably want to know is where I was born, and what my lousy childhood was like, and how my parents were occupied and all before they had me, and all that David Copperfield kind of crap, but I don't feel like going into it, if you want to know the truth.(p. 1)

From just that first sentence what kinds of inferences can your students make? Can they sense Holden's self-indulgence? Do they understand that he suspects they may really not "want to know the truth"? What kinds of predictions can they make about his story? Accuracy here is less important than the attempt: Their trying to guess what might happen can motivate them to read on.

It is, of course, but a short remove from this kind of study of opening lines to ask your students to create their own opening lines. They don't have to know their whole novel or even its central messages; rather, they want to invite their readers, to help them into the story. They may want to introduce their imagined protagonist. Will they have him or her use a word or phrase that later will be frequent, like Holden's "and all" or every contemporary teen's "you know"? Will they hint at a future incident, a past one? Will they try to set a mood? Sharing their writing in small groups or with the entire class may excite them to write more. Who knows? You might get a novel from someone, or at least a short story.

Though Salinger's use of language is better than that of most authors whose works are widely read by adolescents, he is far from alone. A number of fine writers string words and phrases along in truly graceful ways. Let's briefly consider the work of three such writers: Alice Hoffman, Richard Peck, and Judith Guest.

1. *At Risk* by Alice Hoffman (306 pp.). Hoffman's *At Risk* may be one of those books about a youngster, eleven-year-old Amanda Farrell, that has a somewhat longer shelf life than many novels read by adolescents: It's about AIDS. When she was six, Amanda had an appendicitis operation, and, when things went wrong and she needed a transfusion, she was given contaminated blood. Now she is dying. It is to Hoffman's considerable credit that she does not fall prey to sentimentality or bathos. Her writing is intelligent, even-handed, at times even cautious. But she must, of course, give her characters full range to their emotions: Amanda's father, Ivan, who can barely control his anger and wants desperately to strike out at some one, some thing; her mother, Polly, who mixes her love for her daughter with the knowledge that her last days cannot be suffused with self-pity; and younger brother, Charlie, who only barely can understand why his best friend will no longer come to play with him.

Two brief passages will suggest Hoffman's skill. The first comes early in the novel, when Amanda is ill but no one knows with what:

> 'You'll be better in the morning,' Polly says.
> It's what she always says when the children are sick, and they always believe her. But this time Polly is wrong. Just after dusk the rain will begin, but it won't bring any relief. In the morning, the last day of August and the hottest on record, Amanda will still be shivering beneath two cotton quilts.(p. 26)

Two chapters later Ed Reardon, the longtime family doctor and the surgeon who performed Amanda's appendectomy, has given the bad news to a disbelieving Ivan:

> Later, as he drives home, Ivan will pull over to the side of the road, not far from where Polly and the children like to pick wild raspberries every summer. He has been crying ever since he left Ed Reardon's office, but now he begins to howl. It is a terrifying sound. It comes from deep inside him, but it doesn't seem to belong to him, he can hear it from the outside as if it were somebody else's pain . . .
> For five years Ivan has been losing her without knowing it. Every time he sent her to her room for being fresh, every time he missed a gymnastics meet, every hour he has spent looking at dead stars, he has been losing her.
> And now, on a Thursday morning, as blackbirds light on the brambles that grow alongside the road, he has lost her.(pp. 57-58)

2. *Unfinished Portrait of Jessica* by Richard Peck (162 pp.). Few young adult novelists rival Richard Peck as a blue-chipper. All of his 17 novels for young readers are still in print (a rare achievement in this volatile market), all enjoy considerable popularity not only with teenaged readers but also with their

teachers and librarians, and all are written well. His *Unfinished Portrait of Jessica* introduces a young girl whose father, whom she loves unconditionally, has left her mother; Jessica is on the father's side. When she visits him in Mexico, she plans to stay with him no matter what the consequences. But that portrait is not quite yet finished. In a prefatory note Jessica recalls that Mexico house:

> Burned into my memory is a house rising among the rocks above a bay. It stands in another world from mine, like a dream in primary colors, and yet it refuses to let me leave. Every hot day of summer recalls winter there. The sea wavers in heat. The sun throws combs of light through the palm leaves.
>
> It's a house in a land where something is always dying in plain sight, and yet nature heals. It creates sand from ashes, and soil from sand, and then flowers to screen and promise. There's salt in the sand there, salt from the sea, and so the terraces crumble at their edges. Even the earth is liable to open at your feet just where you were sure of your ground.
>
> The house has a very Mexican name, *Amor y Muerte* - Love and Death. But I knew nothing of love and death the first time I went there. I was fourteen. (p. 2)

3. *Ordinary People* by Judith Guest (256 pp.). The highly acclaimed *Ordinary People* was Judith Guest's first novel and what an auspicious beginning it has. She writes about the Jarrett family—successful lawyer Calvin; Beth, who as wife if not always as mother, nears perfection; Conrad, the second son, the one who tried to commit suicide and has just now returned from four months in a mental hospital; and always in the background, Conrad's older brother Buck, who was killed a year earlier in a boating accident. Guest alternates chapters in the telling of the story, the first from Conrad's point of view, then from Calvin's, then from Conrad's, and so forth and—significantly—never from Beth's.

Lying in bed soon after he has returned home, Conrad is trying to summon enough courage to begin the day, a difficult task:

> Straining, he can barely hear the early-morning sounds of his father and mother organizing things, synchronizing schedules at the other end of the hall. It doesn't matter. He doesn't need to hear, and they would certainly not be talking about anything important. They would not be talking, for instance, about him. They are people of good taste. They do not discuss a problem in the presence of the problem. And, besides, there is no problem. There is just Phase Two. Recovery. A moving forward. (p. 4)

Later, after a family Christmas that doesn't quite work, Calvin reviews the situation, even wondering about the car his affluence had permitted him and Beth to buy for Conrad:

> Something was missing, something terribly wrong, but it was not just the car. It was the whole day. Well, what do you expect? We are a family, aren't we?

And a family turns inward towards itself in grief, it does not go in separate directions, pulling itself apart. Like hell it doesn't. Grief is ugly. It is isolating. It is not something to be shared with others, it is something to be afraid of, to get rid of, and fast. Get those months, days, hours, minutes out of the way, it can't be quick enough.(pp. 117-118)

Just these brief passages reveal the writing quality of these authors. Your students will no doubt select other passages and other authors. The key matter is that they focus some of their classroom attention on language, on the way an author tells the story, introduces characters, develops themes, indicates setting. Writing is a craft, after all, the tools of which are words. Good students of literature must examine how the words are put together.

Conclusion

It's time for a brief review. *The Catcher in the Rye*, I think, richly merits a place in the secondary school literature curriculum. It is an important book, worth study not only in its own right but also in conjunction with numerous other important works. Among these are young adult novels, including those I've mentioned but hardly limited to them. I believe that a focus on *Catcher*, the core novel, the one all students read, and additional small-group attention to such other novels as I've described in these pages (or those you would prefer to use) can be a rewarding classroom experience for your students and for you.

References

Blume, J.(1975). *Forever*. New York: Bradbury Press.
Briders, S. E.(1980). *All together now*. New York: Harper & Row.
Bridgers, S. E.(1987). *Permanent connections*. New York: Harper & Row.
Cormier, R.(1974). *The chocolate war*. New York: Dell Laurel-Leaf.
Crutcher, C.(1989). *Chinese handcuffs*. New York: Greenwillow Books.
Guest, J.(1977). *Ordinary people*. New York: Ballantine Books.
Hoffman, A.(1988). *At risk*. New York: Berkley Books.
Lipsyte, R.(1991). *The brave*. New York: Harper Collins.
Lipsyte, R.(1967). *The contender*. New York: Harper & Row.
Paulsen, G.(1991). *The Monument*. New York: Dell Laurel-Leaf.
Peck, R.(1991). *Unfinished portrait of Jessica*. New York: Delacorte Press.
Pfeffer, S. B.(1991). *Most precious blood*. New York: Bantam Books.
Salinger, J. D.(1964). *The catcher in the rye*. New York: Bantam Books.
Scoppettone, S.(1991). *Happy endings are all alike*. Boston: Alyson Publications.
Zindel, P.(1987). *The amazing and death-defying diary of Eugene Dingman*. New York: Bantam Books.

Chapter 5

Family Relationships As Found in Arthur Miller's *Death of a Salesman* and Cynthia Voigt's *The Runner*

RUTH CLINE

Introduction

The American family has been the source of study and concern in the past few decades. The structure of the family is changing with more divorces, single parent homes, children born outside of marriage, and unmarried people living together. The evidence indicates that communication within families is often lacking entirely or is not at a level that is meaningful. This lack can be the result of external causes such as alcohol abuse, parents working away from the home, or an inability of family members to show empathy or concern for each other. Because of the widespread nature of these home conditions, it is safe to assume many students in an average classroom are experiencing this lack of communication in their own families.

Young people need models of good communication to help them understand its importance. Teachers may help these students understand themselves and their families by looking at how characters in literature interact with family members. Knowing how a fictional character acts and reacts may give insight to a student in a similar situation. Students may find alternatives for decisions about life-issues through their understanding of literature.

Arthur Miller's award-winning play *Death of a Salesman* is regarded as a classic of American literature and is often studied in high schools. Although Cynthia Voigt has written several novels that would make great companions to this piece, I have chosen her book *The Runner* for this discussion.

The Family as Portrayed in *Death of a Salesman*

Arthur Miller, a well-known American playwright, was interested in the haunting influence of a guilty past on the present. He introduced this theme in *All My Sons*, his first successful play, which was produced in 1947, and he pursued the theme in *Death of a Salesman*, which was written in 1949. The play has been performed countless times, including a long run on Broadway, film adaptations, and a 1984 television presentation featuring Dustin Hoffman as Willy that won critical acclaim.

Willy, the Father

Willy Loman at age 63 is a worn-out salesman, one who opened new territories for his company but now takes his valises in and out of the car without making a sale. "He drives seven hundred miles and when he gets there no one knows him any more, no one welcomes him" (p. 57). He has an obsession about "being liked," and thinks his son Biff should be a salesman because "people always like him."

Willy feels "boxed in" by the closeness of the apartments, the streets lined with cars, and "not a breath of fresh air in the neighborhood" (p. 17). Willy becomes increasingly more and more nostalgic about the past. Although he and his wife, Linda, talk to each other, they don't really communicate. For instance, when Linda buys a new kind of cheese, Willy says, "I don't want a change. I want Swiss cheese. Why am I always being contradicted?" (p. 17). This seems like an overreaction to a simple thing.

Willy had an affair with a woman in Boston, and the fact that Biff came into the hotel room and realized what was going on has haunted Willy ever since. Since Linda, his wife, is sweet and concerned about his well-being, Willy is also suffering from guilt about his behavior. The incident also influences Willy's relationship with Biff in that he is not sure how to deal with his son. As a result, Willy puts on an act with Biff and the others, pretending that everything is going well. In reality, Willy's sales territory has been cut back, his salary has been taken away, and he is borrowing money from Charley, pretending he has earned it.

Willy's Uncle Ben, a fast-talking kind of con man, is part of many of Willy's dreams. Ben is constantly luring Willy into adventures and "get rich quick" schemes. Although Ben has died before the play starts, he appears to Willy in many scenes as almost another identity for Willy.

At the end Willy decides to carry out his "perfect proposition," his suicide, with the mistaken idea that it will benefit his family, but especially Biff.

Biff, the Son

Biff feels like life is passing him by. Every spring when the new colts arrive and the farm starts greening up, he feels that "I ought to be makin' my future. That's when I come running home . . . everytime I come back here I know that all I've done is to waste my life." Biff is personally attractive and a hard worker, one who had high promise in high school because of his athletic ability. Now at age 34, Biff is working on a farm and has "yet to make $35 a week" (p. 16).

One of the questions raised in the play is why Biff never realized his potential. As the play unfolds the reader becomes aware of several influences. One is that

Willy didn't reprimand him when he became aware that Biff had stolen a school football. Later Biff stole some lumber for a project at home and his father made light of it. Again there is an eroding of Biff's moral fiber. When Biff found out he was in danger of failing his high school math course, he went to Boston to talk to his father about it. There he found his father in his hotel room with a girl. Biff was devastated and refused to take his father's advice about school.

In the play when Biff comes home to start life again, he makes a job appointment with Oliver "who always liked him." To Biff's chagrin, Oliver doesn't remember him and won't even talk to him. Biff steals Oliver's fountain pen and leaves. Biff wants to tell Willy the truth, not just about Oliver but about how he feels about life, but his brother Happy talks him out of it. When Biff tells Willy that he is leaving for good because they will never understand each other, Willy accuses Biff of being spiteful. When Biff confronts Willy with evidence that Willy plans to kill himself, Biff cries and Willy is amazed to realize that Biff loves him.

Happy, the Other Son

Happy is well-built and sexually appealing, but he drinks too much and is not a commendable character. He picks up some girls in the restaurant where he and Biff are going to meet Willy for dinner, and Happy convinces them all to leave the restaurant without Willy. It is a cruel thing to do, especially considering the fragile ego that Willy has and how anxious he is to make Biff feel good. Happy talks Biff out of being truthful with Willy, and like his father, refuses to face the possibility of failure or compromise. Happy has been in Biff's shadow most of his life and his actions can be seen as a way to gain favor with his father. He shows mild concern about his father's condition.

Linda, Willy's Wife

Linda has compassion for Willy and sees the agony he is enduring because of his lost dreams. She sees that his ambitions far exceed his results, and it is hard for him to reconcile himself with failure. She tells her sons, "I don't say he's a great man. Willy Loman never made a lot of money. His name was never in the paper. But he's a human being, and a terrible thing has happened to him. Attention must be finally paid to such a person" (p. 56).

When Linda is mending her silk stockings, Willy becomes agitated and tells her to stop it. Linda is unaware that Willy had given her silk stockings to his Boston paramour, and it reminds Willy of how Biff reacted blurting out, "You gave her Mama's stockings."

Linda is pleased that the boys are going to take their father to Frank's Chop House that evening, and she is furious when she learns that the boys pick up some girls instead and leave Willy alone in the restaurant.

Throughout the play, Linda consistently turns back Willy's attempts to admit his failures. She continually denies his shortcomings. She respects his worth and tries to build up his confidence. When she is talking to the boys, however, it is obvious she understands the problems Willy is having, but her denial may inhibit his attempts to come to terms with himself.

The Family as Portrayed in *The Runner*

Cynthia Voigt introduced us to the Tillerman family in her two previous novels, *Homecoming* and *Dicey's Song*. In these books we learn about the four Tillerman children, who have never known their father and whose mother abondoned them. They find their Grandmother Tillerman, a crusty woman, abrupt in her views and forbidding in her appearance. The reader wonders what happened in the grandmother's life to make her so wary of people. We learn about her and the family background in *The Runner* (1985), a prequel to the two previously published books.

The Runner is set in 1967, four years after Liza, who becomes the mother of the Tillerman children, left home with her boyfriend, Frank. Liza's older brother, Johnny, went to college on a scholarship and hardly ever returns home. The younger brother, Bullet, is a high school student and the focus of the novel. The father at age 60 is intolerant, psychologically abusive, and "boxes people in." He did this to Bullet's older brother, but Johnny fought back and was literally driven from home. Bullet is constantly on guard when he is with his father, aware of nuances in his father's voice that he almost hopes will offend him.

Bullet

Bullet has learned that running is a release for his feelings. He runs his own nine mile, cross-country course, pushing himself until he is afraid he will throw up his supper. Instead he stands straight and "locked his throat tight" (p.9). That description gives us insight into Bullet's character: He wills himself to do or not to do almost anything. When his father commands Bullet to get a haircut before he is welcome to sit at his dinner table again, Bullet has his head shaved. His father is furious, as Bullet knew he would be, and tells Bullet he can not sit at the table with them or have food prepared by his mother until his hair has grown out again. All this means to Bullet is that he will run before dinner and fix his own meals. No big deal!

Bullet is not afraid of work. He will get up at five in the morning to work for two hours in the field before going to high school. Bullet has also worked on a crabbing boat with Patrice since he was only thirteen. Although it is hard work, he and Patrice have opportunities to talk, Patrice being one of the few people with whom Bullet converses.

Bullet has little tolerance for his classmates, whom he considers shallow. Because Bullet's hair is long, he is teased by some of his classmates. When one bully calls him "Tiller-girl" because of his long hair, Bullet fights him and blackens both of the boy's eyes. Bullet intervenes, however, when a food fight erupts in the school cafeteria and helps stop the mess.

Even though Bullet has won track championships, he does not want to assist a young black man, Tamer, with cross-country running when the coach asks him to do it. It is when he learns his friend Patrice is part black that Bullet realizes he is being a bigot and consents to help Tamer.

Voigt presents Bullet as a young man who is alienated from most people. He hardly speaks to his father, he communicates in nonverbal ways with his mother, and he has little to say to his classmates, his teachers, or his coach. If it were not for his work with Patrice, Bullet would be isolated altogether in his own world.

Bullet's Father

Bullet's father is aptly described in the following words: "The old man got hold of ideas and kept them, clenched tight in his fist, as if that made them true" (p. 10). Bullet says his old man "builds boxes around people," making them do what he wants them to do. He uses the farm as an example of this. Bullet can use the farm as both a draft deferment for the Vietnam War and a job, but it would mean working with or for his father. He is sure he could not do that. The old man had taken over the farm from his wife's father, but Bullet thinks the farm had "taken over the old man," who never really liked it.

His father's need for control extended to doling out dabs of money for groceries or refusing to take his wife to the store, making her go in Johnny's boat, which would take two to four hours, depending on the wind. Bullet teases his mother by calling her "Maw, which the old man said was common as dirt, as well as illiterate and ill-enunciated" (p.18).

Bullet's Mother

Bullet's mother is caught between her belligerent husband and her rebellious son, afraid to speak up in defense of her son and yet not wanting to side with her husband. The home is often tense with unspoken arguments, curt demands, and unanswered requests.

The mother likes working in the garden or sitting in Johnny's boat with the tiller in her hand. Bullet reflects about her: "There was something about her, something proud and bold and brave and strong—the old man couldn't break her, couldn't drive her off. Not if he lived to be a hundred" (p. 11).

Bullet gets along with his mother. They communicate in silent ways with looks or smiles. The mother is sympathetic with her son and wants him to get along with the father, but she doesn't dare express these feelings. She would like to intervene for Bullet but she doesn't. She calls him "You" or "You, boy," when he is about to do something he shouldn't. "He could read her and she could read him—which was the closest they came to talking" (p. 18). The mother risks the anger of her husband by going to the high school track meets when Bullet is competing. Then she heads for home before Bullet can speak to her.

Relationship Between Bullet's Parents

Bullet's parents do not communicate with each other in the story. "His old man was a nothing, nothing but right answers and holding onto his precious farm" (p. 7). The father didn't allow Bullet's mother to get a driver's license. He expects her and others who sit at his table to be dressed for dinner. Although the farm belonged to the Hacketts, his wife's family, the old man is the master of it now and acts like it has always been his: "The old man slapped his name on her, slapped his name on the land, and owned everything. Only, the way he acted and talked, the farm owned him and he hated it. What a life" (p. 11).

The tension in the Tillerman home increases through the novel: "The air in the room got very still, like an iceberg forming all at once. Bullet looked up briefly: his father stared at his plate, his mouth working; his mother stared at the middle of the table, just waiting" (p. 184). The parents didn't talk to each other or to their son.

When Bullet enlists in the army, he tries to think of some way to give money to his mother so she will be able to fix Johnny's old boat. Bullet knows, once he leaves, that his father will act like Bullet had never lived there.

When the call comes that Bullet has been killed in Vietnam, his mother uses a cleaver to cut the phone wire, takes the phone to town, and throws it through the phone company window.

Comparisons Between *The Runner* and *Death of a Salesman*

The father in *The Runner* tries to ignore his son and avoids talking to him. The father in *Salesman* has high hopes for his two sons, Biff and Happy. Willy is especially concerned about Biff, whom he once thought had such a promising future. Bullet's father does not communicate effectively with anyone; Willy talks a lot, but he does not recognize the difference between truth and lies. He lives in an unreal world much of the time.

Class Discussion

Bullet talks about "the box" that his father puts around people. Teachers could ask students to describe "the box" that Bullet feels his father has put him in. Why can't Bullet talk to his parents? Why can't Bullet's parents talk to each other? What could change the environment in the home? These same questions could be asked of Willy and his two sons.

Describe Bullet's relationship with his classmates and coach. Why did Bullet enlist in the army? Why did Biff steal Oliver's pen? How do one's parents affect their children? How would you like either story to end? Write a new ending for either story.

Writing Assignments

What would happen if Willy were Bullet's father? Would they get along? Try to imagine a scene where the two of them were talking. What would they say to each other?

The sons in the two selections are very different from each other. Bullet is younger, still in high school, but he has much more determination than Happy and Biff. Give examples from the text that illustrate the differences in these boys and their character. Try to imagine the boys in a particular setting. How would they interact? If Bullet had come into Frank's Chop House for dinner the night Biff and Happy were there with Willy, what would he have done? Do you think Biff or Happy would enlist in the army for the Vietnam War?

Compare the mothers from the two selections. In what way were they different? The same? What might a conversation between them be about? Who would dominate the discussion?

Using circles for the main characters in each of the selections, draw lines to show the interaction between the characters. Is each relationship going both directions or just one way? Discuss what would have to happen in each selection to provide for effective two-way communication between the characters. Role-playing or readers' theater presentations of scenes from both selections will help readers identify with the characters.

Conclusion

The Runner and *Death of a Salesman* are two examples of different approaches to the common theme of family relationships. Although *The Runner* is considered young adult literature and *Death of a Salesman* is an adult classic, the selections would work very well together. Each selection provides vivid examples of lack of communication among family members. The ages of the sons vary, but their problems are similar. Using these books with young adults will provide them with case studies of family communication and ample opportunity for discussion. Hopefully, it will help the young reader think about his or her family relationships and how to improve them.

Other Young Adult Novels that Deal with Family Issues

Many young adult novels have plots or subplots that revolve around the family, family problems, and family relationships. Suggested titles and annotations are included here for teachers to encourage their students to read widely on this topic. It would be interesting to use some of the novels set in other countries to help American students understand how their version of family life fits into a continuum of relationships. Since the reference book, *Focus on Families* (Cline 1990), includes chapters, fiction, and informational bibliographies on pertinent family topics (traditional families, single-parent families, stepfamilies, extended families, divorce, adoption, and child abuse), the books listed here are included because they were not part of the *Focus* publication.

1. *Blue Heron* by Avi (186 pp.). Maggie is almost 13 and has gone to a cabin in the woods for her summer vacation to get acquainted with her stepmother and stepsister. Her father is somewhat uncommunicative, and Maggie seeks refuge from her feelings by observing a blue heron and nature. Maggie tries to determine her responsibilities in this new family.

2. *The True Confessions of Charlotte Doyle* by Avi (210 pp.). Charlotte is a 13-year-old girl who takes passage on the Seahawk, leaving England in 1832 and heading for America. She is the only passenger and gets caught in the intrigue between the crew and captain. The intense encounter with her family when she finally arrives in Providence shows the contrast in expectations, behavior, dress, and speech of young girls at that time and today. How would Charlotte's return home be different if this story took place today? (Newbery Honor Book)

3. *Midnight Hour Encore* by Bruce Brooks (263 pp.). A talented cellist lives with her father in Maryland. Finally, at the age of 16, she asks her father if he will take her to meet her mother in San Francisco. This story of a single-parent family shows great love and support for the daughter and is for mature readers.

4. *Permanent Connections* by Sue Ellen Bridgers (264 pp.). Seventeen-year-old Rob is a loser while living with his New Jersey family, but he learns something about responsibility when he goes to live with his extended family in North Carolina. Comparing Rob's character development to Bullet's and Biff's would be an interesting exercise for students.

5. *Stranger, You and I* by Patricia Calvert (152 pp.). The story is told by Hugh, a high school boy, who sees his friend Zee struggle with an unwanted pregnancy. This novel presents one solution about teen-parenting which could be the basis for a thoughtful class discussion on this contemporary issue.

6. *The Education of Little Tree* by Forrest Carter (216 pp.). This is a touching story about Little Tree, a Cherokee Indian boy who is orphaned at the age of five. Brought up by Granpa and Granma,

Little Tree learns the lessons of life as they are taught by his extended family.

7. *Among the Volcanoes* by Omar Castaneda (183 pp.). Guatemala is the setting for this story of a family trying to rise above illness, poverty, and a lack of education. Customs of the village are strong and unyielding. The teens have to learn to adjust to the village and society's ideas.

8. *Other Bells for Us to Ring* by Robert Cormier (136 pp.). Eleven-year-old Darcy learns about life from a friend who is killed when her drunken father pursues her. Child abuse is a contemporary issue with roots in family life.

9. *Tunes for Bears to Dance To* by Robert Cormier (101 pp.). Both of these Cormier novels have younger protagonists, but serious concepts are discussed. In this novel, Henry's parents are struggling with their problems, and he has to make his own decisions about power, money, and morality.

10. *Nekomah Creek* by Linda Crew (191 pp.). Robby, a fourth grader, thinks the school authorities are spying on his family because they are non-traditional: His father, a house-husband, cooks and takes care of the house and children while his mother goes to her job every day.

11. *The Honorable Prison* by Lyll Becerra de Jenkins (199 pp.). A journalist and his family are taken from their home in 1955 (possibly in Bolivia) and held in house arrest for many months. The effects of stress, illness, and financial deprivation on the family are devastating.

12. *Bearstone* by Will Hobbs (154 pp.). Cloyd is an Indian boy who learns a new lifestyle when he comes to live with Walter, a crusty rancher. They learn to respect each other's values, demonstrating intergenerational and racial themes.

13. *Downriver* by Will Hobbs (204 pp.). Eight teenagers are on an Outward Bound experience when they ditch their adult leader and go on a river trip by themselves. Their home lives are varied and part of their problem is in getting along with others.

14. *Changes in Latitudes* by Will Hobbs (162 pp.). Travis, a cool teenager, is vacationing with his mother and two siblings in Mexico while his family is in the midst of disintegrating. A strong theme about environmental issues parallels the family issues.

15. *Can't Hear You Listening* by Hadley Irwin (202 pp.). Tracy, a high school senior, has supportive parents, but she still finds it hard to expose a friend who's addicted to drugs and alcohol. The relationships between Tracy and her parents and her friends are basic to the story.

16. *Kiss the Dust* by Elizabeth Laird (279 pp.). A Kurd family has to leave their pleasant home in Iraq and become refugees in Iran. Twelve-year-old Tara has to take care of the family in the refugee camp when her mother becomes very ill. The hardships of this family give meaning to the news' stories our students read. The expectations of this modern heroine are enormous.

17. *D . . . My Name is Danita* by Norma Fox Mazer (163 pp.). The happy family is penetrated by a young man who claims he is Danita's half-brother from her father's early and forgotten romance. The responsibilities of casual relationships are an underlying theme. Students could compare Willy's affair in *Death of a Salesman* with Danita's father's and the difference in how each man reacted.

18. *Somewhere in the Darkness* by Walter Dean Myers (168 pp.). Jimmy Little, a black 15-year-old, is surprised when his father shows up at the apartment house and takes Jimmy on a trip of his past. Jimmy is being raised by a family friend and experiences a conflict of loyalties. Students might discuss if Jimmy has any obligations to his father who deserted him long ago.

19. *Molly by Any Other Name* by Jean Davies Okimoto (257 pp.). As Molly approaches her 18th birthday, she wants to learn about her birth parents. The topic of adoption and the rights of birth parents and adoptive parents is well done.

20. *Lyddie* by Katherine Paterson (182 pp.). Set in the 1840's in the textile factories in Lowell, Massachussetts, Lyddie—fatherless and in her early teens—learns to be self-reliant. Teenagers could discuss if Lyddie would be one of today's homeless children.

21. *Canyons* by Gary Paulsen (184 pp.). A 14-year-old boy lives with his mother who is searching for a male companion. The mystery of a skull Brennan finds when camping provides the framework for a glimpse of his single-parent home.

22. *Everybody's Daughter* by Marsha Qualey (201 pp.). A 17-year-old girl, a daughter of parents who lived in a commune during her birth, rebels against the disbanded group trying to protect her. Although the family is traditional in a sense, the relationship of the former commune members continues to be a problem for this heroine.

23. *Ice Warrior* by Ruth Riddell (138 pp.). Twelve-year-old Rob struggles to be a part of his new family. He is not realistic about his memories of his birth father, and this gets in the way of his establishing better relationships with his stepfamily.

24. *Blue Skin of the Sea* by Graham Salisbury (215 pp.). Six-year-old Sonny Mendoza is growing up in Hawaii and learns about life from the relatives with whom he has been living since his mother's death. When Sonny goes to live with his father, he hopes for some insights into his mother's character.

25. *Hank* by Jim Sauer (260 pp.). The younger brother wants to help those who are less fortunate. This congenial family is disrupted when tragedy occurs.

26. *Maniac Magee* by Jerry Spinelli (240 pp.). A homeless white boy with remarkable talents learns about many lifestyles and families as he meets people around the city: some old, many black. It would be interesting to find out if students thought Maniac would be accepted in their school.

27. *Shabanu: Daughter of the Wind* by Suzanne F. Staples (240 pp.). This novel depicts the lifestyle of the Cholistan Desert in Pakistan. Here an 11-year-old girl learns about family tradition with limited choice. Students can compare these expectations and traditions with those of American families. (Newbery Honor Book)

28. *The Rain Catchers* by Jean Thesman (182 pp.). A story of extended family life is told by a fourteen-year-old girl who has never known her

father and tries to learn more about her life's story through a visit with her career mother.

29. *On the Road to Memphis* by Mildred Taylor (290 pp.). This novel, a continuation of the Logan family story just as World War II is breaking out, shows strong sibling relationships. The other books about the Logans describe this loving, strong black family in Mississippi and show the changes in their lives as the children mature.

30. *Free to Be . . . a Family: A Book about All Kinds of Belonging* by Marlo Thomas (Ed.) (176 pp.). This book filled with poetry, essays, illustrations, and songs is appropriate for any age. Since family is the theme of the entire book, it illustrates various structures and provides insights into families.

References

Avi. (1992). *Blue heron*. New York: Bradbury Press.

Avi. (1990). *The true confessions of Charlotte Doyle*. New York: Orchard.

Bloom, H. (Ed.). (1988). *Arthur Miller's death of a salesman: Modern critical interpretations*. New York: Chelsea House.

Bridgers, S.E. (1987). *Permanent connections*. New York: Harper & Row.

Brooks, B. (1986). *Midnight hour encore*. New York: Harper Trophy.

Calvert, P. (1987). *Stranger, you and I*. New York: Charles Scribner's Sons.

Carter, F. (1986). *The education of Little Tree*. Albuquerque: University of New Mexico Press.

Castaneda, O. (1991). *Among the volcanoes*. New York: Lodestar Books.

Cline, R.K.J. (1990). *Focus on families*. Santa Barbara: ABC-CLIO.

Cormier, R. (1992). *Tunes for bears to dance to*. New York: Delacorte Press.

Cormier, R. (1990). *Other bells for us to ring*. New York: Delacorte Press.

Crew, L. (1991). *Nekomah creek*. New York: Delacorte Press.

de Jenkins, L.B. (1988). *The honorable prison*. New York: Lodestar Books.

Garland, S. (1992). *Song of the buffalo boy*. New York: Harcourt, Brace, & Jovanovich.

Hobbs, W. (1991). *Downriver*. New York: Atheneum.

Hobbs, W. (1989). *Bearstone*. New York: Atheneum.

Hobbs, W. (1988). *Changes in latitudes*. London: Pan Horizons Publishers.

Irwin, Hadley. (1990). *Can't hear you listening*. New York: Collier Macmillan.

Koon, H.W. (Ed.). (1983). *Twentieth century interpretations of death of a salesman*. New York: Prentice-Hall.

Laird, E. (1992). *Kiss the dust*. New York: E.P. Dutton.

Mazer, N.F. (1990). *D . . . My name is Danita*. New York: Scholastic.

Miller, A. (1949). *Death of a salesman*. New York: Penguin Books.

Myers, W.D. (1992). *Somewhere in the darkness*. New York: Scholastic.

Okimoto, J.D. (1990). *Molly by any other name*. New York: Scholastic.

Paterson, K. (1991). *Lyddie*. New York: E.P. Dutton.

Paulsen, G. (1990). *Canyons*. New York: Bantam Books.

Qualey, M. (1991). *Everybody's daughter*. Boston: Houghton Mifflin.

Riddell, R. (1992). *Ice warrior*. New York: Atheneum.

Salisbury, G. (1992). *Blue skin of the sea*. New York: Delacorte Press.

Sauer, J. (1990). *Hank*. New York: Delacorte Press.

Spinelli, J. (1990). *Maniac Magee*. Boston: Little, Brown, & Company.

Staples, S.F. (1989). *Shabanu: Daughter of the wind*. New York: Alfred A. Knopf.

Taylor, M. (1990). *On the road to Memphis*. New York: Dial.

Thesman, J. (1991). *The rain catchers*. Boston: Houghton Mifflin.

Thomas, M. (Ed.). (1987). *Free to be . . . a family: A book about all kinds of belonging*. New York: Bantam Books.

Voigt, C. (1985). *The runner*. New York: Ballantine (Fawcett Juniper).

Chapter 6

Using Young Adult Literature to
Modernize the Teaching of *Romeo and Juliet*

ARTHEA J. S. REED

Introduction

Romeo and Juliet is frequently the first Shakespearean play taught in the high school curriculum. It is an excellent choice for introducing teenagers to Shakespeare because they can relate to its plot, characters, and themes. The play's action is fast-moving and easily understood. The characters are realistic and their motives are clear. The themes are as current as they were in Shakespeare's time: parent-child conflict, teenage love, friendship and peer pressure, and suicide. More advanced students can deal with the complex social and literary themes of hostility and its effects on the innocent, the use of deception and its consequences, and the effects of faulty decision making.

Similarly, able readers can study how the characters function within the drama and can examine how Shakespeare uses language to develop plot, characters, and themes. They can delve into the play's classical tragic themes: the role of fate and fortune, the inevitable nature of tragedy, and the isolation of the tragic hero.

By using contemporary young adult literature along with Shakespeare's *Romeo and Juliet*, students can better understand the play. In addition, they can examine how contemporary writers use characters to carry the plot's action and utilize language to develop characters and themes. They can also begin to understand the universality of great literature as they discover the classical themes of tragedy in contemporary young adult fiction.

This chapter will be divided into four sections: (1) before reading *Romeo and Juliet*, (2) while reading *Romeo and Juliet*, (3) after reading *Romeo and Juliet*, and (4) extending the students' learning. Each section will contain numerous ideas for teaching the play and employing adolescent literature to bring the play to life for contemporary readers. It is recognized that no teacher can employ all of the suggested ideas but instead, can pick and choose among them to meet the specific goals and objectives of his or her course.

Before Reading *Romeo and Juliet*

Shakespeare's plays were to be performed rather than read. In fact, most were unpublished until after his death in 1594. When Elizabethan audiences heard the prologue, introducing "the two hours' traffic of our stage," they already were aware of the story of *Romeo and Juliet*. The tale was popular in Elizabethan times, with many versions available. The best known was Arthur Brooke's narrative poem *The Tragicall Historye of Romeus and Juliet* (Reed, p. 4). Therefore, Shakespeare's audience was not fooled by the comic beginning of the play when Sampson and Gregory opened it with swashbuckling action and humor. Even without hearing the prologue, they knew that by the end of the play the "star-crossed" young lovers would "take their life" and "bury their parents' strife" (Prologue, 6-12). Our students should have the same advantage. We can introduce them to the play in numerous ways.

Introducing the Plot

Although the plots are not exactly the same, students can read modern versions of *Romeo and Juliet* to help them understand the feud between the Capulets and the Montagues and the teenage love story of Romeo and Juliet. There are numerous young adult novels that revolve around the plot of teenage lovers from different worlds.

Teenage Lovers from Around the World

1. *Summer of My German Soldier* by Bette Greene (199 pp.). This is the story of a young American Jewish girl who falls in love with a German prisoner of war during World War II.

2. *Fair Day, and Another Step Begun* by Katie Letcher Lyle (157 pp.). Based on a medieval love ballad, a young girl seeks the love of the man who has impregnated her.

3. *Across the Barricades* by J. Lingard (159 pp.). The story is set in Belfast, Ireland and revolves around a Protestant girl and a Catholic boy who fall in love despite their parents' objections. This is a Romeo and Juliet romance with a political angle.

4. *Song of the Buffalo Boy* by Sherry Garland (249 pp.). The reader learns about the ridicule heaped on Amerasian children in Vietnam and the family traditions involving arranged marriages.

Students can also view films that present modern versions of a tragic love story. Bette Greene's *Summer of My German Soldier* is available in video tape, for example. Additionally, students might view one of the movie versions of the play prior to reading it. The most popular and accessible one is S. Franco Zeffirelli's *Romeo and Juliet* (1968). Since Zeffirelli's screenplay changed a good bit of the play, the changes he made will make interesting discussion as students read the original. And, finally, because *Romeo and Juliet* is frequently performed, students may be able to see a production of the play prior to its reading.

Teachers can also tell the story to the class. If you are a good storyteller you can bring the plot of *Romeo and Juliet* to life for the students. Or, you can introduce each act of the play by asking leading questions: The plot begins with a teenage boy who is smitten but rebuffed by a lovely young girl named Rosaline. Suppose you were in a similar situation and you knew that the person you cared for was going to be at a party to which you were not invited. What might you do? Would you crash the party? Well, that's what Romeo does.

One of the subplots of *Romeo and Juliet* is the feud between the Montagues and the Capulets. Students are often intrigued by the concept of a feud. Students can investigate other feuds in history, such as the ones between the Campbell and MacDonald Scottish clans or the one between the Hatfields and McCoys in Appalachia. They can read about feuds in literature. In *West Side Story*, for example, the feud is between ethnic gangs. In Mark Twain's *Huckleberry Finn* the students can read about the feud between the Shepherdsons and the Grangerfords. Students can examine the effects of the feuds and present information about them in oral reports or creative dramas to the class.

Introducing the Themes

An interesting way to organize a unit in which *Romeo and Juliet* is taught is thematically. Teachers can introduce the difficult theme of the isolation of the tragic hero by having students read young adult novels before reading the play.

Isolation of the Tragic Hero

1. *I Am the Universe* by Barbara Corcoran (136 pp.). Katharine Esterly, an eighth grader, has to write a composition entitled, "Who Am I?" at a time when her mother has to have a brain tumor removed.

2. *The Chocolate War* by Robert Cormier (191 pp.). Jerry Renault finds himself "disturbing the universe" alone in an all boys' school.

3. *The Magic Box* by Olga Cossi (191 pp.). Mara Bennetti changes from an immature teenager who hates her mother into a concerned, grown-up daughter through an intense series of events.

4. *Two Blocks Down* by Jina Delton (148 pp.). This novel explores the

emotional decline of Star, a lonely seventeen-year-old.

5. *Beyond the Divide* by Kathryn Lasky (264 pp.). Fourteen-year-old Meribah decides to accompany her father on the '49 Gold Rush, leaving the Pennsylvania Amish community where she has been shunned for attending a non-Amish funeral.

Ambitious students could tackle the same assignment using either of these classics: Harper Lee's *To Kill a Mockingbird* or Arthur Miller's *Death of a Salesman*.

Students can be divided into small groups with each group reading one of the works listed to examine the tragic hero in the novel or play. After they have read and discussed these works, they can read *Romeo and Juliet* and compare Shakespeare's characterization of the tragic hero with that of the authors of the more contemporary works they have read. They might deal with questions such as the following:

* What makes the hero tragic?
* Why is the hero isolated? From whom?
* How does this isolation affect the hero's behavior?
* Could the hero have avoided this isolation? How?
* Would the outcome of the novel or the play have been different if the hero had not been isolated? Why? How?

Other thematic units can be developed. Below is a thematic list of more contemporary books and authors which can be used along with *Romeo and Juliet* in exploration of other specific themes:

Hostility and Its Effects on the Innocent

1. *Blubber* by Judy Blume (153 pp.). Jill, an upper class fifth grader, torments Linda, better known as "Blubber," because of her weight and her oral report on whales.

2. *Farewell to Manzanar* by Jeanne W. Houston and James Houston (160 pp.). The true story of a Japanese-American child's survival at the Manzanar internment camp during World War II.

3. *Across the Barricades* by J. Lingard. In modern-day Belfast, a Protestant girl and Catholic boy fall in love despite family opposition.

4. *The Witch of Blackbird Pond* by Elizabeth Speare (249 pp.). Set in Colonial America, "Kit" not only deals with feeling unloved and alone

in a house of strangers but has to withstand accusations of being a witch.

5. *Words by Heart* by Ouida Sebestyen (144 pp.). The story of an African-American family who suffers discrimination in the American Southwest in the early part of the twentieth century.

Teenage Suicide

1. *Ordinary People* by Judith Guest (256 pp.). A sensitive teenager, Conrad Jarrett, is recovering, both physically and emotionally, from his suicide attempt.

2. *So Long at the Fair* by Hadley Irwin (202 pp.). Joel spends a week at the State Fair trying to figure out why Ashley, his best friend, committed suicide.

3. *Because of Lissa* by Carolyn Meyer (192 pp.). Four teenagers decide to make some good come out of Lissa's suicide by establishing a school hotline for troubled students.

4. *Remembering the Good Times* by Richard Peck (181 pp.). Three teenagers, two boys and a girl, strike up a friendship that ends in tragedy.

5. *How Could You Do It, Diane?* by Stella Pevsner (192 pp.). Bethany finds her older stepsister's body after she commits suicide and is left with the struggle of trying to figure out why.

6. *About David* by Susan Beth Pfeffer (176 pp.). After David kills his parents and himself, his close friend Lynn is left to figure out why he could do such a thing.

Decision Making

1. *Leroy and the Old Man* by William Butterworth (154 pp.). When Leroy's no-good father offers him a chance to be a numbers runner in New York City, Leroy must decide between right and wrong.

2. *The Outsiders* by S.E. Hinton (156 pp.). Ponyboy Curtis, a fourteen-year-old Greaser, ultimately discovers that life is rough all over, even for the Socs, and that he can choose what he wants out of life.

3. *Grounded* by William Jaspersohn (244 pp.). Joe runs away from home because of his father and meets another teenager who helps him face up to some unpleasant realities.

4. *The Contender* by Robert Lipsyte (167 pp.). Alfred Brooks must choose between gang life or be different from what his environment cultivates.

5. *I Never Loved Your Mind* by Paul Zindel (144 pp.). Two bright but lost high school students drop out of school in order to search for meaning to life in a world that they find unbearable.

The Generation Gap

1. *Ask for Love and They Give You Rice Pudding* by Bradford Angier and Barbara Corcoran (151 pp.). Robbie Benson, a very rich and lonely teenager, lives with his less-than-doting grandmother and dying grandfather while his mother recovers from her alcoholism.

2. *Everything is Not Enough* by Sandy Asher (155 pp.). Seventeen-year-old Michael's future has been all mapped out for him—by his parents.

3. *Home Before Dark* by Sue Ellen Bridgers (150 pps.). Stella, the oldest child in a family of migrant workers, refuses to leave the cabin—her only real home—to move into her stepmother's larger house in town.

4. *Dinky Hocker Shoots Smack* by M.E. Kerr (192 pp.). Dinky does not have a drug problem but feels her mom is too busy helping other kids with drug problems to notice her.

5. *Crossing Over* by Jesse McGuire (184 pp.). A group of teenagers deal with their inability to express their true feelings to their parents and themselves.

The Role of Friendship and Peer Pressure

1. *The Moves Make the Man* by Bruce Brooks (280 pp.). Jerome, an outstanding student and an excellent basketball player, has been selected as the token black to integrate the Wilmington, North Carolina schools in the Fifties. He meets Bix, and through their friendship, each learns more about the other and himself.

2. *Killing Mr. Griffin* by Lois Duncan (243 pp.). Five teenagers fall prey to peer pressure and its negative effects.

3. *The Friends* by Rosa Guy (203 pp.). Fourteen-year-old Phylissia, a West Indian, and Edith, a child from Harlem, eventually become friends. The friendship is difficult due to the girls' many differences.

4. *The War on Villa Street* by Harry Mazer (192 pp.). In an attempt to escape the pain of his drunken, abusive father, Willis runs into Rabbit Slavin's gang on Villa Street.

5. *Scorpions* by Walter Dean Myers (216 pp.). Twelve-year-old Jamal Hicks might have a gun, but it doesn't help him lead the Scorpions and it doesn't prevent the older kids from pressuring him into selling drugs.

The Use of Deception and Its Consequences

1. *I Am the Cheese* by Robert Cormier (233 pp.). Adam Farmer, a young teen, struggles to regain his identity.

2. *Gentlehands* by M.E. Kerr (144 pp.). Buddy outclasses himself when he falls for the well-to-do Skye Pennington during the same summer his gentle grandfather is accused of being a Nazi murderer.

3. *The Masquerade* by Susan Shreve (184 pp.). Seventeen-year-old Rebecca's father is arrested for embezzlement, and her mother suffers a nervous breakdown.

Teenage Love

1. *Forever* by Judy Blume (220 pp.). Katherine meets, falls in love, and decides to have her first sexual experience with Michael, her forever love.

2. *Acts of Love* by Maureen Daly (164 pp.). Retta's family is poor but genteel, whereas Dallas is basically the head of his family since his father is a broken man. In spite of their differences and a family moral dilemma faced by Dallas, the teenagers are drawn to each other.

3. *My Love, My Love, or, the Peasant Girl* by Rosa Guy (119 pp.). A poor girl in the Antilles nurses to health a wealthy Creole injured in an

auto accident. The theme of this love story is clear: Color and class division are difficult to bridge.

4. *The People Therein* by Mildred Lee (271 pp.). This is a touching love story about a crippled girl and a recovering alcoholic that takes place in late-nineteenth century Appalachia.

5. *When We First Met* by Norma Fox Mazer (192 pp.). Jenny, a high school senior who has never experienced romance, falls in love at first sight. When she finally meets Rob, the object of her affection, she is appalled to learn that his mother was the drunk driver who killed her sister two years earlier.

6. *That Night* by Alice McDermott (184 pp.). Sheryl's mother decides that Sheryl will drop out of school and give the baby up for adoption without consulting the father; she seriously underestimates his love.

Another approach to teaching thematically is to allow each student to select and read any one of the aforementioned books and attempt to track in a reader's response journal the development of the theme. Then, as students read *Romeo and Juliet* they can track the development of the same theme in the play. Afterwards, students can compare how the authors of the contemporary works and Shakespeare developed the theme.

Students can also read or view modern versions of the play that deal with many of the themes. The closest parallel in terms of multiple themes is the musical *West Side Story*. This musical, which is available in script or video, introduces most of the major themes found in *Romeo and Juliet*: parent-child conflict, teenage love, friendship and peer pressure, and suicide. In addition the more complicated, literary themes of hostility and its effect on the innocent, the use of deception and its consequences, and the effects of faulty decision making are also important in the musical. However, the classical tragic themes are not a part of *West Side Story*. Instead of the role of fate and fortune, *West Side Story* addresses the role of hate and prejudice. Students can discuss why the modern version leaves out these themes as they read Shakespeare's play. This is a good way to introduce them to the Elizabethan belief that one's life is controlled by elements external to the individual that is so important in Shakespearean drama.

Introducing the Characters

It is best to introduce the characters in a straightforward manner. You can begin by explaining to the students that the characters can be divided into two groups. Each group represents one of two feuding families who are well-known and prosperous in their community of Verona. The first family we meet is the

House of Montague, the family of Romeo, who is the son of the household. The second family is the House of Capulet, the family of Juliet, who is the daughter of the household. All of the characters are related to one or the other of these families. It is helpful to list the characters and their relationships on an overhead or handout that can be kept by the students.

House of Montague

Romeo: son of Montague, isolated, passionate, idealistic, naive, has premonitions but does not act on them, helpless.

Mercutio: kinsman to Prince and friend of Romeo, witty, honorable, intelligent, loves word play, amiable, could be voice of reason but underestimates Romeo's passion, foil to Romeo, his death makes the tragedy inevitable.

Benvolio: Montague nephew, friend of Romeo, peacemaker.

Friar Laurence: Romeo's counselor, loved and respected, attempts to do what is "right", marred reasoning, misplaced virtue.

House of Capulet

Juliet: daughter to Capulet, takes the lead in the romance, lyrical use of language, has premonitions but does not act on them, isolated, only one in play to guess the outcome.

Tybalt: Juliet's cousin, foil to Romeo, passionate, prideful, easily provoked, high-spirited, hot-blooded, fiery nature, inflexible, single set of absolutes.

Nurse: Juliet's nurse, stereotypical, arrogant, garrulous, ignorant, bawdy, uncultivated, old and infirm, fickle, wants the "best for Juliet" (translated: wants Juliet married to anyone), looks at love as "animal lust," comic.

Capulet: Juliet's father, impatient, loves Juliet but is misguided in his love, garrulous, inflexible, old, looks at love as a good match.

Paris: a count, betrothed to Juliet, foil to Romeo.

Introducing Literary Techniques: Comedy and Tragedy

Since *Romeo and Juliet* is a play that has elements of both Elizabethan comedy and tragedy, students can investigate the dramatic techniques of each genre. Divide the class into two groups—one group to research the elements of comedy and the other to research the elements of tragedy. After locating the elements of comedy and tragedy, students can be directed to modern comedies and tragedies to help them understand these elements. Two young adult novels that will work well for comedy follow.

1. *Who Put That Hair in My Toothbrush?* by Jerry Spinelli (220 pp.). A teenage brother and sister are continuously taunting one another with practical jokes.

2. *The Snarkout Boys and the Avocado of Death* by Daniel Pinkwater (156 pp.). A group of adolescent boys take on their parents and their teachers.

Two young adult novels, mentioned earlier, that will work well for tragedy are 1) *About David* by Susan Beth Pfeffer and 2) *Remembering the Good Times* by Richard Peck. Students may also be able to relate the elements of comedy and tragedy to other books they have read or films they have seen. This will help them better understand the elements in Shakespeare's play.

Foreshadowing

Young readers often do not recognize the literary technique of foreshadowing which allows authors to develop plots. Students can be successfully introduced to this technique by reading them the first chapter of Lois Duncan's *Killing Mr. Griffin*. The chapter begins with the words, "It was a wild, windy, southwestern spring when the idea of killing Mr. Griffin occurred to them." It ends with a bird crashing into the classroom window and dropping "like a feather-covered stone to the ground below." In between the students in Mr. Griffin's English class argue with him about an assignment to write a final song for Ophelia in Shakespeare's *Hamlet*. Susan, the unhappy heroine of Duncan's story, thinks to herself at the end of the chapter:

> 'Poor thing . . . Poor little thing. Poor bird, Poor Ophelia. Poor Susan.' She had a sudden, irrational urge to put her head down on the desk and weep for all of them, for the whole world, for the awful day that was starting so badly and would certainly get no better.
> From his seat behind her she heard Jeff Garrett mumble under his breath, 'That Griffin's the sort of guy you'd like to kill.'

After reading aloud this opening chapter, made even more appropriate because of the classroom assignment of Hamlet, ask the students what they predict will happen during the rest of the novel.

*   What will happen to Mr. Griffin?
*   Who will be involved?
*   What about Susan, what will happen to her?

The students will be able to guess a good bit of the plot. Ask them how they know so much about it.

*   What clues did they get from the first chapter?
*   Why does the chapter begin with the weather?

    *   Why is the bird killed?
    *   Why is it important that the students are reading *Hamlet*?
    *   How does Lois Duncan foreshadow Griffin's murder?

The students will now have a clear understanding of the technique of foreshadowing and you can introduce one or more examples of it from *Romeo and Juliet*.

> O God, I have an ill-divining soul!
> Methinks I see thee, now thou art so low,
> As one dead in the bottom of a tomb. (Juliet, III,v,54-56)
> Or if you do not, make the bridal bed
> In that dim monument where Tybalt lies. (Juliet, III,v,202-203)

Structure and Dramatic Techniques

Most students are unaware of the structure of Shakespeare's plays. It is important to explain to them that each of his plays is divided into five acts, which are divided into scenes. The rising action occurs in the first two acts, the climax or turning point in the third act, and the falling action in the final two acts.

In addition, it is important to introduce students to some of the dramatic techniques used by Shakespeare: chorus, prologue, soliloquy, asides, and blank verse. The chorus can be found at the start of the play in the prologue. One of the most famous soliloquies of all time is Romeo's love speech under Juliet's window at the beginning of Act II, Scene ii. An example of an aside can be found shortly after this speech immediately following Juliet's own profession of love when Romeo says to the audience:

> Romeo: [Aside] Shall I hear more, or shall I speak at this? (II,ii,37-38)

Introducing Language Techniques

Students who are just becoming acquainted with Shakespearean drama often have problems with the language in the play. Since he used the language to develop his characters, to introduce humor, and to carry the plot, it is important that students learn how to recognize the techniques of language Shakespeare employs. To show students that other authors use language in similar ways, you can present models from contemporary novels. Following are some examples of how you can help students understand how authors use language:

Developing Characters. Introduce students to a work like Robert Cormier's *The Chocolate War*. Have the students compare and contrast the language of the villain, Archie, and the hero, Jerry. Ask questions such as these:
    *   How does their language tell you more about their personalities?
    *   How does their language identify their social class?
    *   How does their language help you predict the outcome of the story?

Point out that they will find the same technique employed by Shakespeare in Romeo and Juliet. For example, the nurse's peasant speech and her attempt to imitate her betters:

> Yes, madam. Yet I cannot choose but laugh
> To think it should leave crying and say, "Ay."
> And yet, I warrant, it had upon its brow
> A bump as big as a young cock'rel's stone;
> A perilous knock; and it cried bitterly.
> "Yea," quoth my husband, "fall'st upon thy face?
> Thou will fall backward when thou comest to age,
> Wilt thou not, Jule?" It stinted and said, "Ay." (I,iii,50-57)

The friar's moralization:
> Virtue itself turns vice, being misapplied,
> And vice sometime by action dignified. (II,iii,21-22)

The gentrified talk of Capulet:
> And too soon marred are those so early made
> Earth has swallowed all my hopes but she;
> She is the hopeful lady of my earth. (I,ii,13-15)

The intellectual banter of Mercutio:
> Romeo! Humors! Madman! Passion! Lover!
> Appear thou in the likeness of a sigh;
> Speak but one rhyme, and I am satisfied!
> Cry but "Ay me!" pronounce but "love" and "dove";
> Speak to my gossip Venus one fair word,
> One nickname for her purblind son and heir
> Young Abraham Cupid, he that shot so true
> When King Cophetua loved the beggar maid! (II,i,7-14)

The fiery, insolent speech of Tybalt:
> What Dares the slave
> Come hither, covered with an antic face,
> To fleer and scorn at our solemnity?
> Now, by the stock and honor of my kin,
> To strike him dead I hold it not a sin. (I,v,57-61)

The love-struck, figurative language of Romeo:
> But soft, What light through yonder window breaks?
> It is the east, and Juliet is the sun!
> Arise, fair sun, and kill the envious moon,
> Who is already sick and pale with grief.
> That thou her maid art far more fair than she.
> Be not her maid, since she is envious.
> Her vestal livery is but sick and green,
> And none but fools do wear it. Cast it off. (II,ii,1-9)

The naivete of Juliet:
> 'Tis but thy name that is my enemy.
> Thou art thyself, though not a Montague.
> What's Montague? Is it nor hand, nor foot,
> Nor arm, nor face. O, be some other name
> Belonging to a man.
> What's in a name? That which we call a rose
> By any other word would smell as sweet.
> So Romeo would, were he not Romeo called,
> Retain that dear perfection which he owes
> Without that title. Romeo, doff thy name;
> And for thy name, which is no part of thee,
> Take all myself. (II,ii,38-48)

Developing Metaphors

Introduce students to some contemporary novels which use metaphoric language in their titles:

1. *Blinded by the Light* by Robin Brancato (215 pp.). A teenager becomes a member of a religious cult, and his family attempts to get him out.

2. *Jacob Have I Loved* by Katherine Paterson (228 pp.). Because Sara Louise believes that she is the despised Esau and her adored twin is the beloved Jacob, she lives in a constant state of conflict.

3. *Bridge To Terabithia* by Katherine Paterson (155 pp.). Leslie and Jess create their own imaginary kingdom of Terabithia. After Leslie is killed swinging across a creek on a vine, Jess builds a bridge to Terabithia and his new maturity.

4. *A Solitary Blue* by Cynthia Voigt (204 pp.). Jeff's mother abandons him for her "more important work," leaving him with his remote, perfectionist father. Jeff comes to understand his parents as he sits in a boat in the marsh near his mother's South Carolina home.

5. *The Pigman* by Paul Zindel (192 pp.). Mr. Angelo Pignati, "the pigman," is a lonely old man who helps make two sophomore's lives more meaningful.

Students can discuss what they believe the metaphors in the titles of the books mean. Students can also search for metaphors in the young adult books they are reading. Prior to having students read *Romeo and Juliet* you can point out and discuss some of the metaphors in the play:
> It is the East, and Juliet is the Sun! (Romeo, II,ii,3)

Two of the fairest stars in the heaven,
Having some business, do entreat her eyes
To twinkle in their spheres till they return. (Romeo, II,ii,15-17)
Alas, poor Romeo, he is already dead:
Stabbed with a white wench's black eye; run through
The ear with a love song; the very pin of his heart
Cleft with the blind bow-boy's butt-shaft . . . (Mercutio, II,iv,13-16)
Gallop apace, you fiery-footed steeds.
Towards Phoebus' lodging! Such a wagoner
As Phaeton would whip you to the west
And bring in cloudy night immediately. (Juliet, III,ii,1-4)

Developing Puns

Students love puns but often have difficulty recognizing them in Shakespeare because they are unclear about the meanings of the words. Since puns use words in unusual, unexpected ways, punning requires a good vocabulary. And that is one of the best reasons to teach it. Begin by acquainting students with puns they will understand. Once you get going, they are likely to be able to find their own puns.

Paula Danziger loves puns. All of her books are filled with them. Here are a few from *Earth to Matthew*:

'Well,' Matthew continues, 'I have a question about chickens.'. . .

Matthew grins again, showing his dimple. 'Why did the chicken cross the new playground?'

Shaking her head, Mrs. Stanton thinks about how hard the class has been working and about how a few minutes of joking is all right. 'Mr. Martin, tell us. Why did the chicken cross the new playground?'

'To get to the other slide' is the answer . . .

Raising his hand, Joshua Jackson looks at her. 'Eggsactly what did you mean by that? I thought that was an excellent yoke.'

'An eggshellent joke. It broke me up.' Lizzie Doran giggles.

'I don't want to be hard-boiled about this, but dozen everyone think it's time to get back to our regular class?'

Mrs. Stanton calls the class to attention. 'Now, let's get serious.' (pp. 24-25)

After the students have shared their puns, they can be introduced to some in *Romeo and Juliet* and instructed to keep a list of others as they read.

Mercutio. Nay gentle Romeo, we must have you dance.
Romeo   Not I, believe me. You have dancing shoes
           With nimble soles; I have a soul of lead
           So stakes me to the ground I cannot move.
Mercutio. You are a lover. Borrow Cupid's wings
           And soar with them above a common bound.

Romeo	I am too sore enpierced with his shaft
	To soar with his light feathers; and so
	bound I cannot bound a pitch above dull woe.
Mercutio.	And, to sink in it, should you burden love-
	-Too great oppression for a tender thing.
Romeo	Is love a tender thing? It is too rough.
	Too rude, too boist'rous, and it pricks
	like thorn.
Mercutio.	If love be rough with you, be rough with love;
	Prick love for pricking, and you beat love
	down. (I,iv,13-28)
	An old hare hoar,
	And an old hare hoar,
	Is very good meat in Lent;
	But a hare that is hoar
	Is too much for a score

When it hoars ere it be spent. (Mercutio, II,iv,141-146)

Choosing Names

The concept of naming and how things are named is important in many religious traditions. Madeleine L'Engle deals with naming in her time trilogy books: *A Wrinkle in Time, A Wind in the Door*, and *A Swiftly Tilting Planet*. Many high school students were introduced to these books in late elementary school or middle school. If students are familiar with the books, you can ask them to find examples of the importance of naming.

You can also discuss with students why names are important. You can deal with given names, and how what we are named may help define who we are or who our parents hope we will become. At this point, you might discuss some of the names in *Romeo and Juliet* as examples: Why is Mercutio Mercutio and Benvolio Benvolio? Students can look in the dictionary for words from which these names might be derived. They will find such words as "mercurous" and "Mercury" when they look for Mercutio. This may help them understand why Mercutio is named as he is.

You can ask them some questions about these characters:
*   Given their names what do you expect Mercutio will be like?
*   What will Benvolio be like?
*   Do you think that Shakespeare believes that names are important?

Now, read to them some passages from the play about naming and discuss whether or not Shakespeare agrees with what he has his characters say.

'Tis but thy name that is my enemy.
Thou art thyself, though not a Montague.
What's a Montague? It is nor hand, nor foot,
Nor arm, nor face. O, be some other name
Belonging to a man.
What's in a name? That which we call a rose
By any other word would smell as sweet. (Juliet, II,ii,38-44)
As if that name,
Shot from the deadly level of a gun,
Did murder her; as that name's cursed hand
Murdered her kinsman. O, tell me, friar, tell me,
In what vile part of this anatomy
Doth my name lodge? Tell me, that I may sack
The hateful mansion. (Romeo, III,iii,102-108)
It was the nightingale, and not the lark . . .
It was the lark, the herald of the morn;
No nightingale. (Juliet, III,v,2; Romeo, 6-7)

While Reading *Romeo and Juliet*

Providing students with the introductory material suggested above should make reading the play much easier. In this section methodologies for helping students read *Romeo and Juliet* through creative drama, writing, and discussion will be suggested.

Creative Drama Activities
Since Shakespeare wrote for the stage, the more you can make his stagecraft a part of the students' reading, the more they will enjoy the play.

Students can practice their own dramatic techniques and be introduced to the themes of *Romeo and Juliet* by using Robin Brancato's one act play "War of Words." Students can practice the following informal creative drama techniques with this play and then utilize them as they read *Romeo and Juliet*.

Choral Reading. Assign several students to each part in Brancato's one-act play. The students practice reading the play with each character represented by a chorus of students. The class presents the play chorally with every member involved.

Readers' Theatre. Assign individual scenes to small groups of students; each group should have one student per character in the scene. Each group should rehearse their scene. Each scene is then read in order by the groups with every student participating.

Story Theatre. Students are assigned to groups with two students for each character in the scene. Each group practices their scene with one student reading the part orally and the second acting it. The scenes are then acted and read in order by the class.

Oral Reading. Students who are good readers can be assigned complete scenes to rehearse and read to the class. They can use the teacher's oral reading of a scene as a model.

Once the students have practiced these techniques using a contemporary play, they can transfer their skills to informal dramatic readings of *Romeo and Juliet*. Informal dramatic reading of scenes of Shakespeare's play can be interspersed with professional recordings of scenes from the play (many different recordings are available).

Writing and Discussion Activities

Writing and discussion activities reinforce students' understanding and learning. Students can participate in one or more of the following activities:

1. Allow students to select one of the young adult novels suggested in "Before Reading *Romeo and Juliet*, Introducing the Themes." Have them read the young adult book and compare it to *Romeo and Juliet* as they read the play.

2. Students can record in a journal the chronological plot sequence of the contemporary book and of *Romeo and Juliet*. A class timeline of the chronological sequence of the play can be kept in the classroom.

3. Students can keep a diary of one of the characters in the contemporary novel and another diary of one of the characters in the play. Students should record not only what the character is doing but also what the character is thinking and feeling. During the reading of the play, one student representing each character can be asked to read the diary entry to a small group or to the class each day. Students can discuss how the characters are developing throughout the play.

4. In their journals, students can trace a young adult novel's character's development noting the chapters in which the character's traits are developed, how language is used to develop the character, how the character interacts with other characters, how the character changes and what makes the character change, and how the character relates to the themes of the novel. After doing this for a character in a young adult book, the students can do the same for a character in Romeo and Juliet.

During the reading of the play students can work in small groups based on the character they select. The group can plot a character relationship chart and discuss how the character is developed.

5. If students have selected a young adult novel based on one of the major themes in *Romeo and Juliet*, they can write in their journals about how the author of the young adult novel develops that theme. Later, as they read Shakespeare's play, they can write about how he develops the same theme. Also, they can keep track of how the characters they are studying relate to the theme. Students can discuss the selected theme with a group of students who are investigating the same theme.

6. Students can attempt to find some of language usage described above in their young adult novels. They can transcribe in their journals examples of language that develops character, puns, and metaphors. When they read *Romeo and Juliet*, they can keep similar journal entries. They can share examples of language usage in small groups.

7. So that vocabulary can be developed in the context of the students' reading, they can identify unfamiliar words in both their young adult novels and *Romeo and Juliet*. These can become the focus of their vocabulary study during the reading of the play.

After Reading *Romeo and Juliet*

The activities in which the students participate after reading the play are designed to help them synthesize various aspects of the drama.

Comparative Essays

After students have read both the young adult novel and *Romeo and Juliet* they can do a comparative essay on any of the topics suggested above. For example, compare how Shakespeare and Cormier develop the theme of the isolation of the tragic hero in *The Chocolate War* and *Romeo and Juliet*. Students can then share their papers with a small group of students who have read the same book or dealt with the same theme.

Classroom Drama

Students can work in small groups to develop one or more scenes into a classroom drama, building on some of the creative informal drama techniques used earlier. Students can be divided into small groups with two groups practicing the same scene or each group practicing different scenes. Students should be instructed to decide who will play each role. They should then discuss how each character will act in the scene, how the character will deliver the lines, where the character will stand, how the character will move. They can also discuss how the character's lines develop the plot and the theme, how the character interacts with other characters, how this scene leads to the next scene. The scenes can be videotaped, viewed, and critiqued by the small groups and the class. In the critique, students can discuss how faithful their staging was to Shakespeare's characterization, plot, and theme.

Viewing the Film or Play

Viewing a film or stage version of *Romeo and Juliet* can provide students with an important synthesis. Students can be asked to compare and contrast the version they have read with the one viewed. They can critique the play they have seen in the way they critiqued their own scenes above.

Extending The Students' Learning

One of the reasons for studying the classics is the possibilities they offer for extending students' learning far beyond the original work. Below are some literary extensions that can be used before, during, or after reading *Romeo and Juliet*.

Developing Critics

Students can become Shakespearean critics. Most editions of *Romeo and Juliet* have prefatory remarks and literary commentaries. Able students can read one or more of these commentaries and discuss them in small groups. The group can select a topic discussed in the commentary and go to the library to research the topic to determine how scholars respond to the issue. (If a college or university is nearby, it presents a wonderful opportunity to introduce students to an academic library.) The group can write a group paper exploring the differences in the critics' views.

Discussing Differences of Plot and Theme

After viewing or reading *West Side Story*, students can compare it to *Romeo and Juliet* and discuss why there are differences in the plot and theme.

Studying Literary and Mythological Allusions

Romeo and Juliet is full of literary and mythological allusions. Students can search the play for these and research them in small groups in the library. The results of the research can be shared orally with the class.

Studying William Shakespeare and the Elizabethan Theatre

Students can research Shakespeare, the man and the playwright. They are likely to find interesting the controversy about whether he was the author of the plays. They can present their findings orally to the class. Students can research the Elizabethan theatre and present their findings to the class in alternative formats: construct a replica of the Globe Theatre, create props that might have been used, play a madrigal song, prepare a medieval recipe such as Rose-Petal Bread (Rygiel, p. 114), or make a sculpture or painting indicative of the time period.

Comparing *The Tragicall Historye of Romeus and Juliet*

Students can locate a copy of Arthur Brooke's *The Tragicall Historye of Romeus and Juliet*. They can compare it to Shakespeare's play and discuss the reason for the differences.

Reading or Viewing other Shakespeare Plays

Students can read another Shakespearean comedy or tragedy and compare it to *Romeo and Juliet*. If students are working in small groups, each group can select a different play. They can examine the plays in terms of the classical elements of comedy or tragedy. How does each play deal with these elements? If students prefer, they can watch a film or video of another Shakespearean play and compare it to *Romeo and Juliet* in terms of the elements of comedy and tragedy, use of language, development of plot, characterization, and theme. They can present their plays and how they differ from *Romeo and Juliet* to the class.

Writing Papers on Contemporary Issues

Students can research and write a paper on one of the modern themes of the play: suicide, teenage love, friendship and peer pressure, or parent/child relationships. It is interesting to note how the attitudes have changed since Shakespeare's time.

Students can research and write a paper on one of the literary themes of the play: hostility and its effect on the innocent, the use of deception and its consequences, or the effects of faulty decision making. The papers might be written in terms of modern literary treatment of the theme or the theme in modern history or politics.

Students can also research and write a paper on one of the themes of classical tragedy: the role of fate and fortune, the inevitable nature of tragedy, or the isolation of the tragic hero. These papers might also deal with modern literary treatment of the theme or the theme as seen in modern history or politics. In addition, students could discuss one or more of the themes as depicted on television or in film.

Exploring Similar Themes

Students can search their literature anthology for works that explore similar themes. They can develop a bibliography for each theme and read and discuss other works related to the theme.

Conclusion

Romeo and Juliet is a particularly accessible Shakespearean play for adolescents since it contains many of the characteristics of a good young adult novel. The protagonists are young and exhibit the developmental tasks of their age group: They rebel against their parents; they succumb to peer pressure; they are emotional and egocentric; and they do not see beyond the moment. The plot is fast-moving and filled with action, excitement, and romance. Subplots provide humor and help readers gain additional information about the characters. The readers often know more about the protagonists than they know about themselves. The themes are as contemporary today as in Shakespeare's time and are meaningful to adolescent readers.

Because there are so many parallels between good contemporary young adult fiction and *Romeo and Juliet*, the pairing of the play and adolescent literature is an effective teaching technique. By reading young adult books and comparing them to *Romeo and Juliet*, adolescents can gain a better understanding of the play, Shakespearean theatre, and Elizabethan England.

References

Angier, B. & Corcoran, B. (1977). *Ask for love and they give you rice pudding*. New York: Bantam Books.

Asher, S. (1987). *Everything is not enough*. New York: Delacorte Press.

Bernstein, L., Laurents, A. & Sondheim, S. (1958). *West side story*. New York: Random House.

Blume, J. (1975). *Forever*. New York: Bradbury Press.

Blume, J. (1974). *Blubber*. New York: Dell Laurel-Leaf.

Brancato, R. (1991). War of words. In D.R. Gallo (Ed.), *Center stage*. New York: Delacorte Press.

Brancato, R. (1978). *Blinded by the light*. New York: Alfred A. Knopf.

Bridgers, S.E. (1977). *Home before dark*. New York: Bantam Books.

Brooks, B. (1984). *The moves make the man*. New York: Harper & Row.

Butterworth, W. (1980). *Leroy and the old man*. New York: Four Winds Press.

Corcoran, B. (1986). *I am the universe*. New York: Atheneum.

Cormier, R. (1977). *I am the cheese*. New York: Pantheon (Dell).

Cormier, R. (1974). *The chocolate war*. New York: Pantheon (Dell).

Cossi, O. (1990). *The magic box*. New York: Pelican Publishing Company.

Daly, M. (1986). *Acts of love*. New York: Scholastic.

Danziger, P. (1991). *Earth to Matthew*. New York: Delacorte Press.

Delton, J. (1981). *Two blocks down*. New York: Harper & Row.

Duncan, L. (1978). *Killing Mr. Griffin*. Boston: Little, Brown, & Company.

Garland, S. (1992). *Song of the buffalo boy*. New York: Harcourt, Brace, & Jovanovich.

Golding, W. (1954). *Lord of the flies*. New York: G.P. Putnam's Sons.

Greene, B. (1973). *Summer of my German soldier*. New York: Dial.

Guest, J. (1977). *Ordinary people*. New York: Ballantine Books.

Guy, R. (1985). *My love, my love, or, the peasant girl*. New York: Henry Holt & Company.

Guy, R. (1973). *The friends*. New York: Henry Holt & Company.

Hinton, S.E. (1967). *The outsiders*. New York: Dell Laurel-Leaf.

Houston, J.W. & Houston, J.D. (1990). *Farewell to Manzanar*. New York: Bantam Books.

Irwin, Hadley. (1988). *So long at the fair*. New York: McElderry Books.

Jaspersohn, W. (1990). *Grounded*. New York: Bantam Books.

Kerr, M.E. (1978). *Gentlehands*. New York: Bantam Books.

Kerr, M.E. (1972). *Dinky Hocker shoots smack*. New York: Dell Laurel-Leaf.

Lasky, K. (1986). *Beyond the divide*. New York: Dell Laurel-Leaf.

Lee, H. (1961). *To kill a mockingbird*. New York: Harper & Row.

Lee, M. (1980). *The people therein*. Boston: Houghton Mifflin.

L'Engle, M. (1979). *A wind in the door*. New York: Fararr, Straus, & Giroux.

L'Engle, M. (1978). *A swiftly tilting planet*. New York: Farrar, Straus, & Giroux.

L'Engle, M. (1962). *A wrinkle in time*. New York: Dell Laurel-Leaf.

Lingard, J. (1973). *Across the barricades*. New York: Grosset & Dunlap.

Lipsyte, R. (1967). *The contender*. New York: Harper & Row.

Lyle, K.L. (1974). *Fair day, and another step begun*. Philadelphia: J.B. Lippincott Company.

Mazer, H. (1990). *The war on Villa Street*. New York: Dell Laurel-Leaf.

Mazer, N.F. (1982). *When we first met*. New York: Macmillan.

McDermott, A. (1987). *That night*. New York: Farrar, Straus, & Giroux.

McGuire, J. (1990). *Crossing over*. New York: Ivy Books.

Miller, A. (1951). *Death of a salesman*. New York: Bantam Books.

Meyer, C. (1990). *Because of Lissa*. New York: Bantam Books

Myers, W.D. (1988) *Scorpions*. New York: Harper & Row.

Paterson, K. (1980). *Jacob have I loved*. New York: Harper & Row.

Paterson, K. (1977). *Bridge to Terabithia*. New York: Thomas Y. Crowell.

Peck, R. (1986). *Remembering the good times*. New York: Dell Laurel-Leaf.

Pevsner, S. (1989). *How could you do it, Diane?* New York: Clarion Books.

Pfeffer, S.B. (1990). *About David*. New York: Dell Laurel-Leaf.

Pinkwater, D. (1982). *The snarkout boys and the avocado of death*. New York: Lothrop, Lee, & Shepard.

Reed, A.J.S. (1987). *A teacher's guide to the signet classic edition of William Shakespear's Romeo and Juliet*. New York: The New American Library.

Rygiel, M.A. (1992). *Shakespeare among schoolchildren: Approaches for the secondary classroom*. Urbana, Illinois: The National Council of Teachers of English.

Sebestyen, O. (1979). *Words by heart*. Boston: Little, Brown, & Company.

Shakespeare, W. (1942). *Romeo and Juliet*. In W.A. Neilson and C.J. Hill (Eds.), *The Complete Plays and Poems of William Shakespeare*. Cambridge: Houghton Mifflin. (originally published 1609).

Shreve, S. (1980). *The masquerade*. New York: Alfred A. Knopf.

Speare, E. (1961). *The witch of blackbird pond*. Boston: Houghton Mifflin.

Spinelli, J. (1984). *Who put that hair in my toothbrush?* Boston: Little, Brown, & Company.

Twain, M. (1940). *The adventures of Huckleberry Finn*. New York: Heritage Press.

Voigt, C. (1983). *A solitary blue*. New York: Atheneum.

Zeffirelli, F. (1968). *Romeo and Juliet*. Paramount Home Video, VHS, 138 mins.

Zindel, P. (1990). *I never loved your mind*. New York: Bantam Books.

Zindel, P. (1968). *The pigman*. New York: Harper & Row.

Chapter 7

Leaving Home to Come Home: The Hero's Quest in *Great Expectations* and Three Young Adult Novels

LEILA CHRISTENBURY

Introduction

Charles Dickens' *Great Expectations* may become the *Silas Marner* of the late 20th century, a 19th century British novel that has become a staple of the literature curriculum of American secondary and even middle school language arts classes. For whatever difficulties it may present a young reader, *Great Expectations* is widely known and widely used in American schools. In varying incarnations, (abridged, excerpted, and sometimes even reworded, if not wholly rewritten), the story of Pip and his quest to become a gentleman in Victorian England is, at this writing, extensively taught and extensively read. While the original 1861 novel is long (almost 400 pages in most editions) and Dickens' vocabulary and syntax is daunting for many students, teachers and English departments continue to assign *Great Expectations*, a novel which some consider among Dickens' very best works.

While there are many themes in *Great Expectations*, one of the most powerful—and most archetypal—is that of the hero leaving home in order to come home. The self-knowledge that Charles Dickens' Pip earns is, additionally, similar to the self-knowledge earned by the main characters in three acclaimed young adult novels, and pairing the novels can be helpful to our students for their understanding and consideration. What Pete in Cynthia Rylant's *A Fine White Dust*, Russel in Gary Paulsen's *Dogsong*, and Sonny Bear in Robert Lipsyte's *The Brave* learn is akin to what Pip learns in *Great Expectations*: Home is not only the place one starts from and the place one necessarily leaves; it is also, essentially, the psychic destination.

Great Expectations: Background and Summary

Great Expectations first appeared in the periodical *All the Year Round*, 1860-61, and was subsequently published in book form. Alert readers notice the serialization flavor of the chapters; there are dangling endings and gripping openings to move readers along. Written nine years before Dickens' death, the novel originally ended sadly, but, upon the advice of Dickens' friend, the writer Edward Bulwer-Lytton, the present happy ending was substituted.

To summarize briefly, *Great Expectations* is the story of young Philip Pirrip, know as Pip. An orphan living in the country with his violent sister and kindly blacksmith brother-in-law, Pip is sensitive and good hearted. Both he and his brother-in-law, Joe, however, are rather brutalized by Mrs. Joe, who is prone to outbursts of temper and physical violence.

Pip's horizons are widened by his contact with the mad Miss Havisham, perhaps the most famous character in *Great Expectations*, who asks that Pip come to her house and serve as a playmate for her beautiful niece, Estella. Miss Havisham was deserted on her wedding day. In perpetual mourning, she dresses in her ancient and tattered wedding gown and in general, centers her life upon the devastating event of her abandonment.

Pip, of course, is fascinated by the eccentric woman and, along the way, falls in love with the disdainful Estella. Estella has been schooled by Miss Havisham to scorn love and use her beauty as a weapon against faithless men. Pip's love for Estella gives him the desire to better himself, and when he becomes the recipient of money from a mysterious source, he goes to London—with great expectations—to become a gentleman.

Being a gentleman is not, however, all it is advertised to be, and Pip not only loses his moral bearings, he also becomes ashamed of his village origins. He eventually learns that the money that enabled him to go to London is not from Miss Havisham but from a grateful escaped convict, Magwitch, whom Pip encountered and helped many years ago. At any rate, Pip loses all of the money, and by the novel's end, a wiser and older Pip returns to the village to reconcile with Joe and reunite with Estella who, widowed after an unhappy marriage and wholly changed in attitude, is now ready to marry him.

Critical Assessment of *Great Expectations*

As described by critic Diana Neill, *Great Expectations* exhibits all of the characteristics of its author, Charles Dickens:

> Dickens is the Victorian age in fiction, or a large part of it. He shared its faults of taste, its love of melodrama, its exuberant vitality, its belief in the sharp division of humanity into sheep and goats. He shared, too, the innate optimism of the period. His novels...are morality plays in which the good angels win the battle for the soul of man, which is just what the majority of the Victorians were sure they would. (p. 175)

Certainly the characters of the eccentric Miss Havisham and her aloof niece Estella, the slimy Jaggers, the brave Joe, are well drawn, and Pip himself, traced from boyhood to manhood, makes a painful and yet illuminating journey away from his origins and into what he and others hope will be a better life. There is, as Neill notes, melodrama, optimism, and morality in *Great Expectations*.

Part of the appeal of the novel is also in the growth and learning of a young character, the forceful plotting, and the clear moral message. Some of the description is truly wonderful, the dialogue is effective, and there is a certain suspense throughout centered upon the money that enables Pip to pursue his great expectations. Despite the gap between late 20th century American culture and England of the Victorian age, students recognize the rather universal theme of leaving home to better oneself, if not precisely the concept of becoming and living like a gentleman.

Challenges to Teaching *Great Expectations*

Challenges teachers have with *Great Expectations* begin with its length and language. Getting students to read all 400 or so pages and, further, to negotiate Dickens' vocabulary and syntax, can be tough assignments. Certainly teachers can overcome the length question by having students read only parts of the novel, by using abridged versions of the novel, or by spending some time in class reading the novel aloud. Additionally, the vocabulary question can be dealt with by having students read versions of the novel where words are glossed or by encouraging students to use their language skills and to define words by context rather than by consultation with the dictionary. Because of the range of vocabulary Dickens uses, having students learn or study all of the unfamiliar words and terms in *Great Expectations* is a sure route to student revolt and certainly decreases the enjoyment of the novel.

Another challenge of *Great Expectations* involves the female characters in the novel. Teachers and students with feminist sensibilities may also be rather appalled at Dickens' women: From the crazed Miss Havisham (whose psychosis revolves around a faithless man) to the cruel Estella (who has been trained to enthrall and then punish men) to the loud and brutal Mrs. Joe (who routinely terrorizes both her brother and her husband) to the saintly Biddy (who loves Pip but demurely keeps to her place in the village), the main female characters in *Great Expectations* present fairly unpleasant extremes. Discussing stereotypes and archetypes may be helpful; certainly the male characters in *Great Expectations* share some of the extremes the females only too vividly personify.

A final challenge regarding *Great Expectations* involves plot. It takes some imagination to accept the relative improbability of Pip being so wholly adored by the convict Magwitch that he would be the recipient of a small fortune. The death of Mrs. Joe is odd, though getting her out of the way is clearly necessary to the later plot, and the believability of Miss Havisham and Estella can stretch credulity. Dickens, however, carries most of this off, and students may be puzzled but not necessarily repelled by these stereotypes difficulties. And, of course, class discussion of how these aspects of the plot could be altered might open further exploration of *Great Expectations*.

Teaching *Great Expectations*

Character and theme are two promising avenues for considering the novel. Certainly comparing and contrasting the female characters (Miss Havisham and Mrs. Joe, Estella and Biddy, or all four) and the male characters (the good Joe and Herbert and the less than admirable Orlick, Jaggers, Magwitch, and/or Pumblechook) can be helpful to students. Students can consider how the characters are alike and how they are different. Students can speculate on the characters' motivations, add dialogue, or create new scenes in which the characters operate.

In addition to the theme of leaving home to come home, discussed briefly above, there are other themes running through *Great Expectations*:

* money as a reflection of merit
* the concept of the gentleman vs. the working man
* the contrast between the "purity" of the country and the "corruption" of the city
* the quest for values
* the search for self
* the "great expectations" of any young person
* roles of men and women in Dickens' novel
* the importance of friendship

Students can discuss, write about, or otherwise consider any of these themes or others that they see in *Great Expectations*.

Students can use the novel, finally, to consider themselves in circumstances similar to Pip's. Relating themselves and their circumstances to the novel, students could speculate on any of the following:

1. How would they react to being reared by someone like Mrs. Joe? Why? Would they feel differently or the same if she were *not* their sister? Why?

2. How would they react to a Miss Havisham? An Estella? If they encountered Magwitch in their neighborhood, would they help him? Why or why not?

3. If they were given a large amount of money, say $100,000, what specifically would they do with it? Why?

4. Would they want to marry Estella as Pip does at the end of *Great*

Expectations? Why? Why not?

5. How would they feel at the end of the novel if they were Biddy? Joe? Could they write a different version of the dialogue these characters have?

6. How appealing do they find different types of work? What would be the modern equivalent of Pip's professional choices (i.e., blacksmith or law clerk)?

Great Expectations and A Mythic Theme

Pip leaving home to find himself—and to find that home far superior than what he left it for—is a great theme in myth and archetype. Although Pip is not on a quest such as a Ulysses or a Beowulf or a Sir Gawaine (or even a Dorothy in *The Wizard of Oz*), he does, as all mythic heroes do, leave the familiar, the home place, the tribe, to venture out toward a test. The test is life-affirming and character-building, and the values of home stand the hero in good stead when he or she returns, victorious and wise.

In Pip's case the test also involves the callow rejection of his origins for the false allure of his new life. Our hero, in this case, learns bitter lessons and returns home chastened, giving those he once felt beneath him "humble thanks for all you have done for me, and all I have so ill repaid" (p. 443). Home and the people of home, specifically Biddy and Joe, represent the values that money and the life of the city could not successfully replace. The "great expectations" of Pip become the songs of experience he sings at the end of the novel.

Nothing is quite as Pip imagined it: The fortune came from a criminal, a source he could not even have guessed; his handling of his new life was disappointing; the gentleman he tried to become was shallow and trivial; the people he felt he has risen above turned out to be his moral superiors. When Pip comes home, he returns with new knowledge and, in a way he could never have anticipated, finally fulfills the promise of his "great expectations."

This mythic theme, of leaving home to come home, of leaving the tribe on a quest that does nothing less than reaffirm the values of the tribe, is part of *Great Expectations* and a great deal of other literature. Pairing *Great Expectations* with a young adult novel—Cynthia Rylant's *A Fine White Dust*, Gary Paulsen's *Dogsong*, or Robert Lipsyte's *The Brave*—can help students bridge from more contemporary work to Dickens and can provide some illumination on the theme of leaving and returning, of leaving home to come home.

Pairing Young Adult Novels with *Great Expectations*

A Fine White Dust

A Newbery Honor Book, an ALA Notable Children's Book, and an ALA Best Book for Young Adults, *A Fine White Dust* by Cynthia Rylant is a strong, tightly written novel that can be read successfully by middle schoolers. While the main character does not physically leave home, he tries to, and, in the trying, learns that the values of home are stronger than he had ever realized.

Pete, a middle-schooler whose interest in religion has never been shared by his parents or his best friend, Rufus, finds himself even more alienated from those he loves when the Preacher Man comes to town to lead the summer revival. Pete's experience is strong and solitary: He feels drawn to religion in a way no one around him appears to understand, and while he does not condemn his parents or Rufus, Pete moves away from them psychologically.

The novel comes to a climax when the Preacher Man asks Pete to leave town and join him on his revival circuit. Although Pete is young and leaving would mean pain to his parents and friend, Pete, after much agonizing, secretly decides to go. He leaves a note in his bedroom, clandestinely packs his belongings, and waits one night for the Preacher Man to pick him up. Pete waits for three hours to no avail. As it turns out, the Preacher Man leaves town without his young disciple and, unexpectedly, in the company of a young, local woman. Pete is left behind, and the Preacher Man has disappeared, never to return to the scandalized town he has left behind.

For Pete, the betrayal is devastating: He was ready to leave home for what he considered a higher good. Pete finds, however, in the wake of the sadness of the Preacher Man's leaving, not to mention the questionable company in which he has left, that Rufus and his parents are, despite their religious non-beliefs, utterly trustworthy: "Like, I *knew*, positively, that I could always count on them. Maybe their ideas about the world were different from mine, but I knew they'd still stick by me" (p. 99). Pete buys Rufus a used guitar and his parents a framed picture of the family and recognizes, fully and finally, that their good is beyond religious creed. Pete has tried to leave home and, in a way, has actually left and returned. And, like the mythic hero, he has also come home with new knowledge:

> One thing I see now that I couldn't see last summer is that after the revival is over, the world is a place that isn't anything like the inside of a church on a hot summer night. It's a world where good guys like Rufus are happy atheists, and nice folks like my parents don't care much about church, and spiritual people like me wander around on earth wishing it was heaven.
>
> It's a world where somebody like the [Preacher] Man can work so hard to save a million doomed sinners but come near killing the soul of one mixed-up kid. (pp. 104-105)

Dogsong

A Newbery Honor Book, Gary Paulsen's *Dogsong* is an elegantly written story of the fourteen-year-old Inuit boy, Russel, who is, at the novel's opening, in crisis. He wants to tell his father but cannot:

> 'Father, I am not happy with myself'...It was not the sort of thing you talked about, this feeling he had, unless you could find out what was causing it. He did not know enough of the feeling to talk. (p. 9)

Russel does know enough, however, to know that he needs to do something about his unhappiness, and his solution is a literal journey away from home, across the frozen Alaskan tundra, on a quest for self-knowledge. Russel seeks to find himself, and the metaphor he uses is the finding of his Inuit song. With the guidance of the blind and old man Oogruk, who in this age of snow machines and white man's inventions and customs knows the old ways, Russel sets out in a dogsled across the ice fields. Oogruk tells him:

> 'You must not go home . . . You must leave with the [sled] dogs. Run long and find yourself . . . Run as long as you can . . . Run with the dogs and become what the dogs will help you become.' (p. 72)

During his journey away from home, Russel has a vision of a warrior from another age and dreams of him and his life. He finds a lamp in the snow that appears to be from the warrior, and, when his food runs out in the frozen wilderness, like his vision warrior, Russel kills a polar bear. During this trip Russel also encounters Nancy, who has fled from her town and, pregnant and half frozen, is stranded on the tundra with her broken snow machine. As Russel fights for survival, Nancy delivers her stillborn baby, and Russel and his sled dogs take her into a village for safety and warmth. The last paragraph of the novel is part of the mythic coming home:

> They drove down the coast, drove on the edge of the sea-ice and land-snow, drove into the soft light of the setting spring sun, drove for the coastal village that had to be soon; the man-boy and the woman-girl and the driving mind-dogs that came from Russel's thoughts and went out and out and came from the dreamfold back.
> Back. (pp. 170-71)

Back, in *Dogsong* as in other novels, is back to home.

The Brave

Written by the acclaimed author Robert Lipsyte, *The Brave* is a sequel to Lipsyte's famous *The Contender*. The novel is the story of Sonny Bear, who, like Russel in *Dogsong*, leaves the tribe in a literal as well as a figurative sense. Sonny is not an Inuit in Alaska but a seventeen-year-old Moscondaga from a reservation in upstate New York. Sonny's white father is dead, his mother is off the reservation—again—with a new boyfriend, and Sonny, who has a strong temper and a restless streak, leaves the reservation to venture into New York City where he hopes to join the Army.

Sonny has done some amateur boxing and, up to this point, has been successfully coached by his Uncle Jake. Jake not only knows boxing but reveres the old ways and talks to Sonny of the tribe's customs, especially the mythic Running Braves, the best of the Moscondaga. For Sonny, escape means getting away from the old ways that Jake seems to dwell on; he thinks as he prepares to leave:

> Won't miss anybody on this raggedy reservation, especially [Jake] a crazy old man waiting for the buffalo to come back. (p. 16)

When Jake realizes Sonny is leaving, he advises him in the old ways, and Sonny, of course, argues back:

> 'No man ever got to be a Running Brave without taking a dangerous journey. Maybe this is it for you.'
> 'No more old stories, Jake.'
> 'Woods, city, don't matter. Got to survive, get strong as the buffalo, speedy as the deer, wise as the owl. Be a leader for your people.'
> 'Sell it to Hollywood.'
> They were in Sparta. Jake stopped for the first red light of the trip. He turned to Sonny. 'You got to follow the Hawk.'
> 'I'll look him up in the phone book.'
> 'Find the Hawk inside you and let it loose and follow it.' (pp. 19-20)

In New York, of course, Sonny finds not so much the Hawk but danger and challenge, and his involvement with other young people in the drug trade leads him to jail and serious injury. Gone are the possibilities of joining the Army, but Sonny's boxing talents resurge, and, in a deal with a former boxer turned police detective, Sonny is encouraged to redeem himself and prepare for a match.

Sonny returns home to the reservation, with Jake, to recover and train. It is then that the images of the Hawk and the Running Brave begin to make sense to him, and he returns to New York. He confronts the drug dealers and is triumphant in the ring, sustained by the image of the Hawk and the Running Brave who "would remember and think and make the right decision for the People" (p. 185). He, too, has left home to come home.

Using *A Fine White Dust*, *Dogsong*, and *The Brave* with *Great Expectations*

The concept of the hero separating from the family, the community, the tribe only to find that that group holds the key to self-knowledge is common to much literature. Focusing on that aspect of *Great Expectations* can help students understand the importance of the story of Pip and why his journey of self-knowledge must start from the village and end there, why his rejection of his origins must be transformed into an embrace of them. Any of the three young adult novels discussed above would make a useful pair with Dickens' work, and students could consider the following questions as they relate to either Pete or Russel or Sonny and to Pip:

1. What is a quest? How is it different for Pip and for Pete? for Pip and for Russel? for Pip and for Sonny?

2. What is the specific journey Pip makes? Pete? Russel? Sonny? How is that journey part of the character's quest?

3. Make a list of what each character seems to want at the beginning of the novel. How is that list different at the end of the novel?

4. What truths have the characters in each novel discovered? To what extent do you think they expected to find those truths?

5. What is the home community like for each of the characters? What person or persons bother them? Don't understand or appreciate them? Are supports for them? Why? When the character leaves and get away from those persons, to what degree is the character's life easier? More pleasant? More difficult? Why?

6. What strengths of character or skills help Pip or Pete or Russel or Sonny find what they are seeking? What weaknesses block them?

7. Who helps the characters in their quest for self-knowledge? Who impedes them? How?

8. What would you say is the central "test" for each character? Why do you pick that one event or incident?

9. What is your definition of a hero? Could you call Pip a hero? Pete? Russel? Sonny? Why? Why not?

10. "Leaving home in order to come home" is a paradox, something which, on the surface at least, does not seem to make sense. It is, however, what happens to all of the characters. Can you discuss why and how?

Conclusion

Adolescent literature is a wide field, and there are a number of novels that could be successfully paired with *Great Expectations*. Certainly one obvious drawback of the choices recommended here is that all of the novels, despite their cultural diversity, feature only male protagonists. (Two possibilities, young adult novels with female protagonists which use a journey motif, are Cynthia Voigt's *Homecoming* and Jean Craighead George's Newbery-winning *Julie of the Wolves*). Using any one of these young adult novels and *Great Expectations*, however, can help students focus on one aspect of Dickens' work and, perhaps, come to a better appreciation of Pip's quest for self-knowledge as he, like Pete and Russel and Sonny, leaves home to come home.

References

Dickens, C. (1962). *Great expectations*. New York: Macmillan. (originally published 1861).

George, J.C. (1972). *Julie of the wolves*. New York: Harper & Row.

Lipsyte, R. (1991). *The brave*. New York: Harper Collins.

Lipsyte, R. (1967). *The contender*. New York: Harper & Row.

Neill, D. (1964). *A short history of the English novel*. New York: Macmillan.

Paulsen, G. (1985). *Dogsong*. New York: Bradbury Press.

Rylant, C. (1986). *A fine white dust*. New York: Bradbury Press.

Voigt, C. (1981). *Homecoming*. New York: Atheneum.

Chapter 8

Reading from a Female Perspective: Pairing *A Doll House* with *Permanent Connections*

PATRICIA P. KELLY

Introduction

As we broaden the literary canon to include more female and minority writers, we must also change the ways we look at that literature as well as the traditional literature in the curriculum. At the risk of becoming embroiled in a variety of personal definitions of feminism that readers might have, I am using some principles of feminist literary criticism that I think apply to literature study in English language arts classes.

If one of the purposes of literature is to help readers see themselves and their relationships with others, then some literature selected for study should provide positive role models. For a feminist perspective, Cheri Register uses Wendy Martin's definition of such role models as females who are "self-actualizing, whose identities are not dependent on men" (p. 20). Although this need for good female role models in literature should undergird our selections from the early elementary years on, I developed this unit for 11th or 12th graders. According to Robert Carlsen, it is at that level that students begin reading literature as a way of searching for both personal and societal values. In this uncertain, transitional period of their lives, they seek literature that lets them explore the sociological and psychological struggles of characters in situations that may soon be theirs as young adults (pp. 29-30).

Carlsen's contention that 11th and 12th graders read to make personal connections is consonant with recent feminist critics who are more interested in having literature provide "realistic insights into female personality development, self-perceptions, and interpersonal relationships" than in looking at discrimination or equity issues (Register, p. 21). Such a feminist reading approach also fits nicely into reader-response theory and practice. Neither didactic nor dogmatic, a feminist reading, like a reader-response approach, encourages students to connect their own experiences with those of the characters; and in the sharing of these personal connections, readers relive, resee, reinterpret, and redefine their understandings of growing up female. Literature study provides a context for young men and women to discuss the sociological and psychological struggles of female characters.

Rationale for the Literary Selections

While it is true that high school boys will generally not select literature they view as being for girls, the materials and activities in this unit are ones that connect, although briefly, male-female relationships across a thousand years. To set the context for the unit, I begin with "A Work of Artifice" by the feminist poet Marge Piercy, with which students can compare the status of females from the ancient Chinese culture to today's societal expectations.

Rather than continuing with a modern selection, we next read a classic work, Henrik Ibsen's *A Doll House*. My experience has been that students are more willing to begin their exploration of these sensitive issues by looking at them in a distant time and place. Written in 1879, Ibsen's play marked the beginning of realism as we know it today in literature, the depiction of ordinary characters struggling with psychological problems brought on by the social and economic contexts in which they live. Called "social realism," this type of drama reflects what feminist literary critics see as a purpose of literature study: "the need for female readers to see their own experiences mirrored in literature" (Register, p. 15).

We then read from a feminist perspective Sue Ellen Bridger's young adult novel *Permanent Connections*. Of course, the order of the two works can easily be reversed, but I prefer using the modern, youth-oriented selection as a follow up. After reading and discussing *A Doll House*, some students may tend to dismiss the feminist issues as irrelevant in today's context. A feminist reading of Bridger's novel helps students see those issues in a situation and with characters to which they can readily relate.

Setting the Context for Feminist Reading

To introduce "A Work of Artifice" by Marge Piercy, I bring to class a bonsai tree or pictures of a bonsai tree and a giant evergreen tree. With these visual aids, I graphically describe the process of making a bonsai by severely cutting the roots and top of a young evergreen, dwarfing and twisting its shape over time into something unnatural but "artistic." The point is to keep a bonsai as small as possible but still alive. The most treasured, smallest ones are hundreds of years old. Students discuss their views of both the natural beauty of the mountain evergreen and the "artistic" beauty of the bonsai. They draw comparisons with other things they know; for example, wild daisies along the roadside and an arrangement of silk flowers, a regular hairdo and the multi-colored hairdo of a punk rocker, or the new naturally brown jeans and the many varieties of stonewashed ones. Whatever their comparisons, they are looking at their definitions of beauty.

As I read the poem aloud, students listen. Because the first 16 lines describe a gardener tending a bonsai, students readily understand the reading, having just seen that process, but the last eight lines shock them with their personal implications: "With living creatures/one must begin very early/to dwarf their growth:/the bound feet,/the crippled brain,/the hair in curlers,/the hands you/ love to touch."

With the poem on the overhead, we read it again. Students usually want first to discuss the specific examples in the five lines following the colon. Having understood the gardener's process, they normally connect immediately their knowledge of the Asian bonsai to the ancient Chinese custom of binding young girls' feet and at the same time begin seeing the current figurative implications. The next examples jump to the present: women and education; women and beauty, particularly the commercial appeals to enhancing one's appearance. Once students have explored the issues in those lines, they consider the picture of the giant tree unprotected from the elements and the cared-for bonsai. What is the price of safety? What is the irony in the gardener's words: "It is your nature/ to be small and cozy,/domestic and weak;/how lucky, little tree,/to have a pot to grow in"? They consider the connection between the gardener's views and a feminist reading of the lines.

When students raise questions about the title, I tell them that two synonyms for *artifice* are *art* and *trick*. As students think about how both of these definitions can be applied to this title, they point out both the artistry and the trickery of nature in developing a bonsai. The next task is to apply those definitions to the last five lines about females.

This poem raises some issues that students will encounter in the other literary selections for this unit. But through the reading and discussion, they have also begun the process of reading from a female perspective.

A Doll House by Henrik Ibsen

As a prereading activity for Ibsen's *A Doll House*, I ask students to consider the following two modern scenarios by writing their feelings about each. Then they try to connect the two situations in some way beyond the simplistic observation that each has a father as a character.

> *Susan is an A student who wants to go to college to study architecture. Her younger brother Eric, has no interest in attending college but wants instead to go to a trade school to become a mechanic. Their father makes Eric go to college to study mechanical engineering but he fails. At that point, their father believes it is unnecessary to send Susan to college because she already has a successful job as a secretary in an architectural firm.

*Because David's father had to work as a young man, he did not have the opportunity to play football—a lifelong dream for him. He now insists that David play football even though his son dislikes the violence of the game. During the season, David has difficulty keeping up with his studies and the extracurricular activities he prefers. Because David has a car and other financial advantages that his father never had, his father does not understand David's attitude.

One connection between the two scenarios is the issue of power over another human being, power that manifests itself through controlling money and, therefore, behavior. Students will express this issue in a variety of ways, but essentially their connections will reflect such a central theme, one of the major themes in *A Doll House*.

Activities for Each Act of *The Doll House*

Although the entire play can be assigned after the prereading activity, I prefer the following reading, writing, and discussion approach with each act. After students read the first act (either individually or in groups), they write both "What Is the Most Important Line?" and "What Is My Character Thinking?" activities in their reader's logs and bring these to class for discussion the next day. The discussions are thus more focused, and the logs also help students build understandings that aid their further reading of the work.

The Most Important Line. Rather than giving students study questions to guide their reading, I ask them to select what they think are the most important line(s) in each act and then write the lines and their reasons for selecting them in their reader's logs. I like a whole class discussion for the students' sharing of their selections and reasons because the students benefit from hearing the wide range of choices and discussing them. Even in Act I student choices always range widely from Nora's declaration, "I was tired so often, dead tired. But still it was wonderful fun, sitting and working like that, earning money. It was almost like being a man" to Nora's reply to Kristine Linde, "You're just like the others. You all think I'm incapable of anything serious" to Helmer's numerous references to Nora as a "sulky squirrel," "little bird," or "little prodigal." By Act III the students' selections of lines touch on virtually every important speech. This strategy provides an in-depth discussion of each act with little teacher direction and totally avoids the teacher-question/student-answer approach.

Characters' Inner Thoughts. Because a drama occurs much as real situations with no omniscient author probing the minds of the characters but with the story evolving through action and dialogue alone, a play is an excellent literary vehicle to use to speculate about what characters may be thinking. As students read each act, have them keep a diary of a character they select. Students should write at least five sentences (responses) that their selected character might have been thinking or doing during each act, that were not actually said or done on stage, designating the places these silent responses might have occurred. For instance, what might Nora be thinking during the following interchange near the beginning of Act I? And, on the other hand, what might Helmer be thinking?

> HELMER: . . .Spendthrifts are sweet, but they use up a fright-
> ful amount of money. It's incredible what it costs a
> man to feed such birds.
>
> NORA: Oh, how can you say that! Really, I save everything
> I can.
>
> HELMER: Yes, that's the truth. Everything you can. But that's
> nothing at all.

The audience learns shortly that Nora is not a spendthrift but pretends to be, begging for more money from her husband, working although unknown to him, diligently saving in every way she can, all to repay a debt she incurred to save his life. Surely a woman in Nora's situation has many thoughts she does not express aloud. The same, of course, is true of any character in fiction or person in real life. We rarely say everything we actually think. As the plot of *A Doll House* evolves, the other characters—Kristine Linde, Dr. Rank, and Nils Krogstad— bring new relationships and perspectives, but much is left unsaid or happens offstage. For example, what is Dr. Rank thinking when he declares his love for Nora in Act II? Although Nora indicates that she wishes he had let their relationship continue as it had been, what might she actually be thinking? Although Nils Krogstad and Kristine Linde's renewed relationship develops offstage, how might that have happened?

Students find Act III filled with "unspoken" dialogue even though this is the place where the confrontations openly occur: Helmer's rejection of Nora just minutes after he wishes he had a reason to lay down his life for her, his forgiveness of her when Krogstad's second letter saves Helmer from disgrace, and Nora's leaving what she has come to see as an oppressive situation. Although Nora says little during Helmer's rejection and forgiveness speeches, she surely must have raging and conflicting thoughts. When Nora tries to explain her leaving to Helmer, he struggles to understand but must have many unvoiced questions or even retorts.

A play provides rich opportunities for such speculative writing that has a basis, however, in the facts of the story. This activity also helps students understand the concept of subtext in literary-critical theory. In a dramatic production, an actress says her lines based on what she believes her character is thinking and feeling, and she reacts to others' dialogue based on those interpretations. Performers try to know their characters by imagining a life for them beyond the words of the play, the text. These interpretations of feelings and motivations are the subtext for a performer.

I allow 10 to 15 minutes at the end of the class following the "most important line" discussion to explore characters' inner thoughts as students have perceived them. I often begin by targeting a major scene and asking for the unspoken lines that students have written about the scene. Whether there is variety or agreement of perspectives about the subtext, the students enjoy going beyond the written text and comparing their perceptions. Although more time can be allocated to this discussion, I prefer to emphasize the "most important line" activity as the basis for the literary analysis. Students frequently interject into that discussion some of their speculative responses in support of why certain lines are important. When students submit their reader's logs (my students' reader's logs are loose-leaf notebooks so that I carry home only the applicable responses, not a ton of paper), I have them identify one unspoken response that they prefer from each act. They use their own criteria for the selection— imaginative, perceptive, well written, and so forth. Students like to use highlighters for marking their selections. In this way, they are reading their own logs evaluatively. While I check broadly to see that the assignments have been completed, I focus my written comments to them (always positive, personal, and/ or questioning) on one of the three highlighted, or otherwise indicated, student preferences.

Concluding Activities for *A Doll House*

A Sociometric Map. Because the relationships in *A Doll House* are complex, a sociometric mapping, or graphing, of the interactions and feelings is a useful activity. First, I explain to students that sociologists who study people's behaviors within groups often chart their perceptions of interpersonal interactions. A play provides an opportunity to look at relationships in much the way they happen in real life because there is no omniscient author giving the reader additional information.

Then I give each small group, large sheets of white unlined paper and a box of colored markers. The whole class decides the color codes for basic emotional relationships they see in the play; for example, green for jealousy, red for hatred, blue for love, yellow for distrust, or brown for dependency. On a drafting sheet, each group then lists all characters, placing each in a circle. Through discussion they begin to decide the kind and direction of the emotional relationships. To explain the nature of the task, I sometimes use the following strategy.

Place the characters *Cinderella, stepmother,* and *stepsisters* on the board in a triangle; circle each. What is the predominant feeling that Cinderella has for her stepmother? Hatred? Draw a red arrow from Cinderella to her stepmother. Is the feeling mutual? If so, put an arrow point at the other end also. Is jealousy a consideration later in the story? Who feels jealousy and who is it directed toward? Draw green arrows.

In a small group students may choose to further define the codes with perhaps a dotted blue line for devotion, which they see as different from love. Once they are satisfied with their relationship decisions, they draw a final map, including a key at the bottom to aid the interpretation. We display these relationship maps, and the whole class looks at places of agreement and difference, discussing the basis for the decisions. This analysis is usually quite lively.

Ranking Questions. Because my overall approach uses few direct teacher questions, for the next activity, I ask students to evaluate the relative importance of questions that might be asked about the play. First, each student ranks the questions that follow as to their importance to the play with 1 for the most important, 2 the next, and so on. In this way students make some personal commitment before entering the small group discussion.

1.   Why did Nora forge the bank note? Would you have done the same?

2.   What is the irony in the way that Helmer reacts to Krogstad's first letter? Then to the second letter?

3.   What are the reasons for Nora's decision to leave?

4.   Why do you think Dr. Rank is included in the play?

5.   What is a major theme in the play?

The aim of the small group discussion is to come to a consensus which encourages a vigorous exchange of ideas. Here the discussion itself is more important than the results because students are weighing arguments, going back to the text in many cases, and evaluating the impact of certain elements on this one piece of fiction. Allow approximately half an hour for the discussion. Each group then puts its final ranking on the board so that the whole class discussion can center on differences. Students are always gratified to see that other groups ranked questions in ways they argued for but lost in their own group.

Becoming the Dramatist. At the end of the above class discussion, I prepare students for their last assignments with the play. I tell them that there are two versions of the play's title. Ibsen titled his play *A Doll House*, but most contemporary stage and film productions are called *A Doll's House*. Students first write what they see is the difference and select the one they prefer. The next day I divide the class according to the students' preferences and have the two sides debate the differences in the messages. Students raise such points as: If the possessive is used, Nora is the "doll" in the house provided for her. If, however, where Nora and Torvald live is a "doll house," then both of them are dolls, shaped by societal forces.

After this debate I sometimes have students either individually or in groups generate some new elements for the play: a new title; a modern setting; another character; and a scenario for an additional act—such as, what happens to Nora. If students have had a similar assignment with a different literary work, I may omit this activity. However, I always arrange an after-school showing of a video production of *A Doll's House* as we begin our class study of the young adult novel *Permanent Connections* by Sue Ellen Bridgers.

Permanent Connections by Sue Ellen Bridgers

After reading *A Doll House* with its obvious feminist message, the next reading is centered in a modern context with situations to which teen readers can readily relate so that they can apply their new understandings to their own lives. Because Sue Ellen Bridger's *Permanent Connections* is the story of an adolescent male but also contains a strong adolescent female character, the novel is a good choice for such a whole-class reading. In addition, adult characters are well drawn and interact in real-life ways.

Rob Dickson, a slightly rebellious but basically good young man, is left to care temporarily for the family that his father worked hard to leave behind in North Carolina. There he meets Ellery Collier, who is also rebelling against being brought to live in the country by a mother escaping a constricting marriage and setting out to make her own life. Intertwined in their stories are another teenage couple and Rob's relatives. The feminist issues are ones encountered every day, often subtle ones, which helps students see their own lives in a new perspective.

Because Marge Piercy's poem and Ibsen's play have introduced the concepts and practice of feminist reading and because students already have the experiences to connect readily with Bridger's novel, I give the students only a brief book talk to generate their interest prior to reading *Permanent Connections*. I distribute the following assignments for their reader's logs (See Figure 8.1)

Figure 8.1

Making Decisions about Characters

As you are reading this novel, you will naturally have reactions toward characters, much as you do in real life when you meet new people. As you interact with new acquaintances on a regular basis, however, your views of them often change. At the points indicated in the novel, stop your reading and make decisions about how you feel about the characters. Give at least one reason why you have made your choice.

Rob Dickson

| Chapters
1 - 15
Why? | like | 1 | 2 | 3 | 4 | dislike | no reaction |

| Chapters
16 - 30
Why? | like | 1 | 2 | 3 | 4 | dislike | no reaction |

Chapters 31 - 45 Why?	like	1	2	3	4	dislike	no reaction
Chapters 46 - 62 Why?	like	1	2	3	4	dislike	no reaction

Add these names to the assignment sheet (or have students write them in their reader's logs) in the above format:
* Davis Dickson, Rob's father
* Carrie Dickson, Rob's mother
* Ellery Collier
* Ginny Collier, Ellery's mother
* Ted Collier, Ellery's father
* Uncle Fairlee
* Grandfather Dickson
* Coralee
* Rosalie
* Travis Williams

These student reactions to the characters serve as an excellent basis for whole-class or small-group discussion whether the book is assigned and discussed in chapters as above or read entirely and then discussed. This personal reaction level is a comfortable starting point for all students, and yet to support their opinions they must deal with the text.

Activities for *Permanent Connections*

My Character's Diary. The other reader's log assignment that accompanies the reading of the novel allows students to focus on one character of their choice by writing diary entries about what that character is doing or thinking. They write one entry after each of the novel's sections in the above activity. A final, evaluative entry is written in which students reflect on their entries and their character:
* Would they have selected a different character if they were writing the diary again? Why or why not?
* What did they like best about their character? The least?
* What do they think happens to their character in the next couple of years?

I group students by the characters they have chosen. Often there is more than one small group for Rob and Ellery. Sometimes I have to merge the relatives or the adult female characters or the adult male characters as groups, depending on the number of students who selected these characters. Because the reader's logs serve as the basis for these group discussions as well as the previous whole-class discussion (in other words, students see that their writing has been useful for them), I do not read and comment on the entire reader's log for each student. Although I check for completion of the tasks, I read the last evaluative diary entry and comment briefly.

Feminist Issues in *Permanent Connections*. Because the novel has male and female characters of varying ages and the gender issues are, as my students say, real life ones, I distribute quotations from the novel and have students write about each one of them. They then select one quotation to explore in some depth before our class discussion. This discussion works best in small groups because some of these issues are new to students; they are just beginning to formulate their ideas and attitudes. The issues may be sensitive to some of them, so their small group is a safer environment for expressing their views, views that may be tentative and neither right nor wrong. (See Figure 8.2)

Figure 8.2
Statements Associated with Feminist Issues
How might each of the following statements be associated with feminist issues? Write briefly on each one, but choose one to explore your thinking in some depth.

1. [Ginny says] "...lately I have been trying to take care of myself. That's what women are most afraid of, you know. Being selfish. It's the ultimate sin." (p. 91)
2. "I am afraid, too," [Ginny] whispered in the darkness. "Hear me, Coralee Dickson, while you are curled like an animal in a hole away from sky and wind and sun. The demons that devour women are all the same." (p. 92)
3. "I just thought I'd reach the time when I didn't have to take care of nothing but me," Coralee said. "I want to have that feeling one day before I die." (p. 117)
4. "I thought that, too," Ginny said. "I married because of it. I did everything I was told because of it. But in the long run being safe meant being in prison. It took a long time, but I came out of it. I guess I thought for years somebody had to open the door for me. I was waiting for that. But the truth is, the door was locked from the inside. Nobody could open it but me." (p. 134)
5. [Leanna says] "... Travis wants us to get married. He says it will make college easier ... He's got in his head how we'll have this cute little apartment instead of living in the dorm ... but I don't know. I was sort of looking forward to being with girls, talking and all like we're doing ... I have to do things on my own sometimes." (p. 151)

These discussions could end the unit; although, throughout the ongoing literature and language study for the rest of the year, I incorporate feminist literary-critical activities. I prefer, however, to engage students in an extension activity at this point.

Expert Group Activities

I hand out the following tasks, which look at feminist issues across literature, and talk briefly about the literary selections to generate the students' interest and to help students make their selections. The difficulty of these tasks varies in order to account for a heterogenous class. (Here I have arranged the tasks in their order of difficulty.) Students are good at self-selecting according to their interests and perceived difficulty.

1. Read *Someone to Love*, a young adult novel by Norma Fox Mazer, which tells of a young woman's first year in college and her self-destructive relationship with a young man. What are the feminist issues in the novel?

2. Read Virginia Hamilton's young adult novel *A Little Love*, in which Sheema searches for her identity in the only ways she knows. Although Sheema may be very different from many readers, how do her life and quest relate to general feminist issues?

3. Read *Nell's Quilt*, a young adult novel by Susan Terris. When Nell's father insists that she marry an older man, Nell takes control of her life in the only way she can. What are the feminist issues in the novel? Although the novel takes place at the turn of the century, are there modern feminist issues in the novel?

4. Read Robert C. O'Brien's *Z for Zachariah*, a young adult novel about sixteen-year-old Ann Burden, survivor of a nuclear holocaust. When a man comes to her farm and attempts to dominate her, Ann must take action to save herself. How is Ann a role model from a feminist literary criticism perspective?

5. Read "I Stand Here Ironing" by Tillie Olsen. What has the mother's life been like? Compare the feminist issues in Marge Piercy's poem "A Work of Artifice" to the issues in this short story.

6. Compare and contrast Nora Helmer in *A Doll House* and Ginny Collier in *Permanent Connections* and Mrs. Sommers in Kate Chopin's "A Pair of Silk Stockings," in which a woman decides to spend the only money she has on herself rather than her children. How are they alike? Different? Are their actions justified? Argue both sides.

7. Relate Emily Dickinson's "Much Madness" (Rob Dickson's favorite poem) to another literary work, such as "The Yellow Wallpaper" by Charlotte

Perkins Gilman. This short story was originally considered a horror story by many editors of anthologies but is now seen as a statement about control of women.

I then establish groups of three to five students. They prepare a 15 minute class presentation to "teach" their findings to the entire class. Groups may use panel discussions, skits, art, music, advertising, charts or other visuals, or whatever they devise to help their classmates understand the feminist issues as they see them portrayed in the literary selections in their assignments. They may also include for comparison other media in which they see similar issues for example, songs, movies, or television shows.

The evaluation of these group projects has two parts. Once students have read their literary selections, they meet in their groups to discuss possible ways they can make their presentations. A recorder keeps a log of the ideas and specific assignments for each student. At the next meeting a different recorder summarizes the work to date and further tasks to be done. This log of the group meetings as well as each student's written self-evaluation of his/her contribution to the group work is submitted when they give their presentation. I use these to evaluate the effectiveness of the group process. Following each presentation, students comment for a few minutes on what they like best or learned from the presentation. Rather than using a checklist for these class presentations, I prefer writing an evaluation, concentrating on positive feedback but also raising some questions that point to areas that could have been improved.

A Feminist Reading of Some Other Young Adult Novels

The essence of any novel cannot be, nor should be, captured in a single theme or issue. Writers set out to tell good stories not to deliver messages. But because good stories are drawn from life experiences, themes and problems are interwoven into the fabric of fiction. Therefore, the content of each of the novels below is much more inclusive than the feminist perspectives in them. My intention is that the discussions may help to demonstrate how I focus on feminist concerns in a variety of novels and may also serve as a starting point for students who want to pursue further reading from a female perspective.

Notes for Another Life by Sue Ellen Bridgers
Among the complex male and female relationships that Bridgers explores in this novel are those of three generations of women. Karen Jackson has left her children for Bliss, their paternal grandmother and a traditional homemaker, to rear. Karen's successful career leaves no room in her life for teenage children, but she seems unaware of the pain she causes them. Ironically, her daughter Wren

is a talented pianist and, like her mother, may someday be confronted with some difficult career and family choices.

In other ways though Karen, not her family, is the victim. After her marriage to Tom, they return to his mother's home, where she busies herself with relatives, committees, children, and potluck dinners. When she gets a job, everyone assumes they need money, for otherwise a woman did not work. Soon Karen is managing everything as Tom sinks into depression and pills. From one perspective it has taken a great deal of courage for Karen to rebel against what society expected her to do. From another, however, she is weak for not assuming responsibility for her family. For women like Karen and Nora in *A Doll House*, there are no easy answers.

Stotan! by Chris Crutcher

Although predominately a novel of male bonding and told from a male perspective, some feminist issues are interwoven into this complex story of male athletes, their coach, their families, and their girlfriends. Walker dates Devnee, who is pretty and smart but arranges her life, even her choice of college, to fit what she thinks he wants. Ironically, Walker is attracted to Elaine, an athletic, free-spirited girl, who pals around with the guys. But Elaine is a force to be reckoned with as when she openly confronts and humiliates a guy who has spread rumors about her. Perhaps Devnee senses that Walker wants to break off the relationship but does not push him to a confrontation because the status quo is so comfortable. Perhaps she does not. But Elaine is wise enough to know that a relationship with Walker would not work for them and tells him so. These two characters function as female counterpoints.

A different feminist issue raised in the novel is the battered wife syndrome. Nortie's mother has been beaten to the point that she is incapable of protecting her children or herself from further abuse. She continues to live in an intolerable situation because she does not have the strength or courage to leave it. Crutcher draws an intense, realistic picture of this family and raises some questions, for which even psychologists continue to seek answers.

Girl in Buckskin by Dorothy Gilman

Originally published in 1956, this historical novel chronicles seventeen-year-old Rebecca Pumroy's struggle for survival. Orphaned when her parents are killed during the French and Indian War, Becky becomes an indentured servant. Her owner attempts to sell her into marriage, but she escapes with her brother Eseck, who had learned Indian ways during his five-year captivity. He teaches Becky how to survive alone in the woods, how to be self-sufficient and independent, how to hunt and trap and protect herself. When Eseck returns to his adopted Indian tribe, Becky uses her skills to save a wounded man, Shane O'Hara. Though she eventually marries him, she comes to that relationship as an equal: He likes and respects her independence and ability. By refusing to accept quietly the decisions being made by men about her life, by learning to take care of herself in a hostile environment, by pushing herself beyond what she thought her limits to be, Rebecca becomes a strong, proud woman.

Historically accurate in depicting a balanced view of the Indian and white man's behavior during their early conflicts, the novel shows the good and evil, the love and hate on both sides. Readers in seventh through tenth grades can benefit from reading this short novel with a female perspective in a setting usually reserved for male characters.

Catalogue of the Universe by **Margaret Mahy**

Dido May, an unwed mother, has struggled to rear her daughter Angela to feel loved and wanted and worthy. From babyhood, Angela has heard how her father wanted to marry Dido but could not because he was already married. She's heard how he loved them both very much and sent money when he could. Angela, discovering the truth about her father, his weakness and his selfishness, is at first hurt but later realizes the enormity of Dido's love and protection of her all those years. Although the story is told from Angela's perspective, this is a novel of two women: a strong mother who gives her daughter the freedom to grow into an independent young woman.

Dido has single-handedly carved out a space for herself high on a mountaintop overlooking a New Zealand city in the distance. With no indoor plumbing and an old car to negotiate the dangerous mountain road, life is hard. But there is a free spirit in Dido that makes her memorable. She has suffered alone, but in that suffering and in that loneliness she is her own person, living life in a way that suits her rhythms.

Who Invited the Undertaker? by **Ivy Ruckman**

Cathy Purcell must manage as a single-parent after her husband's death. Although she works as a legal secretary, her thirteen-year-old son Dale does not think his mother has the ability to make enough money to handle the family finances. He gets a job and wishes he were older. A boy of any age sometimes thinks he can handle a situation better than a woman, just because he is male and she is female.

However, Dale begins to see his mother in a new light and is proud of her when she and two other single mothers defy the traditional school policy by attending the maturation program with their sons. The three women listen as first a male teacher and then a female principal explain that they have had great success with keeping only fathers with the sons and mothers with the daughters. Threatening to sue the school under the equal protection clause of the Constitution, Mrs. Purcell and the others are seated. Dale's embarrassment at these women's action turns to pride as he sees his mother become a strong person for having stood up against such a sexist policy.

Jackaroo by Cynthia Voigt

With a clear feminist message set in medieval times, Voigt offers Gwyn, the Innkeeper's daughter, as a female who dares to face the cultural restrictions placed on a single woman when she announces she will not marry. Gwyn further takes on the role of Jackaroo, a legendary figure who operates as an outlaw to help the common people. She likes the freedom of a man's clothes and the power of being in control of her own destiny.

Voigt provides a sense of medieval life, particularly for poor women. Though she claims to be neither a feminist nor an antifeminist but instead looks at people first as human beings, her books, particularly *Jackaroo*, contain female characters who like being strong and independent. Students in grades eight to twelve who like historical fiction, Gothic romance, or even fantasy should enjoy this book because it has elements of all these, but Gwyn is no retiring heroine. She is adventurous and fearless, someone who makes decisions and takes action.

Weeping Willow by Ruth White

Tiny Lambert begins high school feeling inferior because her parents are uneducated and she lives in the country. Determined to succeed, she makes friends, studies hard, and assumes the care of her brothers and sisters because neither her mother nor her stepfather seems able to manage family responsibilities. After her stepfather sexually molests her, Tiny's life does not appear to change because she does not allow herself to think about it, instead pushing the memory into a well-hidden spot deep within. But when she realizes the same thing is about to happen to her sister, she takes control and is surprised and gratified that her mother stands beside her—three females confronting the man who has harmed them.

In this touching, tastefully done story, a strong girl becomes a strong woman, a survivor emerging from a chaotic childhood. Almost a period piece with details of teenage life in the 1950s, Tiny's story should appeal to girls in grades eight to ten.

Conclusion

I readily concede that these literary selections might be categorized as typically female books and stories, but my countering contention is that the mainstream curriculum is filled with male-oriented writers and male-oriented views with which female students cope handily. Feminist reading is not just for female students: Male students need to encounter a range of reading perspectives as well. In today's pluralistic society we cannot continue to promulgate narrow views of the literary canon and literary-critical perspectives that disenfranchise readers.

References

Bridgers, S.E. (1987). *Permanent connections*. New York: Harper & Row.

Bridgers, S.E. (1982). *Notes for another life*. New York: Bantam Books.

Carlsen, G.R. (1967). *Books and the teenage reader*. New York: Bantam Books.

Chopin, K. (1988). A pair of silk stockings. *The awakening and selected short stories*. New York: Bantam Books.

Crutcher, C. (1986). *Stotan!* New York: Dell Laurel-Leaf.

Dickinson, E. (1938). Much madness. In M. Bianchi and A.L. Hampson (Eds.), *The Poems of Emily Dickinson*. Boston: Little, Brown, & Company.

Gilman, C.P. (1973). *The yellow wallpaper*. New York: Feminist Press.

Gilman, D. (1984). *Girl in buckskin*. New York: Fawcett Juniper.

Hamilton, V. (1984). *A little love*. New York: Philomel.

Ibsen, H. (1965). A doll house. *Four major plays, 1*. New York: Signet.

Mahy, M. (1985). *Catalogue of the universe*. New York: Antheneum.

Mazer, N.F. (1983). *Someone to love*. New York: Dell Laurel-Leaf.

O'Brien, R.C. (1974). *Z for Zachariah*. New York: Dell Laurel-Leaf.

Olsen, T. (1956). I stand here ironing. *Tell me a riddle*. New York: Delacorte Press.

Piercy, M. (1973). A work of artifice. *To be of use*. New York: Doubleday.

Register, C. (1975). American feminist literary criticism: A bibliographic introduction. In J. Donovan (Ed.), *Feminist literary criticism*. Kentucky: The University Press of Kentucky.

Ruckman, I. (1989). *Who invited the undertaker?* New York: Thomas Y. Crowell.

Terris, S. (1987). *Nell's quilt*. New York: Farrar, Straus, & Giroux.

Voigt, C. (1985). *Jackaroo*. New York: Fawcett Juniper.

White, R. (1992). *Weeping willow*. New York: Farrar, Straus, & Giroux.

Chapter 9

Exploring the American Dream:
The Great Gatsby and Six Young Adult Novels

DIANA MITCHELL

Introduction

Students in English classes are always pleasantly surprised when they get not only to choose a book to read but also to choose from books written in years most of them have been alive. "You mean this author's not dead!" many of them exclaim after hearing brief book talks on six young adult novels that correspond with *The Great Gatsby*, a selection commonly found in American literature classes.

The Great Gatsby has a strong link with adolescent literature having a strong focus on goals or dreams. Since Jay Gatsby's goal of attaining Daisy drives him in many directions, students ought to think about the importance of having dreams or goals and whether they function negatively or positively. Dreams can become obsessions that cause us to turn on people, betray them, or overlook them. Goals can make us so single-minded that we forget about others and the values that were important to us. Thus dreams or goals can corrupt and change us for the worse. On the other hand, dreams or goals can be inspirations that push us forward and help us hang on. They can give us that extra bit of perseverence we need to keep at a task or the comfort we need when our life seems too chaotic to ever accomplish anything.

With the intention of asking students to evaluate dreams or goals and their subsequent affect on the character in mind, I found the following young adult novels available in my high school's library: *The Hero and the Crown, Tiger Eyes, The Moves Make the Man, Izzy Willy-Nilly, A Ring of Endless Light*, and *Jacob Have I Loved*. Each of the books are linked to *The Great Gatsby* because each of the protagonists desire to reach a dream or goal.

Dreams or Goals as Protrayed in Adolescent Literature

Synopses of the Young Adult Novels

1. *Hero and the Crown* by Robin McKinley (246 pp.). Aerin struggles in her efforts to realize her own heritage. She seeks to show her country that her mother's bloodline was not the inferior one that they perceived it to be. Aerin's goal is to prove herself to her country and confront gender limitations by slaying dragons herself.

2. *Tiger Eyes* by Judy Blume (222 pp.). Davey's major goal is to get over her father's death, her own guilt about his death, and to regain some measure of family security after her mother's emotional breakdown.

3. *The Moves Make the Man* by Bruce Brooks (280 pp.). Jerome wants to be good in basketball and have a secure and economically sound family life. He dreams that racism will one day disappear, and people will respond to him as a person independent of the color of his skin.

4. *Izzy Willy-Nilly* by Cynthia Voigt (258 pp.). Izzy loses a leg in a car accident, and her dream is to be accepted by others her age and not be considered a freak because of her injury.

5. *The Ring of Endless Light* by Madeleine L'Engle (324 pp.). Vicki has several dreams and goals: She desires more quality time with her grandfather before he dies, wants to be appreciated for her own qualities, would like to figure out how to know if a relationship is a good one, and intends to learn more from the dolphins.

6. *Jacob Have I Loved* by Katherine Paterson (175 pp.). Louise dreams of a life not dominated by the needs of her twin sister. She decides to get off the island she was raised on and wants to be appreciated for who she is.

Setting up the Unit

Finding and Arousing Interest in Adolescent Literature

Day One—The Book Pass.

As a general rule, it is recommended that teachers read all books prior to their classroom use; however, it is often impossible to accomplish this when teaching multiple texts. Rather than not use books that will be a positive experience for students, there are a few things teachers can do to get a fairly good idea of the content of the books.

Book reviews found in the *ALAN Review*, *Horn Book*, or the National Council of Teachers of English (NCTE)'s *Books for You: A Booklist for Senior High Students* are helpful. Reviewers provide a brief summary and comment on each book's quality. Of course, other teachers and media specialists can give recommendations of books related by theme.

Once possible book options have been identified, an easy way to help students with their selections is to use the book pass (Tchudi & Mitchell, pp. 139-140). Try to acquire multiple copies of at least six different books and put them on the students' desks by seat number. In other words, place the 1st book on the first desk in each row, the 2nd book on the second desk in each row, and so on. Then ask students to read the book on their desk for a set period of time, such as three to six minutes. When the teacher says "Stop," students write down the title of the book, the author, and whether or not they think they would like to read the book. Students then pass the book to the person behind them, with the last student in the row bringing the book to the person in the front seat. Each student should be able to look at and read a little of each book before the end of the hour. Finally, the students rank the books according to their first, second, and third choices. After class, based on choices and availability of books, the teacher assists students with acquiring their books.

Activities for the Young Adult Novels

Days Two and Three—Reading and Small Group Discussion

When different novels are being read by a class, several meaningful classroom activities involving all of the students can occur. To begin, give a class two reading days so that students are able to get deeply involved in their books. Usually, they can finish at least half of their novels in that time. On the third day, split the class into groups based on what the students were reading. If more than five students are reading the same book, break them into two groups. To give them a focus and ensure they all have successful experiences, I hand each group this list of directions and questions and ask students to address as many of them as possible:

1. Each person in the group takes a turn to tell what is happening in the story.

2. As a group, make a list of the issues raised so far in the story. Which do you think are important? According to the protagonist, which would be the most important issues raised thus far?

3. Describe another character's view on an issue in the book. Why does this character think or feel this way? Do you agree or disagree with this character? Why?

4. Discuss a character whose actions you don't understand or one you don't like.

5. So far, what does the protagonist seem to want the most? What is his or her dream or goal?

6. What does the main character seem willing to give up or to do in order to achieve this goal or dream?

7. What are some of the obstacles so far to this dream or goal?

8. What qualities or characteristics of the protagonist make him or her seem strong? Weak?

Each group is required to submit one sheet with their group's responses. Most groups can complete this task in a 55-minute class period, but, if students don't get done, it is not unreasonable to ask them to take the questions home and finish them individually.

Day Four—Issues and Questions

Before class, let students review their answers to the aforementioned questions in their groups. After a whole-class discussion of these questions, all students become fairly familiar with the content of their classmates' other books. Since no other homework is expected and students are well into their respective books, most of them will have their books finished by the end of the week; those needing more time can have the weekend. While they are reading, individuals are required to generate a list of five to eight issues or questions that they would like to talk about in their small groups. Students are required to bring enough copies of these questions for their group members on Day Six.

Day Five—A School Visit

This next assignment encourages students to think deeply about the main character, since they have to take what they know about the protagonist and go beyond that knowledge in order to fit the character into another location. Give groups about 20 minutes to discuss and prepare a presentation about what it would be like if their novel's protagonist visited their school. Each group chooses a spokesperson and splits up the task so that each member participates in an oral presentation lasting three to five minutes.

(The Protagonist) Visits (Name of School) High School

1. How would the protagonist in your novel get along at our high school?

2. What might be unusual about him or her in the context of our school?

3. What kinds of friends would he or she have?

4. What types of things would she or he do on her or his lunch hour?

5. What kinds of clothes would he or she wear? What would he or she think of the school's dress code?

6. What classes would she or he take?

7. What kind of school rules would he or she agree with? Disagree with?

8. What sports, clubs, or activities would she or he be involved in?

This assignment enables students to become familiar with the main characters in the other books so that subsequent whole group discussions make more sense to them. Usually the presentations go into the next day, and students have lots of questions about other groups' characters.

Day Six—Tape Recorded Discussions

Getting ready for the big wrap-up discussion in which the students tackle the questions they have generated (see Day Four) takes a lot of planning but is well worth the time. Cassette recorders and tapes must be found for each group. Since students will be recording their discussions, additional space must be found so that each group can record their group's deliberations without outside interference. A cafeteria, a gymnasium, or a large space where groups can be separated some distance from each other is necessary; if nothing else, outside will work. Tape recording their discussions and the teacher's circulating from group to group will generally keep most students on task.

After students get their group members' questions, the first task is to categorize them. This initial bit of critical thinking makes the discussions go smoother since similar questions and issues can be grouped together. In their groups, they can choose to focus on whichever questions they want by ranking the questions in priority order. After these tasks are completed, students turn on their cassettes and begin their discussions.

It is important that we as teachers get a sense of what students want to know and think about after reading a novel. As teachers, we should become aware of our students' attempts to arrive at a holistic understanding of their novels. To see the compilations of some of the questions and issues my students were concerned with as they examined each of their young adult novels, see Student Examples 9.1-6.

Student Example 9.1
Discussion Questions and Issues for
The Hero and the Crown by Robin McKinley

In this novel, many of my students' questions were aimed at helping them understand the story better. Some questions also show their desire to grapple with societal issues, trying to understand why people behave as they do.

1. People Questions

What are the obstacles Aerin had to face? Describe the many aspects of Aerin's relationship to Talat. What are some of Aerin's major strengths? At the end, how do you think Aerin felt? What about Aerin's feelings of insignificance? Would Tor make a better king than Arlbeth? Was Arlbeth weak as a king? Why did Tor choose Aerin over Galanna? Why did Aerin go to kill Maur without her father's permission? What did Aerin think of her mother? Did Aerin know she always loved Tor? Didn't Aerin feel strange having two lives and two loves?

2. Societal Issues

How is their society different than ours? How did society view the king and his family? What did society think about Aerin's mother? Do the women in their society really differ that much from the women in our society today? Have women always been treated as inferiors, unable to do the same activities as men?

3. Clarification Questions

Why didn't they keep the heartstone? Was kenet toxic? I don't understand the part when Aerin was climbing the stairs and she gets back and finds out she was going through time. Was her uncle in another time? When the dragon was dead, how could it still do evil? What happened at the lake?

4. Philosophical Issues and Speculation

How much of this fantasy is closely related to reality? Could there ever be an ointment that repels fire? Are our destinies written in a book somewhere? What things in this book could really happen? Could a fantasy-land like this exist somewhere today? Is this time period like earth's Medieval time? Could there be another kind of world?

5. Things to Explore in More Depth

The battle with Agsdad. The lake that gave Aerin visions. Luthe's character. The red dragonstone. What the dragon's head symbolizes. The significance of Maur's skull talking to Aerin. How would this book be different if gunpowder had been around?

Student Example 9.2
Discussion Questions and Issues for
Tiger Eyes by Judy Blume

Students who read *Tiger Eyes* wanted to talk about the book's impact and discuss why the characters behaved as they did. Students really enjoyed the book because they could get into Davey's mind and were exposed to her feelings, both good and bad. They thought that everyone's reaction to Davey's father's death was realistic and typical.

1. People Questions

Why is it that Walter can make weapons and can carry a gun, but still think that everything Davey wants to do is dangerous? Why did Davey hide things from her mom? Why didn't Wolf come back at the end? What made Jane start to drink? How did Davey feel about Hugh after she met Wolf? Do others feel that Bitsy and Walter seized too much authority in Davey's family? What was Jason's reaction to his father's death? Why did Davey keep those bloody clothes in a paper bag even when she went to New Mexico?

2. Societal Issues

Let's talk about the fear of death and how people handle a loved one's death. What are kids supposed to do when their parent can't handle problems and sort of flip out? Why are some adults overly protective of children? Alcolholism is hard to understand; why do people turn to it?

Student Example 9.3
Discussion Questions and Issues for
The Moves Make the Man by Bruce Brooks

Understanding people and racism seemed to dominate students' concerns regarding this book.

1. People Questions
A. Bix

Why does Bix send a postcard with no writing on it? Why was it so hard for him to distinguish between lies and truths? Why did Bix run away? Why didn't he get along with his father? What is so interesting about him that makes Jerome want to know him?
B. Jerome

In the beginning, why did Jerome sit and do nothing at the game where Bix played? Why does Jerome have so few friends even around his own neighborhood? Why didn't Jerome put up a fight with the school when he was cut from the team for being Black? Why was Jerome so willing to keep peace and not fight? What kind of impact does Jerome's mother have on him?

2. Societal Issues

Regarding basketball, small town hoops compared to big city hoops. Prejudice today compared to yesterday. Small-town life and the struggles of its inhabitants. Negatives and positives of family life. Would you be willing to be an only Black going to an all-White school? How about an only White attending an all-Black school?

3. Things to Explore in More Depth

Why aren't there more unusual and distinctive professional educators? Truth vs. deceit. How is it that simple lies can lead to the moral corruption of society? Should the coach of Chestnut be fired for his racism? Are moves just faking or are they another kind of truth? The parallels between basketball at our school and in this book.

Student Example 9.4
Discussion Questions and Issues for
Izzy Willy-Nilly **by Cynthia Voigt**

Drinking and driving, a desire to deal with issues that surround friendship and outrage at people who reject their friends were the focus of this group's questions.

1. People Questions

Could people really act like her so called friends toward someone they knew in Izzy's situation? Are people really that shallow? It surprised me that all the kids would stop hanging out with her just because she had only one leg. Why didn't the kids treat Marco the same way they treated Izzy? How can her best friends leave her when someone Izzy barely knows can stay by her side? I really grew to hate Izzy's mom. Why did she try to make her kids feel guilty? Izzy's dad didn't seem to handle this very well—let's talk about his reaction.

2. Societal Issues

Is our society now like the society presented in the book? Don't we have a different attitude about drinking and driving? What things have you done because of peer pressure? What things do we take for granted? What would it be like to be crippled or handicapped?

3. Things to Explore in More Depth

What can we do about drinking and driving? How important are looks really? How can people tell who their true friends are and which ones aren't?

Student Example 9.5
Discussion Questions and Issues for
Ring of Endless Light **by Madeleine L'Engle**

Because there were so many issues in this book, students concerns ranged from the philosophical to the scientific but again with emphasis on trying to understand why people behave as they do. From the list it can be seen that this book touched students deeply.

1. People Questions
   A. Zachary

Does Zachary ever become serious about his life? What does life mean to him? Does his childhood have something to do with it? Why does he try to scare Vicki? Does anyone else dislike Zachary but still feel sorry for him? Can anyone else relate to his need to be destructive? Wouldn't Vicki feel guilty if she broke up with Zachary and he then killed himself?

   B. Vicki

Why does Vicki want to grow up so fast? Why does she continuously say she's not smart when she knows so much about science? Why isn't more focus put on her poetry? Which relationship should Vicki choose? Vicki doesn't seem to enjoy being with Leo, so why does she always do things with him? Does she just feel sorry for him? Which of Vicki's actions do you disagree with? Why does Vicki seem to deal with death so optimistically and calmly?

Why doesn't Vicki tell her family about the dolphins? Do people like Vicki really have a way to communicate with dolphins? How do dolphins feel about the death of one of their own? What do dolphins symbolize? Why can't Adam communicate with the dolphins if he can communicate telepathically with Vicki?

2. Societal Issues
   A. Death
   How should you react to death? Why is Vicki's dying grandfather so calm about life after death? Why are some people like Vicki's sister so scared of death for other people? Why does the family seem to grow closer together because the grandfather is dying? Why does grief make people closer? What happens after death? What is more important—a happy life or a happy death?
   B. Friendship
   What is a true friendship? Discuss the family's relationship with each other. Discuss the intimacy of crying with someone. Talk about young people facing difficult, depressing, or painful situations and their emotions.
   C. Scientific
   Discuss the beginnings of the universe alluded to in the book. How does everyone feel about extra sensory perception (ESP) with the animals and especially with other people? What do others think about meditation and the way they meditated in the story? Talk about animal issues such as dolphin killings. Does cryogenics, where they freeze people, actually exist?

3. Things to Explore in More Depth
   Why is there so much irony is this book? Why does the book end with so many loose ends? Where is the sequel? What frustrations did you have with this book?

Student Example 9.6
Discussion Questions and Issues for
Jacob Have I Loved by Kathrine Paterson

Parent-child relationships and sibling relationships dominated the lists concerning this novel.

1. People Questions
   A. Louise
   Let's talk about Louise's feelings regarding how Caroline treated her and how everything was taken away. Why didn't Louise ever try for anything she wanted until the end of the book? Why did Louise want to be like her father and accepted as if she were male? Why didn't Louise ever tell her parents how she felt? How could Louise hate her sister so much? Could Louise be Caroline if she wanted to be?
   B. Grandmother
   Why was the grandma so rude to everyone? Why was she in the story since everyone thought she was insane? Why did she always pick on Louise?
   C. The Parents
   Why did the parents treat Louise differently than her sister? Why didn't her parents realize how much tension there was between the two girls and do something about it? Why did it take them so long to figure out what was going on between the girls?

2. Societal Issues
   Why do parents sometimes favor one child over another? Why do looks affect the way people interact with you? Why are some people so much more jealous than others? How important are friends? What is loneliness really? What causes some people to hate so deeply?

Using these questions and concerns as their guide, students tape record their hour long discussions and submit their tapes at the end of the hour. Since it is impossible to listen to all of the tapes by the next day, students are asked to reflect on the day's discussion and generate three to five statements about the most significant parts. This could be some insights they gained about a character(s) or issue(s), an understanding of the fact that others viewed a character(s) or event(s) differently than they did, or a part of the discussion they found personally rewarding.

Day Seven—Reflection

For the first 15 to 20 minutes of class, let students share their observations with the other group members. Each group, then, will explain to the class some of the significant things they feel they learned from the previous day's discussion. This reflective activity encourages students to think about their own learning and what, indeed, they gained from reading the novel. The reports are usually also a learning experience for the teacher—my students have almost always come up with comments and insights that hadn't occurred to me. Hopefully, this sharing also piques the interests of the students enough so that they will want to read some of the other novels.

Their lists often show that students don't read books just for our purposes. They want to understand what happened and why before they think about such things as theme, characterization, and setting. If we really want engagement with literature, we need to make room in our curricula to deal with issues and questions that are important to our students. After all, we read to be touched by the literature. I was pleased that the questions my students generated indicated that many of them were moved by their novels.

Making the Links Between
the Young Adult Novels and *The Great Gatsby*

Now that students have had the opportunity to think about and explore a young adult novel in ways that were meaningful to them, ask them to think about their novels in terms of ways that make links with *The Great Gatsby*. It is important to keep in mind that even though the intended link is in terms of dreams or goals, do not try to force students to see it in this way when they are working through their group novel. By forcing our themes and framework on a novel, we limit what students can get from the work and deprive them of the richness of their own perceptions and musings. For homework, ask students to write about the following:

1. In your novel what were the goals and dreams of the protagonist?

2. List all of the things your characters did or were willing to give up to achieve their goals or dreams.

3. From what you know of your characters' actions, what values (such as honesty, being accepted, acquiring possessions, etc.) would you say are most important to them?

4. Do you approve of your characters' value choices? Explain.

5. The American Dream is a term frequently used to try to explain the goals Americans would like to achieve. It probably started out meaning "life, liberty, and the pursuit of happiness" but today it has a much broader meaning. To some Americans the ultimate dream is to own their own home. To others, it's to have a fulfilling job. To still others, it might mean having a rewarding relationship. To most of us the "American Dream" has many components. Your task here is to write a paragraph explaining what the American Dream means to you. Include as many aspects as you can, and explain why these things are important to you.

Day Eight—Defining the American Dream

Students' homework papers are collected at the beginning of the hour, then, in random groupings, students try to come up with one definition for the American Dream. After 10 to 15 minutes, each group reports their definition to the class while the teacher writes the elements of each group's definition on the board or overhead.

When all of the groups have reported and the commonalities of the definitions have been noted, the class writes one definition for the American Dream. Students copy this definition for later use. Finally, ask students to explain which elements of the American Dream were important or not important to their characters.

Day Nine—Reader Response to *The Great Gatsby*

Distribute *The Great Gatsby* and briefly explain that the American Dream is a central issue in this novel. Students will be looking at these characters' versions of the American Dream and what these characters are willing to do to achieve it. Begin by reading the first several pages of the book aloud, so they can get used to the narrative structure and ask any questions about things that confuse them.

As students read the rest of the novel, ask them to write their reactions and responses to each chapter in a literature log. Each day begin class with questions or comments students have about what they have read. To see some of my students' responses, see Student Example 9.7.

Student Example 9.7
Student Response to *The Great Gatsby*

1. "Tom sounds violent. If he wants you to do something, you'll do it. He gets done what he wants done, even if it has to be forceful."

2. "One more piece of information about Gatsby was given, saying that he might have been a descendent of Kaiser Wilhelm. Considering the source of information, this seems highly unlikely."

3. "Why doesn't Daisy say anything to Tom, especially when she knows about his mistress? Are Jordon and Nick seeing each other? Why does the book only hint at this but never states it plainly? Why does Myrtle invite her neighbors to the party. Didn't she want to keep the affair secret? Why does Nick have such a fascination with Gatsby? Why doesn't Gatsby ever get really involved in his parties? Why is Gatsby so 'great'?"

4. "In Chapter Eight Nick says, 'he (Gatsby) paid a high price for living too long with a single dream.' Was the high price the loss of his self respect? If you don't respect yourself, no one else can and you are emotionally 'through.' Maybe he feels he isn't good enough any more and has been living in a dream-world, wasting years away out-of-touch with reality and he can't bear it."

Through their responses in their literature logs the students begin to question and wonder and make "what if" connections. By the time they get to class, they are usually ready to dig into the stuff of the novel and many lively discussions may result. I tell my classes that we are trying to make connections that make sense and that help us see the novel in new ways. It has become a tradition in my class that when a student makes an observation or connection that no one else had thought of before or that really brought part of the novel into focus for us, we say that that observation is "deep." Students feel they have made it in the class when their classmates respond to their contribution with "d-e-e-e-p." It is the highest compliment.

Day Ten—Characters' Names

F. Scott Fitzgerald adds another layer of interest and intrigue to his novel by his choice of the characters' names. Once students have gotten almost all the way through the book, give these directions to your students:

1. After each name below, write down associations or ideas that you can connect with the name.

2. Write a sentence explaining why you think Fitzgerald named each character as he did. For example, if John were one of the character's names, I might write something like this:

John—a common name, a regular guy, a toilet.

The author might have named this character John because John didn't stand out in a crowd and didn't draw attention to himself, but, as you got to know him you could see that he affected everyone's life, representing everything rotten, evil, and dirty.

3.   Please do the same for Daisy, Tom Buchanan, Myrtle Wilson, Nick Carraway, George Wilson, and Meyer Wolfsheim.

Of course, we talk about and share students' views on the significance of the names, and each year I am always pleasantly surprised by some new connection or perception about the names. Once a student looked up the word "myrtle" and explained the connection he saw between the low growing plant and the character of Myrtle. Another student once went beyond the assignment with his response to the name Daisy. He explained that a daisy is a rather plain flower. Although it has white petals and is surrounded by white (as Daisy was), it has a center of yellow because Daisy is a moral coward. He further explained that this Daisy was held up by her green stem, which represented the money that supported or held her up. Again, student responses can be amazing!

Day Eleven—Motifs

After students have shared their work on names, review what a motif is (a recurring feature such as a name, an image, or a phrase in a work of literature such as cars in *The Great Gatsby*) and ask students, in their groups, to make a list of 15 motifs that appear repeatedly in the novel. Some of the motifs my students have generated are as follows: weather; time (clocks, schedules); parties; Gatsby's pool and other water; eggs; light; East vs. West; eyes (glasses, cameras); ashes and dust; alcohol and illegal activities; racism and superiority complexes; rumors, gossip and "noses"; the colors of green, yellow, white, silver, etc.; smoking; wedding and wedding cake images; music and singing; and dishonesty.

Day Twelve

Distribute a class list of the motifs the students generated and have them work in pairs to brainstorm associations, connections, and possibilities of what the words were used to mean in the story. These associations can be shared orally or can be duplicated so students can move on to the next part of the assignment (See Student Example 9.8).

Student Example 9.8
Eyes/Glasses/Cameras/Windows/Dr. Eckleberg's Eyes

You are always being watched; blind authority; God being all-seeing, pupils, round and watchful, seeing through things, observing, and capturing images; visions; sometimes you can be standing right in front of something and not see it; "don't believe it until I see it"; seeing is believing; eyes are the windows to the soul; eyes give emotions away; everyone is watched; secrets are not kept kept but are discussed behind someone's back; and most of the time we see only the surface of people.

Eggs

Thin shells break easily; warmth; people hiding under a shell; walking on egg shells; delicate; hard boiled; shells can crack; eggs can be scrambled; eggs need a shell, must crack to be born; "you're a good egg."

Smoking/Cigars/Cigarettes

Death; air pollution; sophistication; smelly; expensive; elegant; a drug; only ashes and butts are left after you smoke, just as when you use someone there is not much left of them; try to suck life out of cigarettes and people; annoying; harmful; headache; coughing; users think they're cool but are stupid.

Day Thirteen

After reading or hearing the associations and connections their fellow students made with the motifs, students are now asked to make generalizations about why Fitzgerald used these motifs in his novel and what he might have been saying through these motifs. Some generalizations are already implied in the connections and associations list, but student pairs should try to generate at least two generalizations for 10 to 12 motifs.

The buzz in the room begins immediately as students get caught up in the excitement of creating their own meaning for the novel. Instead of the teacher trying to force interpretations, the students actively create their own meanings. Asking students to bring everything they know about the novel to bear on these motifs and associations requires them to use higher level thinking skills. The generalizations the students come up with range from brilliant to weak; the fun however, is in the sharing (See Student Example 9.9).

Student Example 9.9

Generalizations

*   Eggs - Fitgerald might have used egg as a geographical place name to imply that the people living in these affluent places hide behind the shell of luxury so their fragile selves won't be exposed.

    These place names may imply that to be accepted by the very wealthy, a person would have to walk on egg shells so as not to disturb the fragile world of the wealthy.

> *   Smoking/cigars/cigarettes - Fitzgerald might have used this motif to show how the very rich use people up just as cigars and cigarettes are used up. Cigars and cigarettes are lit up, provide brief enjoyment and then become ash just like Gatsby's bright parties.
>
> *   Glasses/eyes/windows/cameras - Becauses glasses, eyes, windows, and cameras are used so much, Fitzgerald does seem to be saying something about our ability to see. Things can be happening right in front of our noses (like Myrtle's affair with Tom) but we refuse to see them. Fitzgerald also may have implied that eyes are always on us, and in reality, we have few secrets from anyone.

If time permits, ask the students to pick the five strongest and the two weakest ones, and explain how the strong ones furthered their understanding of the book and why they felt the other two were weak. By building on the responses of the students, this gets students more involved in thinking about the book than if teachers tell them what the book is supposed to mean.

Day Fourteen—Discussion Essays

Because students have done so much thinking and writing about this novel, I do not feel obligated to have the students write a final essay. What I often do is turn the essay topics into questions that are discussed and then presented orally. Sometimes I'll ask a group to discuss the book from a feminist perspective while another group tries to figure out what made Gatsby "great." I've also had them compare Gatsby's quest to the Arthurian quest. Some students may volunteer to watch the movie version with Robert Redford so they can see what changes were made in the movie as compared to the novel. The possibilities are as broad as your imagination.

Day Fifteen—Yearbook Snapshots

The final project that students are asked to do is quite popular; it's called "Yearbook Snapshots." Have students illustrate their in-depth understanding of four characters in *The Great Gatsby* by imagining what they were like in high school. If they have shown little change in the course of the novel, chances are they haven't changed a great deal in their values and outlooks since high school. Encourage students to capture the essence of the character, their values, beliefs, etc., by carefully creating all of the information that would go under their picture in a yearbook. They should attempt to include as much of the following information as possible:

1. Nickname;
2. Activities, clubs, sports they were in and what years (1,2,3,4);
3. Class mock award such as "class clown";
4. Quotation that shows something about the person and what is important to him or her;

5. Favorites such as colors and foods;
6. Book that has had the greatest impact on him or her;
7. Voted "most-likely-to" what?;
8. Plans after high school.

Also look through magazines for pictures of each of these four characters then mount one picture per page with all the other information neatly written on the page. Make a cover and turn in the completed "yearbook."

Each year students seem to come up with different twists. The last time I did this assignment, several students asked for permission (if you can imagine) to include baby pictures of the characters as many real high school yearbooks do. For some memorable snippets from my student yearbooks, see Student Example 9.10.

Student Example 9.10
Tom Buchanan

Nickname: The Brute;
Sports: Football (1,2,3,4), Football Captain (4); Wrestling (1,2,3,4); Polo (2,3,4)
Clubs: German Club (2,3); Student Council (2,3,4);
Mock Award: Most Macho;
Can be quoted saying: "I deserve it all!"
Favorite Color: Any color except black;
Favorite Food: Any food but quiche;
Favorite Books: *How to Get Ahead in Life without Worrying about Other People* and *The Biography of Attila the Hun*;
Most Likely to: Do what he wants when he wants to do it;
Plans After High School: Make money and live in style.
Daisy Buchanan
Favorite Book: *Presumed Innocent*;
Can be quoted saying: "High school is the best time of your life. You have seven straight hours to talk to all of your friends."
Jay Gatsby
Favorite Book: *Great Expectations.*
Nick Carraway
Favorite Book: *A Tale of Two Cities*;
Can be quoted saying: "If you can't say something nice, then don't say anything."
Myrtle Wilson
Favorite Book: *The Scarlet Letter.*
Jordan Baker
Nickname: Pinocchio.

On the day these are due, have students pass the yearbooks around the class so the other students can appreciate their work. Often I have students give awards for best quotation, best picture, and so forth. After I grade this particular project, I always hang them on the walls. For the first week they are "published," students from every class I teach crowd around the boards at the beginning of the hour and seem to enjoy reading these yearbooks.

Ending the Unit

Day Sixteen—Final Comparisons

To wrap up their work with the two novels, have students get back into their original novel groups and do the following:

Directions: In your small group, compare and contrast your novel of choice with *The Great Gatsby* by answering the following questions.

1. In *The Great Gatsby* what issues are dealt with or brought up that are still relevant today?

2. In your novel of choice, what issues are relevant today?

3. Did you feel that *The Great Gatsby* was basically a negative or a positive novel? Explain. Were there any characters you think would make good role models?

4. Was your novel of choice basically negative or positive? Any positive role models?

5. What did you learn about people, life, and society from *The Great Gatsby*? From your novel?

6. In *The Great Gatsby*, how is the American Dream portrayed? Compare it to the definition the class developed. Which parts of the dream as shown in *The Great Gatsby* do you believe to be worthwhile and which parts do you believe to be unimportant? Explain.

7. In your novel of choice, do you consider the dreams or goals of your characters to be worthwhile? Explain.

8. Briefly contrast the American Dream as portrayed in your novel with the American Dream portrayed in *The Great Gatsby*.

9. Taking all of the above information into account, which of the two books do you believe is a better choice to teach as an all class book in an American Literature course? Explain your reasons.

Needless to say, the discussion in which the groups share their opinions on the above questions is often lively as students debate the merits of the American Dream as portrayed in each book as well as the merits of the books as texts the whole class could use. Some students believe the issues in *The Great Gatsby* are the differences between classes and the way people are treated differently based on their material possessions whereas others see love and trust as the predominant issues.

Many view *The Great Gatsby* as a novel that examined the sometimes negative attitudes of the rich as indicated by these comments: "Through this novel people are able to see that even though these people are rich, they're also corrupt, racist, adulterers, and bigots. In fact, the people viewed as being the better part of society are actually worse than the rest because they don't even realize that what they're doing is wrong." Another student felt *The Great Gatsby* belonged in an American literature class because it gives us "a real look at how the rich live and helps protect us from the jealousy that can be felt toward them."

Many students felt that they could better understand people and what motivated them by reading their young adult novels. Often, they thought that what their characters were willing to give up or do to achieve their goals was often more honest and moral than the things Gatsby was willing to do to capture his dream.

Conclusion

Even though the activities the students are asked to do for *The Great Gatsby* are more guided than the ones for their novels of choice, they don't seem to resent them because they know that their opinions and perceptions are valued. At no time do I as the teacher try to push students to view the book as I do or see if they can guess the answers I have in mind. We work from the material they generate and so when we are finished with *The Great Gatsby*, they feel they have made the book their own by grappling with it in ways that were meaningful to them. Young adult literature speaks to students when teachers sometimes can't.

References

Blume, J. (1981). *Tiger eyes*. New York: Dell Laurel-Leaf.
Brooks, B. (1984). *The moves make the man*. New York: Harper & Row.
Fitzgerald, F.S. (1925). *The great gatsby*. New York: Charles Scribner's Sons.

Gallo, D.R., Chair and the Committee on the Senior High School Booklist. (1985). *Books for you: A booklist for senior high students*. Urbana, Illinois: National Council of Teachers of English.

L'Engle, M. (1981). *The ring of endless light*. New York: Dell Laurel-Leaf.

McKinley, R. (1984). *Hero and the crown*. New York: Greenwillow Books.

Paterson, K. (1980). *Jacob have I loved*. New York: Harper & Row.

Tchudi, S. & Mitchell, D. (1989). *Explorations in the teaching of English*. New York: Harper & Row.

Voigt, C. (1986). *Izzy, willy-nilly*. New York: Atheneum.

Chapter 10

Their Eyes Were Watching God and *Roll of Thunder, Hear My Cry:* Voices of African-American Southern Women

PAMELA S. CARROLL

Introduction

When I informally polled my English teacher friends about which literary works by Southern, African-American writers they teach regularly, the only work that they named without prompt and almost without exception is Zora Neale Hurston's *Their Eyes Were Watching God.* Hurston was born and died in the South. The novel's Florida setting and its language are clearly Southern; its themes are at once Southern and universal. *Their Eyes* begs for modern day readers. Henry Louis Gates, Jr., in an Afterword published in the 1990 Harper & Row edition of the novel describes Hurston's art as "mythic realism, lush and dense within a lyrical black idiom" (p. 190), and acknowledges her role in the "black literary paternity" that Alice Walker claims and Toni Morrison demonstrates.

Just as it seems reasonable that *Their Eyes Were Watching God* is an appropriate choice as this chapter's focal Southern novel, it is also reasonable to select Mildred Taylor's *Roll of Thunder, Hear My Cry* as the focal Southern novel for young adults. *Roll of Thunder* is a work through which the artistic characteristics of Southern literature, the thematic Southern preoccupations, and the sociocultural voice of Southern writers can be taught and learned. Taylor is an African-American who treats Depression-era Mississippi sensitively and creates an invincible, admirable black family whose rich black Southern voices resonate throughout the novel.

Using *Their Eyes Were Watching God* and *Roll of Thunder, Hear My Cry* as primary texts, I have designed an instructional unit that is broad enough in its scope and implementation strategies to provide ideas to high school English teachers without insisting on a rigid approach. The teacher's individual style for delivering instruction and students' learning strengths, needs, and interests must ultimately have a greater influence on the teacher's choices than do suggested unit objectives and activities.

Literary Approach

The activities offered in this chapter assume a teaching stance that is based on a transactive model of reader response theory. This model assigns equal significance and responsibility to the reader and the written text for constructing meaning (Probst, 1988; Rosenblatt, 1988). Student readers will base interpretations of the literary works in part on their personal experience with an existing knowledge of the historical condition of Southern African-Americans. Their original reactions will be refined through direct consideration of two aspects of the works: (1) the specific features that are characteristically Southern and (2) recognition of the social/cultural context of the settings and the political conditions reflected in the works.

Along with this unit on Southern literature, I pose three challenges to teachers: (1) Try to implement an instructional model that draws from reader response theory, (2) encourage students to take responsibility for determining the meaning of the literary texts, and (3) listen to students as they talk about what they are reading.

Equally important will be the teacher's use of activities that integrate all of the language arts—reading, writing, speaking, listening, and viewing—in the study of Southern literature. Elements of each of the language arts should occur often. An aspect of language that is emerging as an area of interest for many educators is metacognition, the ability to reflect on what one knows and to recognize gaps in understanding when gaps exist. In this unit, activities such as the use of self-monitoring comprehension checklists, predict-the-plot exercises, and double-entry journals will contribute to students' development of their metacognitive abilities.

The Novels: A Brief Synopsis of Each

Roll of Thunder, Hear My Cry by Mildred Taylor

This is the story of the Logan family as it struggles to assert its dignity in the face of prejudiced, hateful white neighbors and frightened, distrustful black ones. Cassie, the eleven-year-old protagonist and narrator, learns that her world is distinctly black and white. A bigoted classmate stings her with the slap of discrimination; white racists terrorize her with the rage of hatred.

It is Cassie's family from whom she derives strength and an indefatigable desire for dignity. It is the Logan homeplace that becomes, for the black girl from Mississippi, a priceless inheritance that must be protected. Challenges to both dignity and property are many—the night riders, school censorship, a fire, to name three—yet this novel is not so much about action as it is about people who, with serene courage, overcome forces that work to defeat and dispirit them. The Logan family's story is continued in Taylor's sequels, *Let the Circle Be Unbroken* and *The Road to Memphis*.

Their Eyes Were Watching God by Zora Neale Hurston

This is the story of Janie Crawford's path toward self-realization and fulfillment. Like Cassie in *Roll of Thunder*, Janie lives for years unaware that she is black and, therefore, socially disadvantaged in the Depression-era South. Through love for her granddaughter, Janie's grandmother arranges for teenaged Janie to marry an old man, Logan Killicks, because he can provide Janie with property and security. What he does not provide is love.

Janie despairs in his lonely house and is easily tempted away by flashy, generous Joe Starks. Joe marries her then takes Janie to Eatonville, Florida, a town exclusively for blacks, where he quickly establishes himself as a leader. Soon Janie realizes that she is, again, nothing more than a man's property. She hides her feelings beneath docile acquiescence until Joe dies. Upon his death, she performs the proper grief rituals, then releases her long hair and revels in her freedom, explaining that "Mourning oughtn't to last no longer'n grief" (p. 89).

Soon, Janie takes up with Tea Cake, a roustabout who is her prince, a man who "could be a bee to a blossom" (p. 101), and to whom she becomes totally committed. When Tea Cake is bitten by a rabid dog and Janie must save her life by ending his misery, Janie's sadness is genuine. She attends his funeral in overalls, "too busy feeling grief to dress like grief" (p. 180). Despite the murmurings and accusations of folks when she returns, alone, to Eatonville, Janie lives her remaining days in peace, with dreams of "'goin on de muck'" (p. 122) and the memory of Tea Cake himself etching "pictures of love and light against the wall" (p. 184).

The Instructional Unit

Classroom Organization

The class should be divided into cooperative learning groups of four or five members, depending on class size. During "Round One" the groups read *Roll of Thunder, Hear My Cry*, during "Round Two" they read *Their Eyes Were Watching God*, and during "Round Three" the two novels are compared and contrasted. If students are given class and homework time for reading, the unit should last about five weeks.

Groups' and Individuals' Responsibilities

When the unit begins and group assignments (to be maintained during the unit) are made or chosen, each student and each group receives a new manila folder. Each student keeps all work related to the unit in his or her personal folder. Each group designates a clerk who serves as an organizer or progress reporter. The students' personal folders are also used later for an extension activity.

The students, as they read, decorate the front of their folders with original drawings, collage pictures and word cut-outs, or other artistic expressions related to *Roll of Thunder, Hear My Cry*. The back of the folder is used for the same type of creative activity, but it will reflect responses to *Their Eyes Were Watching God*. The full inside of the folder becomes a canvas for original artwork that is inspired by each student's comparison and contrast of the two novels.

Each student's folder, with all writing related to the required and selected activities, is collected by the teacher for part of the unit evaluation. Overall grades for the unit may be based on the quality of products included in students' activities folders, on their oral, listening and dramatic activities, on their group contributions and products, and on their performance on reading quizzes and/or novel tests. Self-evaluation of learning and attitudes toward the subjects and themes studied during the unit may also be used as important evaluative tools.

Unit Objectives

General Objectives

The general instructional objectives for this unit are listed in ascending order according to Bloom's (1956) taxonomy of the cognitive domain. The final three objectives come from the affective domain (see Krathwohl, 1964).

Upon completion of the unit, students will be able to:

1. Name writers and works of Southern literature for young adults and adult Southern literature (knowledge);

2. Cite four characteristic features that, when combined in a work, account for the regional self-consciousness—the flavor—of Southern literature (knowledge);

3. Discuss actions and consequences of characters' actions in the focal novels (comprehension);

4. Recognize themes that are important in the novels (comprehension);

5. Point out characteristics of Southern literature in the novels, current television shows, and movies that have Southern settings (application);

6. Compare and contrast literary elements (setting, plot, characterization, theme, etc.) of the young adult novel, the adult novel, television

shows, and movies (analysis);

7. Examine each author's treatment of the historical context of her novel in terms of social and racial circumstances (analysis);

8. Make predictions about future events in the novels based on information given by the writer and inferred by the reader (synthesis);

9. Produce an original short work of Southern fiction, giving attention to place, memory, the clash of traditional and modern ways, and language (synthesis);

10. Compare and contrast the authors' use of the Southern voice and determine which is more effective, moving, compelling, readable, and so forth. (evaluative);

11. Evaluate each novel in terms of its artistic quality and its social significance for African-American and white readers (evaluative);

12. Develop an increased appreciation for Southern literature (affective);

13. Develop an increasing appreciation for the artistic qualities and contributions of African-American and women writers (affective);

14. Derive pleasure from approaching texts with an aesthetic stance (see Rosenblatt, 1988) (affective).

Specific Objectives

In addition to the list of general objectives, the following sets of objectives are particularly germane to study of each of the focal novels.

For *Roll of Thunder, Hear My Cry*, students will be able to:

1. Become aware of the history of social and physical mistreatment of African-Americans in the South as portrayed in the novel, including segregation of churches and schools, burnings, tar and feathering, night riders, and economic measures (knowledge);

2. Explain the significance of Cassie's inheritance—a family homeplace—particularly as it relates to the time and social contexts of the novel (comprehension);

3. Identify natural elements used as symbols such as the land, fig tree, thunder, rain, and fire (application);

4. Explain how each of the symbols is used in the novel (analysis);

5. Develop an ending that focuses on T.J. (synthesis);

6. Determine whether Taylor's portrayal of Cassie and the Logan family, in terms of their strengths and weaknesses, is three dimensional (evaluative).

For *Their Eyes Were Watching God*, students will be able to:

1. Increase their understanding of the Everglades and tropical storms (knowledge);

2. Define anthropology, and identify examples of African-American traditions and folklore included in the novel (comprehension);

3. Chronologically plot Janie's life and circumstances (application);

4. Analyze Janie's growth toward self-realization (analysis);

5. Develop an informed position on the place of Black women writers in American literature (synthesis);

6. Analyze the novel in terms of potentially objectionable aspects and respond to Hurston's use of those aspects (evaluative);

7. Evaluate Hurston's contributions to African-American and to Southern literature (evaluative).

Instructional Activities

All activities used to enhance the reading of each novel are filed in a box labeled "Activities Box for (name of novel)." Descriptions and directions for activities are typed and posted on large index cards. The card boxes have three dividers—"Speaking/Listening/Viewing," "Reading/Thinking (Metacognition)," and "Writing"—to indicate which language arts skills are of predominant concern in the activities of the sections. Overlaps occur, reinforcing the idea that language skills are interrelated. Each card is also keyed according to the feature of Southern literature with which the activity is primarily concerned.

Each group is given a box of activities cards. All boxes labeled "For *Roll of Thunder, Hear My Cry*" include identical cards, as do all the boxes labeled "*For Their Eyes Were Watching God.*" Each group's clerk is responsible for keeping track of the group's division of labor. Ideally, individuals will have time to select and complete many of the activities during the study of each novel. Even with time restraints, each group should be sure that responsibilities are divided so that all activities are completed and discussed among group members.

"Round One" Preliminary Activities

The activities boxes, with assignments for enhancing students' reading and studying *Roll of Thunder*, should be given to the clerk who will pass on the information to his or her group members. Group work during "Round One" is initiated with these steps:

1. Each clerk will read all activity cards to his/her group.

2. Individual group members will be responsible for selecting activities to complete and will be held accountable to the group for the successful completion of the selected activities.

3. The clerk will list students' names with their selected activities.

A progress check should be made by the clerk and teacher periodically, at least twice a week. Individuals should also record their selections and file the list in their personal folders.

"Round One" Activities

The teacher prepares cards with directions that are appropriate for his or her own students. The descriptions given are intentionally broad so that they will be easy to modify for the needs of varied classes.

Listening/Speaking/Viewing Activities

1. **Oral Histories.** Students may interview a member of the community or their family in order to gain depth of information about the community's move toward racial desegregation or the impact of the Great Depression on the community. Interviews with the community or family members will be audiotaped. Students will transcribe the taped conversation and will turn in the tape and written transcription for presentation to the group during the study of the novel.

It is recommended that students prepare a list of interview questions and practice using the questions (and an audiocassette tape player) with a classmate. All class members who choose to complete an oral history will be required to meet with the teacher for a 10 to 15 minute mini-lesson on interviewing guidelines during the second day of activities work.

Several books may be used by the students for examples and inspiration:

* *Narrative of the Life of Frederick Douglass: An American Slave* by Frederick Douglass
* *Before Freedom: 48 Oral Histories of Former North and South Carolina Slaves* by Belinda Hermence
* *Hard Times: An Oral History of the Great Depression in America* by Studs Terkel
* *Life Under the Peculiar Institution: Selections from the Slave Narrative Collection* by Norma R. Yetman, (Ed.)

For the teacher, a practical description, "Person to Person: An Oral History Project" is provided by Sam Totten of the Walworth Barbour International School, Israel, in the NCTE publication *Ideas for Teaching Middle and Junior High School Language Arts* (1980).

2. **The Southern Voice.** Bring students together for a whole-class session during which they view and listen to excerpts from popular television shows and movies that feature Southern characters and settings. Have the class discuss characteristics of pronunciation, inflection, and rate of speaking, working to create a list of descriptions of the Southern voice.

Possible television shows and movies include the following:

* "Designing Women"	* "In the Heat of the Night"
* *Driving Miss Daisy*	* "Matlock"
* "Evening Shade"	* *Norma Rae*
* *In Country*	* *Steel Magnolias*

Following this activity, students return to their groups and select one excerpt from Taylor's novel that is particularly rich in dialogue. Group members write a script that imitates and/or extends the novel's dialogue and distribute it among participating group members. After independent practice, the group rehearses and then performs the creative interpretation and extension of the text. If possible, videotape the performance and show it to the whole class during the culmination of the unit.

It is recommended that all students wishing to participate in this activity meet with the teacher for a 15 to 20 minute mini-lesson on the use of video camera equipment. If a media specialist is available, he or she would be a good resource person to invite to the class for delivering the mini-lesson.

3. **Response Discussion Groups.** Donelson and Nilsen (1989) contend: "Nearly everyone agrees that discussing books is valuable. It enables students to exchange ideas, and to practice their persuasive techniques by arguing about and examining various interpretations" (p. 358). While students need to be responsible for the direction of discussions about the young adult novel, the teacher will probably need to establish some guidelines that will help students focus their attention and energy during group—or group-within-a-group— discussions.

A strategy that I have found helpful is to have students use response journals as a place to record their prediscussion ideas about the texts. Discussion can proceed, based on group members' individual readings of the book, from literal to abstract levels. The discussion is then followed by students' writing responses—not initial reactions—but reflections that are informed by group interaction.

A group-within-a-group may designate a member leader, who then decides on a particular focal point for the group's talk. Examples could be the literary elements of characterization, plot, point of view, and so forth, or the characteristics of Southern fiction: attention to place, emphasis on memory, concern with the clash of tradition and modernity, and language that bespeaks the voice of the South.

Reading/Thinking Activities

1. **Choral Reading.** For this activity, two or more students select excerpts from *Roll of Thunder* and rewrite the prose in poem or song form. Students are required to include a repeated refrain. The reworked passage is rehearsed with two or more speakers sharing the responsibility for reading the stanza(s) and refrain. The student-created version is presented to the class (and videotaped, if possible) after it has been rehearsed for and approved by the group.

2. **Character Circles.** This activity encourages students to examine individual characters and the relationships between characters. To complete this activity, students should follow directions similar to those shown in Figure 10.1.

Figure 10.1
Character Circles

A.   In the center of a sheet of unlined paper, draw a small circle that is approximately 1 1/2 inches in diameter.

B.   Write the name of the protagonist (or a focal character of the student's choice) in the center of the circle.

C. Add concentric circles, one for each character who is somehow connected to the focal character. Be sure to write the name of the secondary character who has the closest relationship to the focal one on the circle closest to the center circle.

D. If two characters share an equal relationship with the protagonist, put their names on the same concentric circle.

E. Continue adding characters' names, moving further from the center to indicate relationships that are increasingly distant from the focal character.

The completed diagram not only shows the relationships of secondary characters with the protagonist but also reflects the relationships between secondary characters who occupy positions on the same circles.

The teacher may want to let students who complete a story diagram to share their diagrams with the entire class after they have rehearsed their presentation within their groups. Questions that probe into the relationships represented on the diagram may also be directed to the student:

*Can it be that enemies of the protagonist (or focal character) occupy circles that are closer to him/her than his/her casual acquaintances?

*Are blood relationships always stronger than friendships?

*Do characters' relationships to one another change during the novel?

3. **Point of View.** By examining the author's use of point of view, students can experiment with it by rewriting passages from another perspective. It is important that students choose an appropriate excerpt, a passage in which the reader discovers something new and significant about a character. Following are two choices that work well with *Roll of Thunder, Hear My Cry*:

1. Reread pages 32-33. Pay close attention to Little Man's feelings about the bus. Rewrite the section, telling the same event from Cassie's or Stacey's perspective (retaining the first-person narrative voice). Then shift the perspective to T.J.'s. How would he relate the incident?

2. Reread pages 186-188. If Mr. Jamison had witnessed T.J.'s role in the robbery and killing of Mr. Barnett, how would the scene change? Rewrite it, adding Mr. Jamison's account of the events given as if he were an eyewitness in the events. Or, extend Cassie's role in the passage; instead of merely narrating it, have her speak her mind along with Stacey.

4. **Extension Reading.** In this activity, students go beyond the novel in order to get a better look at the novel. Have students read "Antaeus" by Borden

Deal, a short story that focuses on a displaced Southern boy's sense of the importance of land. Students have the option of making a two to four minute mini-presentation or writing an essay about the significance of homeplace as reflected in the short story. Students then compare the story's sense of place to the novel's, using criteria they develop either independently or with the help of their peers or teacher.

Again, these activities, though dependent first on reading, also develop skills in the other language arts and thus support one of the major goals of the unit.

5. **Structural Overview or Graphic Organizer.** This activity has students construct and continually upgrade a graphic overview of the novel they are reading. The overview may simply reflect the novel's plot structure, highlight a particular character's development, or correlate places with actions associated with them, and so forth. Encourage students to develop overviews based on their own needs for organizing the novel. One may create a cluster diagram related to themes while another fills in a time line. A group member who chooses this activity may make daily review and preview reports to the group, thus allowing peers to benefit from his or her graphic organizer.

6. **Self-monitoring Checklist.** This is an activity to which all group members should be introduced during a mini-lesson in the first few days of the instructional unit. Readers benefit by learning to stop their reading occasionally to ask themselves questions such as these:
*What did I just read?
*Does it connect with what I read before?
*What might happen next?
*Am I confused about any details?

Writing Activities
Students are required to write each day during this instructional unit. The standard daily assignment, one that is shared with the whole class before any group work begins, may follow these guidelines:

1. During the last ten minutes of each reading period, students get their personal folders and record the number of pages read. A new page is used for each reading period, and the heading for the page should include the date.

2. For the first part of the daily reaction, students write a statement of what the text was about. This part draws on students' transaction with the text to construct meanings that are based on textual elements and personal experiences; it is a summary.

3. The second part of the daily reaction is a response to the day's text. This is each student's personal statement of what the text means. This part requires reflection by the student so that personal significance can be a part of the reading event; it is a response. It may also include the student's evaluative statement about his or her progress and attitudes about the reading experience.

4. The third part of the daily reaction is the listing of any unfamiliar vocabulary words, including the sentences and page numbers in which the words occur. This list enables readers to develop their own word study lists.

5. The last daily requirement is a double-entry journal entry. Each student chooses one particularly memorable, provocative, alarming, or confusing phrase, clause, sentence, or segment and writes it, exactly as the author did, on the left side of a page. On the right side, the student comments on the quotation in whatever way seems appropriate.

I strongly suggest that these activities be assigned regardless of whether the reading is done in or out of class.

Other writing activities are available from the "writing" section of the activities box for each novel. Ten generic assignments are described and include examples of ways they might be implemented during the reading of *Roll of Thunder*. (The same set of ten assignments are also appropriate for stimulating written response to *Their Eyes Were Watching God*.) All of the writing activities are also keyed to the particular characteristics of Southern literature with which they are primarily concerned. Again, it is intended that each of these activities is described and posted on a card that is filed in the respective novel's activities box.

Writing Activities for *Roll of Thunder, Hear My Cry*

Newspaper Article (memory and language). Students read several news articles, to infer style and content standards, and then write articles that could appear in the *Strawberry Daily News*. Possible topics include the night the Wallaces and Simses went after T.J. Avery and the time that the land burned (pp. 190-210).

Song/Poem (language). 1) The students write in poem form the prayer Mamma would have said on the night that her husband faced a would-be lynch mob and T.J.'s on the run. (Taylor tells us that Mamma prays but doesn't give us her words.). 2) By using Cassie's question, "Does it have to be?" (pp. 174, 180, 209) as part of a song's refrain, students can write a song "around" Cassie's plaintive query.

Skit/Role Play (memory). A group-within-a-group might want to work together in order to dramatize a specific scene as described by Taylor. Another possibility is to extend or change a scene through role play. Consider these as possible scenes to dramatize:

*T.J., Jeremy, Cassie, Little Man, Stacey, and Christopher John are on the way to their school when they see the white bus heading towards them.
*The Sims' brothers threaten T.J. to keep quiet about the Barnett store incident.
*The day Hammer comes back to town.

Letter (clash of traditional and modern; memory). Students take on the perspective of a character and write a letter to another character in the novel. Possible choices include Momma writing to her colleagues at the Great Faith Church School about why she was dismissed from her teaching job (p. 139) or Papa writing to Cassie about self-respect (pp. 133- 134).

Postcard (place; language). On one side, students decorate a postcard with a scene that is related to the novel. On the other side, students write a card to or from a character. Hammer sends a postcard to the Logan children from his big city home, for example.

Article/Essay (clash; memory). Students develop their expressive or expository writing skills by producing essays that are related to the novel. Possible essay topics include these choices:

*Review the incidents of racist behavior in the novel and discuss one or more in terms of the overall themes and tone of the novel. See pages 5-10, 15, 17-19, 32, 56, 73-75, 83-87, 95-96 and 124 for ideas.
*Discuss what we, in the 1990's, have learned about racial and social injustice.
*Research the history of segregation and desegregation in your community and report on it.
*Discuss the impact of story telling in the novel (p. 111) and relate it to the characteristics of Southern literature that deal with memory and language.

Autobiography (place; memory). Students step into Cassie's place and write her autobiography, including her disappointments and aspirations. Students who choose this activity may wish to check their product against the sequel to *Roll of Thunder*, called *Let the Circle Be Unbroken*.

Obituary (memory). Students propose an obituary for a character who dies or who comes close to death such as an obituary for Big Ma (including reference to the times she has seen), for T.J., or for Mr. Morrison.

Diorama from a Description of Place or Other Features (place; memory). Students review Taylor's details (such as the dinner table, which is usually significant in contemporary Southern fiction), synthesize them into one description, and build a diorama of the scene. Some possible focal points include the Logan home, the church, school, and the road to the school.

Symbols (place; memory; clash; language). A student may work alone or wih a partner to explore symbols used in Taylor's novel. She or he will choose one and write an explication or expression of the value and contribution of the symbol: the fig tree, thunder, rain, fire, or night.

"Round Two" Preliminaries

Upon completing and sharing these activities, each group will be ready to read Hurston's *Their Eyes Were Watching God*. It may be helpful for the teacher to demonstrate Hurston's use of flashback since flashback is not used in *Roll of Thunder*. A direct mini-lesson using the first and last chapter of *Their Eyes* works well. Not only is the narrative framework presented, but the use of heavy dialect is introduced when these sections are used. In this way, the craft and art of Hurston's novel receive immediate attention, and students' responses are given validity.

"Round Two" Activities

The activities boxes used in "Round One" can be recycled for "Round Two." This round again lends attention to the integration of all language arts with a focus on the literary characteristics of Southern fiction. Suggestions offered are just that—suggestions.

Listening/Speaking/Viewing

Living Histories. Students and their teacher can brainstorm to produce a list of names of people in their community who were children during the years of the Great Depression. Select a student committee whose charge is to invite one or more of the persons listed to come and share information about the Thirties with the class. All students are required to prepare a few questions for the speakers before their visit but should not be restricted or obligated to these questions. It is likely that the speakers' remarks will evoke an unanticipated line of inquiry, and students should be encouraged to follow through with the line of thought that the speaker establishes.

The Southern Voice. Language—lush passages fill the pages of *Their Eyes*. The students can choose the sections of dialogue that they think best showcase Hurston's use of the black vernacular then present oral readings to the class.

Response Discussion Groups. By the time students are reading *Their Eyes*, they should be able to sustain conversations about the novel and discern which issues need to be discussed. Because they have considered the historic, economic, and social conditions of the post-slavery South, they have a basis for interpreting the significance of these and other parts of the text: the Washburn place and Nanny's desire to move from it; Logan Killicks and the promise of stability; Joe

Starks as a self-made man whose success separates him from his race; the apprehension that porch sitters feel about Tea Cake, in whom they see many of the negative traits ascribed to their race by outsiders; the tension of the courtroom scene; and Janie's return to Eatonville and memories of her home there.

Reading/Thinking Activities

Choral Reading. As in "Round One," students may wish to select excerpts from *Their Eyes* that would be appropriate to rewrite as songs or poems with a repeated refrain. Also appropriate for enhancing the study of the work would be choral readings of poetry by Alice Walker. One that is often anthologized is "My Sister Molly Who in the Fifties." The rhythm of the poem, along with information about Walker's admiration and loyalty to the memory of Hurston, may contribute to a lesson that extends Hurston's work to the present. Maya Angelou's poetry and James Weldon Johnson's verse sermons would also be fine choices.

Character Circles and Structural Overviews. See directions under "Round One" (pp. 11-23) and follow them, using Janie at the center of the smallest circle. Other structural overviews (for example, a family tree to graphically represent Janie's relationship with the three men of her life) increase the probability that students will comprehend what they read.

Point of View. This aspect may be the most difficult for students to understand of the literary elements in *Their Eyes* because the narrative voice flows in and out of the first and third persons. Students should be led to question not only where Hurston shifts, but to consider why. For this activity, they first reread with a fact-finding stance and then reread again with an aesthetic one.

Self-monitoring Checklist. The directions here are identical to those of "Round One."

Writing Activities

Along with the required daily journal entries (see "Round One") students may choose to do any of the following, each of which is based on the ten generic writing activities suggested for enhancement of *Roll of Thunder*.

Newspaper Article. Students can write an account of Tea Cake's death, Janie's trial, or report on the hurricane damage.

Song/Poem. Some suggestions for students might be "Janie's Blues;" "Joe's Jam;" or "The Tea Cake Shuffle."

Skit/Role Play. Of course, the possibilities are endless but consider these: Tea Cake courting Janie, porch sitters judging Janie as she passes by, or Pheoby and Janie sharing secrets.

Letters. Offer your students these suggestions: Nanny gives Janie advice, Pheoby writes to Janie to keep her up-to-date on Eatonville happenings, or Janie writes to Logan about why she left him.

Postcards. Students can create postcards from Tea Cake to Janie from Jacksonville, Janie to Pheoby from the Everglades, a visitor in Eatonville to a friend.

Article/Essay. Students can choose among these possibilities: Using the first and last chapter, explain the novel's structure; discuss the effectiveness of the structure; give Hurston's perspective, as implied in *Their Eyes,* on the condition of African-Americans in the 20th century; describe Hurston's use of language as meaning, not decoration; present Nanny's world vs. Janie's limited vision and unrestricted horizons; or explain why we do not "hear" Janie's voice in the trial scene.

Autobiography. Students may want to concentrate on Joe's later years; Tea Cake's life; Janie's later years; or life after Tea Cake.

Obituary. Writing possibilities include Nanny's; Joe's; or Tea Cake's obituaries.

Diorama/Description. Students may want to describe the Washburn place; Eatonville; Tea Cake; or Janie's house in the Everglades and construct a diorama.

Symbols. As in *Roll of Thunder, Their Eyes* is rich with symbolism: bees and birds, Logan's house, Joe's zoo acres, the horizon, water, the storm, the porch, first names (Sop de Bottom, Tea Cake, Motor Boat, Stew Beef), and last names (Killicks, Stark, Woods).

"Round Three" Activities

After students read *Roll of Thunder* and *Their Eyes*, they begin the final round of literature-related activities. These experiences promote students' analytic thinking skills by requiring comparisons and contrasts between the novels. The experiences also reinforce responses made during the first reading events and, through reconsideration with added perspectives, enhance the literary experiences.

"Round Three" Issues (comparison and contrast between the novels)

1. Students can examine the narrative structure and language used in both novels (narrative voice, point of view, and so forth).

2. Students can discuss the socioeconomic situations of important characters.

3. Students investigate the significance of homeplace and family.

4. Students explore the clash of traditional and modern values within both novels.

5. Students analyze the inequities, injustices, and/or other human conflicts.

6. Students peruse the historical settings, noting the significance of temporal and geographical features.

7. Students write a letter to the author commenting on their ideas and asking why passages or instances were presented (and others were not). (See "Dear Author" in Kirby and Liner, p. 170)

8. Students notice the importance and relevance of secondary characters. (See "Don't Forget the Little Guy" in Kirby and Liner, p. 174)

9. Students can compare the natural imagery used in both selections.

Supplemental Southern Texts

There are other works that teachers may find valuable as supplements to the Southern literature unit. Teacher may wish to include the entire reading or incorporate excerpts from any of the following:

Classic Literature

1. *I Know Why the Caged Bird Sings* by Maya Angelou. Ms. Angelou's autobiography of her love and trouble-filled childhood. (See P. L. Gauch, pp. 125-129).

2. *Invisible Man* by Ralph Ellison. The disturbing account of a Southern black man who goes underground in the North.

3. *To Be Young, Gifted, and Black: Lorraine Hansberry in Her Own Words* by Lorraine Hansberry. Hansberry's autobiography of her growth as an artist.

4. *Dust Tracks on a Road* by Zora Neale Hurston. Hurston relates how she came to look at the world as an artist and traveller.

5. "I Have A Dream" by Martin Luther King, Jr. King's famous, inspirational speech emphasizing the dream of freedom for all blacks.

6. *To Kill A Mockingbird* by Harper Lee. A heart-rendering look at racial injustices in the pre-Civil Rights South.

7. *Black Folktales* by Julius Lester. Contains several sources of oral histories.

8. *Motherwit: An Alabama Midwife's Story* by Onnie Lee Logan and Katherine Clark. Contains several sources of oral histories.

9. *The Color Purple* by Alice Walker. A novel about black women—and their men—as they face life in the Deep South.

10. *Jubilee* by Margaret Walker. An historical novel about life in the South.

11. *Black Boy* by Richard Wright. Wright's autobiography of his childhood in the South.

12. *Native Son* by Richard Wright. Wright's horrifying account of a black man's violent struggle in a white man's world.

Young Adult Novels

1. *Sounder* by William Armstrong. The memorable story of a young Southern farm boy whose prize possession is his dog, Sounder.

2. *Home Before Dark* by Sue Ellen Bridgers. Fourteen-year-old Stella Mae Willis has spent most of her life living out of an old, beaten-up station wagon and moving, with her migrant family, from one harvest to another. (See Carroll, pp. 10-13).

3. *Black Like Me* by John Howard Griffin. A chilling account of Griffin's experiences of traveling the South disguised as a black man.

4. *Skeeter* by K. Smith. Two white Tennessee boys are drawn by the love of hunting to old, black, Skeeter.

5. *The Secret of Gumbo Grove* by Eleanor E Tate. A young girl complains in her history class about not studying black heroes. (A Parents' Choice Award Winner)

6. *Thank You, Dr. Martin Luther King, Jr.* by Eleanor E. Tate. A companion novel to *The Secret of Gumbo Grove*.

7. *The Gold Cadillac* by Mildred Taylor. Daddy drives the car to visit family in the South; the Northern license plate on the golden car stirs trouble.

8. *Come a Stranger* by Cynthia Voigt. Mildred thinks she is expelled from ballet camp because she is black.

9. *Not Separate, But Equal* by Brenda Wilkinson. Malene and six other blacks integrate a public high school in Georgia during the 1960s.

The writers of these supplemental works make African-American experiences accessible to white readers—and all readers—in the 1990s. The excerpts will contribute to readers' readiness for understanding the sociocultural contexts of *Their Eyes Were Watching God*.

Conclusion

By introducing our students to Taylor and Hurston, we offer them a peak at an America that is neither always the beautiful nor the damned. With *Roll of Thunder, Hear My Cry* we help students become engaged in realistic fiction that is easy to read yet difficult to forget. With *Their Eyes Were Watching God*, we challenge students to become involved in another's dialect, another's world, and we can promise great rewards for those who accept the reading challenges.

When we choose to supplement our American literature texts with Hurston's not-yet-anthologized work, we help rectify the error of overlooking for years her place in American, and particularly Southern and African-American literature. For too long we have dismissed Hurston's optimistic, dignified voice as insignificant. We have listened as her contemporaries condemned Hurston for choosing to focus on beauty wherever it is flourishing instead of joining the protest against social ills. By teaching students about Southern literature and regional preoccupations through Taylor's fiction then having them apply what they have learned to Hurston's art, we will introduce students to writers whose words tell the stories of the South, writers whose literature celebrates the voice of the South.

References

Angelou, M. (1990). *I know why the caged bird sings*. New York: Random House.

Angelou, M. (1990). *I shall not be moved*. New York: Random House.

Angelou, M. (1978). *And still I rise*. New York: Random House.

Armstrong, W. (1969). *Sounder*. New York: Harper & Row.

Bloom, B. (Ed.). (1956). *Taxonomy of educational objectives: Handbook I: The cognitive domain*. New York: David McKay.

Bridgers, S.E. (1977). *Home before dark*. New York: Bantam Books.

Carroll, P.S. (1990). Southern literature for young adults: The novels of Sue Ellen Bridgers. *The ALAN Review*. 18 (1), 10-13.

Deal, Borden. (1961). "Antaeus." In J.S. Simmons and M. Stern (Eds.), *The short story and you: An introduction to understanding and appreciation*. Lincolnwood, Illinois: National Textbook Company.

Donelson, K. and Nilsen, A.P. (1989). *Literature for today's young adults, 3rd ed.* Glenview, Illinois: Scott, Foresman, & Company.

Douglass, F. (1989). *Narrative of the life of Frederick Douglass*. New York: Anchor. (originally published in 1845).

Ellison, R. (1947). *Invisible man*. New York: Random House.

Gates, H.L., Jr.. (1990). Zora Neale Hurston: A negro way of saying. Afterword in Z.N. Hurston, *Their eyes were watching God*. New York: Perennial Library of Harper & Row.

Gauch, P.L. (1984). Good stuff in adolescent fiction. *Top of the News*. 40 (winter), 125-129.

Griffin, J.H. (1961). *Black like me*. Boston: Houghton Mifflin.

Hansberry, L. (1969). *To be young, gifted, and black*. New York: Signet.

Hermence, B. (1990). *Before freedom: 48 oral histories of former North and South Carolina slaves*. New York: Penguin Books.

Hurston, Z.N. (1942). *Dust tracks on a road*. Philadelphia: J.B. Lippincott Company.

Hurston, Z.N. (1990). *Their eyes were watching God*. New York: Harper & Row. (originally published in 1937).

Johnson, J.W. (1985). The creation. In J.E. Miller, Jr., C.C. de Dwyer, and K.M. Wood (Eds.), *The United States in literature, 7th ed.* Glenview, Illinois: Scott, Foresman. (originally published in 1927).

King, M.L., Jr. (1992). I have a dream. *African-American literature: Voices in a tradition*. Austin: Holt, Rinehart, & Winston.

Kirby, D. and Liner, T. (1988). *Inside out: Developmental strategies for teaching writing, 2nd ed.* Portsmouth, New Hampshire: Boynton/Cook Publishers.

Krathwohl, D., Bloom, B., and Masia, B.B. (Eds.). (1964). *Taxonomy of educational objectives: Handbook II: The affective domain*. New York: David McKay.

Lee, H. (1960). *To kill a mockingbird*. Philadelphia: J.B. Lippincott Company.

Lester, J. (1991). Black folktales. In R.W. Baron, O.L. Logan, and K. Clark. (Eds.), *Motherwit: An Alabama midwife's story*. New York: Plume.

Logan, O.L. and Clark, C. (Eds.). (1991). *Motherwit: An Alabama midwife's story*. New York: Plume.

Morrison, T. (1987). *Beloved*. New York: Alfred A. Knopf.

Morrison, T. (1974). *Sula*. New York: Alfred A. Knopf.

Probst, R. (1988). *Response and analysis: Teaching literature in junior and senior high school*. Portsmouth, New Hampshire: Boynton/Cook.

Rosenblatt, L.M.. (1989). The transactional theory of the literary: Implications for research. In C.R. Cooper (Ed.), *Researching response to literature and the teaching of literature: Points of departure*. Norwood, New Jersey: Ablex.

Smith, K. (1989). *Skeeter*. Boston: Houghton Mifflin.

Tate, E.E. (1990). *Thank you, Dr. Martin Luther King, Jr*. New York: Bantam Skylark Books.

Tate, E.E. (1987). *The secret of Gumbo grove*. New York: Bantam Books.

Taylor, M.D. (1990). *The road to Memphis*. New York: Dial Press.

Taylor, M.D. (1987). *The gold cadillac*. New York: Dial Press.

Taylor, M.D. (1981). *Let the circle be unbroken*. New York: Bantam Books.

Taylor, M. (1976). *Roll of thunder, hear my cry*. New York: Bantam Books.

Terkel, S. (1970). *Hard times: An oral history of the Great Depression in America*. New York: Pantheon (Dell).

Totten S. (1980). Person to person: An oral history project. In C. Carter and Z. Rashkis (Eds.), *Ideas for teaching English in the junior high and middle school*. Urbana, Illinois: National Council of Teachers of English.

Voigt, C. (1986). *Come a stranger*. New York: Atheneum.

Walker, A. (1982). *The color purple*. New York: Harcourt, Brace, & Jovanovich.

Walker, A. (1972). My sister Molly who in the Fifties. In *Revolutionary Petunias and Other Poems*. New York: Harcourt, Brace, & Jovanovich.

Walker, M. (1967). *Jubilee*. Boston: Houghton Mifflin.

Wilkinson, B. (1987). *Not separate, but equal*. New York: Harper & Row.

Wright, R. (1937). *Black boy*. New York: Harper & Row.

Wright, R. (1940). *Native son*. New York: Harper & Row.

Yetman, N.R. (Ed.). (1970). *Life under the peculiar institution: Selections from the slave narrative collection*. New York: Holt, Rinehart, & Winston.

Chapter 11

Alienation from Society in
The Scarlet Letter and *The Chocolate War*

ELIZABETH ANN POE

Introduction

Although *The Scarlet Letter* is probably one of the most frequently required and widely taught classics in high schools today, many students do not enjoy their encounter with this text and remember it with dismay. I base this statement not only on the students I observed and talked to when I was teaching high school English but also on my conversations with preservice English teachers in my Methods for English Teachers course. The prevailing feeling seems to be that this challenging novel needs to be taught in a way that will engage teenage readers who feel it has little to do with them and contemporary society.

Interestingly enough, when I used this novel with a class of pregnant teens and teenage mothers, all of whom were impatient to graduate and therefore fixed a high premium on relevant materials, they read *The Scarlet Letter* with enthusiasm and sympathy. Despite Hawthorne's antiquated language and long-winded explanations, something in the novel spoke directly to them. Due to their own painful experiences, they understood the alienation of Hester Prynne. They applauded her conviction to do what she believed was right—conceal the identity of the child's father. They also felt relief that their punishment for breaking a societal sexual taboo and conceiving an illegitimate child was not as severe as Hester's. Their own experiences provided an entry into this difficult novel that other teens did not have.

The Chocolate War, on the other hand, is a young adult novel to which teens readily relate. Also about alienation, this novel deals with peer pressure and standing up for one's beliefs. The tenth graders with whom I used this novel sympathized with Jerry Renault and understood his dilemma. They liked reading this novel, considering it an accessible, thought-provoking, meaningful piece of literature. Their responses to the novel have been shared by many teens, making this a classic novel in the field of adolescent literature.

There are some interesting possibilities for using these two literary works as companion pieces, particularly in a situation where it is a curriculum requirement that all students read *The Scarlet Letter*. Although they have several overlapping themes, the alienation of each novel's central character seems like a viable entry point into each work because teenagers are well-known for their feelings of alienation. I have written elsewhere (Poe 1992) of the effectiveness of allowing small groups of students to read several novels simultaneously, but in this case I would have all class members read each novel at the same time. I would begin with *The Chocolate War* because it is the more accessible of the two and students' shared experiences with this novel can serve as a bridge to *The Scarlet Letter*.

Introducing *The Chocolate War*

Before introducing the novel, I would ask students to write journal entries about peer pressure. How does it feel when peers try to make them do something they do not want to do? I would also ask them to write, either from personal experiences or from their imaginations, how it feels to be left out or isolated from friends or schoolmates. These entries will undoubtedly generate several days worth of discussion.

In a third pre-reading journal entry, I would ask students to tell me if they have ever heard of a book written by Robert Cormier called *The Chocolate War*. Some students may have read this previously or seen the movie made from it. If this is the case, I would assure them that their familiarity with the work will add to their forthcoming experience with the text; it is a book that bears multiple readings. I suspect that most of the students will have heard that this is a good book and be eager to read it.

Reading *The Chocolate War*

After distributing copies of *The Chocolate War*, I would tell the students they will be reading on their own and discussing the novel in small study groups. I would assign or allow students to select, which ever seems most appropriate for a given class, study groups of four to six students. Each group would divide the novel into five sections of between 30 to 50 pages each and read one section per night. Immediately upon completing the reading assignment, each student would make an entry in his or her reading log (journal). This entry would be a response to the pages just read. It would not be a mere summary of the reading assignment but an expression of the reader's emotional reaction to what he or she has read. I also hope the reader will ask questions, make predictions, draw personal connections, bring in literary associations, or discuss whatever the novel makes him or her think or feel.

Each small group will have a daily opportunity to share group members' responses to the previous reading assignment and discuss that section of the book. I would read and respond to journal entries, be available to answer questions, and periodically join in small group discussions. After discussing the assigned reading, students would use the rest of the period to read the next section and write their journal responses. It will probably take about two weeks to read the book.

Plot Summary of *The Chocolate War*

As students read, they will enter the world of Jerry Renault who is a freshman at Trinity School, a Catholic boys' school. Trinity is tyrannized by the Vigils, a Mafia-like group masterminded by a student named Archie. School authorities are aware of the Vigils, but by choosing to ignore them they condone their existence. The Vigils delight in devising "assignments" which students must carry out. For example, Jerry's assignment is to refuse to sell chocolates during the school's annual fund-raiser. This unheard of behavior draws his teacher's wrathful contempt and threatens to undermine the success of the sale as other students see that it is possible to defy their teachers' authority. Jerry, of course, is extremely distressed by the situation. Then an extraordinary event occurs. Thinking that a successful chocolate sale will enhance his career, Brother Leon, a temporary administrator, actually elicits the assistance of the Vigils. Archie pledges his support, knowing that he now has the administration in his powerful grasp. Jerry's assignment changes—Archie now orders him to sell the chocolates.

But Jerry decides to remain true to himself and resists further manipulation by the Vigils and pressure from the teachers. Defying his new Vigil assignment, Jerry continues to refuse to sell the chocolates. The entire school, except for his friend Goober, turns against Jerry. He is sabotaged in class and at football practice, beaten up in the locker room, harassed with phone calls, ostracized at school, set up for defeat in a brutal boxing match, and finally lowered to the animal violence he abhors, making him just "another violent person in a violent world" (p. 183). In the end, lying in a pool of his own blood, Jerry no longer believes he should have stood up for his convictions. He wants to tell Goober to go along with the crowd; "otherwise, they murder you" (p. 187).

The novel's bleak ending makes it both controversial and thought-provoking. Some adults consider such a seemingly hopeless ending inappropriate for adolescent readers and fear the novel will encourage conformity. However, my experience with teenagers reading *The Chocolate War* tells me that the novel generates many questions that students want to discuss with peers and teachers. Some of these questions may be raised by students as they read, but concerns about the plot and reactions to the characters generally dominate journal writings and small group discussions. Therefore, after the students have read the entire book and discussed it in small groups, it is a wise idea to spend several days discussing it as a whole class.

After Reading *The Chocolate War*

I would begin such a discussion by asking the students what they thought about *The Chocolate War*. In the past, most students have expressed a general liking for the book because it seems realistic to them. When I press them for specifics, they say the characters act and talk like real teenagers, even though the book does seem dated in some ways. A few say they were "grossed out" at points, but that just made the book more realistic.

We talk about the characters and whether they know people like those in the story. Many of them have had experiences with bullies of some sort, although not as organized as Archie, and are eager to talk about this. Some of them have had unpleasant dealings with teachers and administrators, making it easy to identify with the more timid characters. Students generally admire Jerry and sympathize with his dilemma, but some think he is stupid for not giving in and getting beaten up.

We discuss the other characters and why they do what they do. Many students feel betrayed by the adults who allow the Vigils to persist in their cruelty. They are angered by Brother Leon's ambition. And they are puzzled by the hypocrisy of the monks in this religious teaching order. All this generates lively discussion and the sharing of many personal experiences that support or contradict situations presented in the novel.

If students do not mention the book's ending, I ask them what they thought of it. There usually does not seem to be any question that Jerry is devastated by his experience. This is distressing, but most students still think he was right to stand against the Vigils and the evil they represent. They hope they would have the courage to do the same in a similar situation. Discussion about similar situations they may be faced with brings up a variety of circumstances involving peer pressure. This is a real force in their lives, and they seem relieved to talk about it.

Discussing peer pressure can easily dovetail with a discussion of alienation, Jerry's consequence for resisting peer pressure. I think most teenagers have had some experience with feelings of alienation from their friends or family, even if only temporarily, so they are already sympathetic. To stress Jerry's extreme sense of isolation, we might try some role playing and reader's theater activities. Several scenes from the novel work well for this: Jerry's initial refusal to sell chocolates when he has been ordered to, the silent treatment he receives from the other boys and the teachers, and the final scene in the gym. I would have students work in small groups again to find such scenes.

Once they have identified a scene, they can either develop it into a reader's theater performance or work out a role playing activity with it. They would have the choice of doing their own reading or role play in front of the class or exchanging activities with another group so that each group performs the other's reading or role play. After each group reads or role plays in front of the class, we would discuss Jerry's sense of alienation from his society at Trinity. While the students are pondering the effects of social isolation, I would ask them to write a journal entry in which they imagine what it would be like to be alienated from one's community for one's entire life. With this question, we would begin our study of *The Scarlet Letter*.

Introducing *The Scarlet Letter*

After discussing their responses, I would ask the students if they have ever heard of a book called *The Scarlet Letter*, and if so, what they have heard about it. Their answers form the basis of a class discussion after which I would introduce the novel. I would tell them *The Scarlet Letter* is a mystery that takes place in Puritan New England and that I want them to figure out as much as they can about what happens. As with *The Chocolate War*, they will write daily journal entries and will work in small groups, but we will also work frequently as a whole class since this is a more difficult novel.

Reading *The Scarlet Letter*

I would begin by reading the first chapter aloud (please note that I skipped "The Custom House") and asking them what they think. Students are usually confused and frustrated by Hawthorne's language and are often quite vocal about these feelings. So we would talk about why Hawthorne writes this way and share what we know about the Puritans in New England. Then we would proceed to spend the next several weeks unraveling the plot of *The Scarlet Letter*. Due to the complexity of the text, small group and class discussions would probably center mainly around answering students' literal level questions about the novel.

As they read, students enter Hester Prynne's world of prisons, scaffolds, and scarlet letters. They come to know her daughter Pearl, her secret husband and self-proclaimed physician Roger Chillingworth, and her partner in adultery Reverend Arthur Dimmesdale. They experience the taunting of the village children, the scorn of the Puritan women, and the harshness of the government officials. Slowly, they piece together the plot and come to understand the characters involved.

As they read and discuss, students may begin to draw comparisons between Hester and Jerry. I would not emphasize comparisons just yet, however. I would rather have students focus on understanding *The Scarlet Letter* before dealing with the two novels as companion pieces. Activities such as journal entries describing and explaining their reactions to the major characters or writing diary entries for one of the characters can deepen students' involvement as they read.

After Reading *The Scarlet Letter*

After students have completed the novel, they would write a response to the whole book. I encourage them to write their reactions to what happened in the novel, their thoughts and feelings about the characters, any associations the incidents in the story might have elicited, or anything else that the novel made them think of. We would discuss these responses, first in their small groups and then as an entire class. Their feelings about the characters may be quite intense. They will often have further comments about Hawthorne's writing style and the harshness of the Puritan community. We would explore these responses in class discussions, learning from one another as we share our questions and ideas.

At this point, students would have the opportunity to do projects related to *The Scarlet Letter*. Some of them might want to conduct library research on what life was like in Puritan times. Others might want to report on Hawthorne's life. A few ambitious souls might want to read "The Custom House" and tell the class about it. A few might be interested in exploring some of the literary symbols in the novel such as Hester's formal cap, the town and the forest, or the colors red and black. Others might want to contemplate new meanings the "A" might take on in contemporary society such as Aids, drug Addict, illegal Alien, Abortion, or even Adolescent. A debate about whether or not the book should be required of everyone wishing to graduate from high school would be interesting, as would be a debate over whether or not it should be censored and withheld from high school readers. Some students might want to create a role playing situation similar to the ones they did for *The Chocolate War*. Artistic students might want to draw or paint a character or scene from the book. Students, if encouraged, would come up with other ideas as well. They would have class time to work on these projects and would take turns sharing them with the rest of the class.

The Scarlet Letter and *The Chocolate War* as Companion Pieces

Following the project presentations, I would ask the students to compare and contrast *The Scarlet Letter* and *The Chocolate War*. Working in small groups, students would revisit each novel. Their task would be to list ways in which the novels are similar and ways in which they are different. Each group would report its findings to the whole class, and we would compile a class list of similarities and differences. Here is what such a class list might look like:

Similarities

* Jerry and Hester were both ostracized by their peers.
* Jerry and Hester both felt alienated from their societies.
* At least one character associated with the church is corrupt and hypocritical.
* Religious symbolism appears in each novel: The football goalposts in the opening scene of *The Chocolate War* look like three crosses; the meteor that appears in the night sky when Hester, Pearl, and Dimmesdale are on the scaffold is reminiscent of the portentous star of Bethlehem.
* Jerry and Hester both had a lot of inner strength to stick with their convictions.
* Both books deal with evil forces of some sort: Archie and Chillingworth represent these forces.

Differences

* Writing styles.
* Characters' manner of speaking.
* Each novel begins very differently: Cormier draws the reader in immediately by saying "They murdered him"; whereas, Hawthorne gives an elaborate description of the prison door.
* The effect of social isolation on both characters is different: Jerry is first a hero, then ostracized, and finally victimized; whereas, Hester is first scorned, then ostracized, and ultimately admired.
* Jerry and Hester's feelings about what they have done at the end of each work differ.
* The extent of our knowledge about what happens to each character after the main part of the story ends is different: We know a little of what happens to Hester after Dimmesdale dies, but we don't know what happens to Jerry after he is beaten up in the gym.

Writing Activities Involving Both Novels

Using our lists as springboards, I would ask the students to do a writing project (as individuals, pairs, or groups) which involve both novels. Here are some possibilities:

1. Write a paper discussing which book you liked better and explain why you chose that one.

2. Hawthorne is a descendent of the Hawthorn who was involved in the Salem witch trials. He wrote *The Scarlet Letter* to show how wrong his ancestor was to persecute those women. Suppose 200 years from now a descendent of Archie's decides to write about the Vigils and Trinity School. Write the story you think he or she might tell.

3. Pretend you are Jerry Renault and several years after the tragedy at Trinity, your English teacher assigns *The Scarlet Letter* and asks you to write a personal reaction to it. What will your paper say?

4. Both *The Chocolate War* and *The Scarlet Letter* have been the target of censors. How would you defend the inclusion of each of these novels in the high school curriculum?

5. After reading Richard Armour's parody of *The Scarlet Letter* in *The Classics Reclassified*, write a parody entitled either The Chocolate Letter" or "The Scarlet War."

6. Write an essay in which you compare and contrast the theme of alienation in *The Chocolate War* and *The Scarlet Letter*.

7. In a formal essay, compare and contrast the decisions Jerry and Hester had to make and the consequences of those decisions.

8. Write a sermon in which you explore the comments each author might be making on religious authorities.

9. Write an essay in which you discuss the effects of social isolation on Jerry and Hester.

10. Write an essay in which you discuss the characters who taunt and those who support Jerry and Hester.

11. Pick a topic of your own and write an essay in which you compare and contrast *The Chocolate War* and *The Scarlet Letter*.

Culminating Activity

These papers would be presented to the class, and we would discuss their relevance. As a culminating activity, I would ask the students to write an evaluation of the paired novel approach in which they explain why or why not it is a good idea to read them as companions. I would grade this final piece of writing based on the thoroughness and thoughtfulness of the assessment and count it as a final essay test.

This final writing assignment would, of course, be of great interest to me. Student evaluations would help me determine the extent to which the study of a classic American novel was enhanced by pairing it with the study of a contemporary young adult novel. From the students' comments, I would know what to revise, alleviate, or embellish next time I taught these, or other young adult and classic novels as companions.

Other Young Adult Books that Deal with Alienation

Of course there are many young adult books that deal with alienation and could be used in conjunction with *The Scarlet Letter*. I might want to have students choose several of these to read independently or in small groups before we begin or instead of reading *The Chocolate War*. The same strategy could be used following the reading of *The Scarlet Letter* for students particularly interested in the theme of alienation. Some young adult novels that might work well with this are *Journey of the Sparrows* by Fran Buzz and Daisy Cubias, *Chinese Handcuffs* by Chris Crutcher, *Sticks and Stones* by Lynn Hall, *Night Kites* by M.E. Kerr, *Good-bye Tomorrow* by Gloria D. Miklowitz, and *Words by Heart by Heart* by Ouida Sebestyn. For a list of works dealing with other themes found in *The Scarlet Letter*, refer to "A Teacher's Guide to the Signet Classic Edition of Nathaniel Hawthorne's *The Scarlet Letter*."

Conclusion

If, at the end of the unit, most of the students leave with positive feelings about their experiences with these two works; if they do not groan at the mention of *The Scarlet Letter*, a work that I think has much to offer them as adolescent readers; and if they express a desire to read more young adult or classic literature, I would feel satisfied. In addition, I hope that the experiences they would share studying and discussing these novels may alleviate, even if only temporarily, some of the feelings of alienation that seem to be a normal, but troublesome, part of adolescence.

References

Armour, R. (1960). *The classics reclassified*. New York: McGraw-Hill.

Buzz, F. and Cubias, D. (1991). *Journey of the sparrows*. New York: E.P. Dutton.

Cormier, R. (1974). *The chocolate war*. New York: Pantheon (Dell).

Crutcher, C. (1989). *Chinese handcuffs*. New York: Greenwillow Books.

Gordon, K. (Dir.). (1988). *The chocolate war*. Forum Home Video, VHS, 95 mins.

Hall, L. (1972). *Sticks and stones*. New York: Follet (Dell).

Hawthorne, N. (1983). *The scarlet letter*. New York: Penguin USA (Signet).

Kerr, M.E. (1987). *Night kites*. New York: Harper & Row.

Miklowitz, G.D. (1987). *Good-bye tomorrow*. New York: Delacorte (Dell).

Poe, E.A. (1992). Intensifying transactions through multiple text explorations. In Nicholas J. Karolides (Ed.), *Reader response in the classroom: Evoking and interpreting meaning in literature*. White Plains, New York: Longman, 155-163.

Poe, E.A. (1991). A teacher's guide to the Signet Classic Edition of Nathaniel Hawthorne's *The Scarlet Letter*. New York: Penguin USA.

Sebestyen, O. (1979). *Words by heart*. Boston: Little, Brown, & Company.

Chapter 12

The Beast Within: Using and Abusing Power in *Lord of the Flies, The Chocolate War,* and Other Readings

BARBARA G. SAMUELS

Introduction

Lord of the Flies by William Golding has been frequently taught in secondary schools because it offers such a good model of novel structure, character development, and symbolism. The novel forces students to grapple with sophisticated ideas. Students easily understand that the actions of the novel and the techniques of characterization represent the larger message that Golding is trying to impart: a view of the human soul.

Themes of the novel involve ideas of control, power, order, evil, and identity. For teens who are involved in developmental tasks of forming their own identity and philosophies, the questions raised by this novel force serious thought about the nature of individual and group behaviors. At the same time, although the novel was published for an adult audience, the protagonists are pre-adolescents whose language and thoughts are within the frame of reference of teens. It is a novel whose obvious parallels are with other survival novels but whose themes lend themselves to consideration with other young adult novels as well.

A deeper understanding of the uses and misuses of power in a group can be developed by involving students in an exploration of a variety of books that explore some of these issues. By comparing and contrasting the ways in which people interact in these novels and non-fiction books, students can begin to formulate their own philosophies of individual and group behaviors. Over a period of six to nine weeks, this unit suggests that students explore these ideas first by comparing two books, and then by reading at least one additional title that addresses some of the same issues.

Setting Up the Core Novels:
Lord of the Flies and *The Chocolate War*

This unit suggests a core reading and discussion of two books, *Lord of the Flies* and *The Chocolate War*, by all students in the class. Depending on the abilities and needs of the students in the class, the reading of the two core books may precede or be followed by supplementary reading of at least one additional young adult book that makes interesting comparisons. Although either core book may be read first, teachers may prefer to start the unit with a reading and discussion of *The Chocolate War* because the events and situations may seem more real to students than the scenario in *Lord of the Flies*.

Obviously, the list of possible titles for further study is broad, but suggestions described later in this unit include the following: *Bless the Beasts and the Children, Killing Mr. Griffin, Downriver, Scorpions, Alive* and "War of the Words." Each of these titles brings another dimension to the concept of individuals getting along with others and the ways in which power and control are exercised in groups. Considering the commonalities and the differences in these books will lead to heightened awareness of how people relate to those who exercise power in different ways. After discussion of each of the supplementary titles in small groups, the whole class might come together to share the insights each group has gotten from its study and discussion. In the course of these discussions and activities, students might address other genres including poems, short stories, and films on related issues as well.

Lord of the Flies by William Golding

Marooned on a paradise island of sand and surf, near an enchanting lagoon ringed with pink granite, palm trees, and coconuts—and without adult supervision—a group of British boys set out to establish a society based on the law and order they have always known. Because he is bigger and has the conch, in the same way that the adults directing them earlier had a megaphone, Ralph is chosen as the leader. In the meeting that he chairs, the boys organize themselves to provide for shelter, food, and rescue.

But in William Golding's classic parable, *The Lord of the Flies*, the trappings of a cultured society quickly begin to crumble as first the rescue fire is neglected, then the responsibility of building the shelters falls to just a few as others refuse to help, and finally the "littluns" begin to fear "the beastie" that lurks in the night. Killing for meat is the first consideration, but then a boy is accidentally burned to death when a fire roars out of control. Simon is beaten to death by the hunters, hungry for the blood of "the beast." And Roger's savage lust for power and blood leads to Piggy's death when he sends a boulder down to crush him.

Unlike the typical survival story in the tradition of *Robinson Crusoe* and *Swiss Family Robinson*, the utopian island of this novel becomes the setting for a story designed to demonstrate the innate evil in human beings. The "civilized" British boys become bestial savages who murder and hunt each other just like the "civilized" adults who eventually rescue them.

The Chocolate War by Robert Cormier

This is the story of Jerry Renault who challenges the pressures of an evil teacher, Brother Leon, and a manipulative gang leader, Archie. To maintain his power, Archie imposes "assignments" on selected students who become his victims. Brother Leon calls upon Archie and his gang, the Vigils, to support him in selling an oversupply of chocolates purchased in Brother Leon's attempt to grab power in the school administration. Jerry's assignment is to refuse to sell the chocolates. But Jerry refuses to participate in the selling of chocolates after his assignment is completed. By saying no, Jerry stands up against the entire student body at Trinity High, the only person to challenge the seemingly invincible power of evil Archie, the Vigils, and Brother Leon.

The Abuse of Power in Both Novels

As a story of the abuse of power in a Jesuit school, *Chocolate War* presents a strong parallel to *Lord of the Flies*. Although the novels are very different in setting, both are about peer pressure and the nature of evil in human beings. Like Jack, the leader of the hunters in *Lord of the Flies*, Archie in *The Chocolate War* manipulates and controls the members of the Vigils. "The law of the Vigils was final, everyone at Trinity knew that" (p .32). Archie invents laws and rules to suit his plan, handing out assignments to the boys. Noone dares to challenge him except Jerry.

Even worse than Archie is Brother Leon, the power-hungry teacher and adminstrator of the school. In the end, when Jerry is engaged in a physical battle for his honor and his life, the entire student body is caught up in the group's shouts for blood. Mob behavior takes over and Archie seems triumphant. Jack, too, in *Lord of the Flies* initiates evil by demanding that all the boys do the hunting dance and chant, "Kill the beast! Cut his throat! Spill his blood!", the savage dance that leads to Simon's murder. Caught up in the hysterical group feeling, the boys follow Jack's lead as they move more and more toward savagery. Like Emile Janza, the bestial fighter in *The Chocolate War*, Roger carries out Jack's dirty work. Unable even to throw stones at other boys at the beginning of the novel, Roger levers the boulder that kills Piggy in the end.

In both novels, the manipulations of evil leadership lead to scenes of animal brutality and incitement of the larger group demanding bloodshed. Both novels suggest that there is an inherent evil in human beings that leads them to perform acts of violence and terror.

Ralph and Jerry present an interesting comparison of leadership as well. Although Ralph accepts responsibility as leader on the island, he is not necessarily the type of personality one usually associates with leadership. He is very dependent upon the wisdom of his advisor, the logical and ordered Piggy. Ralph never seeks the leadership, but he is willing to take on the role because he is older and has the conch. While Ralph wishes that the adult world had a way to signal them and make contact, he organizes the boys into groups to maintain the rescue signal fire and to build shelters. He believes that the boys must attract the notice of passing planes or ships because they will die if they are not rescued.

In *The Chocolate War*, too, there is an unlikely protagonist. Jerry is a quiet loner, the kind of teen who passes through the halls of school unnoticed, until he is told by the Vigils to refuse to sell the chocolate candy. Jerry dares to be different, insisting, for reasons he isn't even clear about himself, on not complying with the evil forces around him. When his "assignment" is completed and he has the opportunity to make his own decision, he still refuses to sell the chocolates. Being an individual is his way of demonstrating that he is alive. Jerry doesn't seek to be a leader, either. He just continues to hold on to his own values. "Jerry is not a noble hero seeking to right injustice. He's a slightly confused kid who thinks that in some way his stand against Archie and Leon will prevent him from falling into the kind of stagnant existence he sees his widowed father leading" (Giannelli, p.80).

Both novels focus on the forces that operate in society to make one conform to a group. Just as Ralph and Piggy are ultimately isolated by Jack's group of hunters because they see the long-range implications of an organized community that keeps a fire going and builds shelters, so too Jerry is isolated at Trinity High when he refuses to go along with the group chocolate sale. In both novels, the protagonists learn about the nature of corruption and viciousness in the world.

A Response Centered Classroom

In a response-centered classroom, students are encouraged to become personally involved with the issues in their reading and to respond to the novels based upon their previous experiences and their emotional reactions to the characters and situations in the books. A variety of activities may help young adults to focus on some issues of individual and group behaviors, to make some connections between the novels and their lives. To set the framework for the discussions while reading the two core books, teachers might choose to involve students in some or all of the following prereading activities.

Prereading Activities for the Two Core Novels

1. Brainstorming. Before reading each of the core novels, students might brainstorm about the basic conflicts in these novels:

   * What would they do if they were stranded on an island?
   * What would they need to survive?

     * How would they select a leader? Would they even need a leader?
     * List some of the rules that a group would have to make in that situation?

Students reading *The Chocolate War* might discuss the impact of peer pressure in their own school:

     * Have they ever taken a position on something contrary to peer pressure? Is there, for example, pressure to drink alcohol at parties, to take drugs, to engage in sexual activity?
     * In what ways does peer pressure affect an individual's decisions?

2. Using Picture Books to Make Connections. Start students thinking about *Lord of the Flies* and *Chocolate War* by reading aloud from one or two picture books: *Where the Wild Things Are* by Maurice Sendak and *Where's the Beast* by Keith Baker. In Sendak's story, Max sails off to be king of the wild things after his mother sends him to his room for misbehaving. *Where's the Beast?* is a boldly colored, simply written picture book in which a tiger discovers that the beast he sees when he is looking into the water is really himself. The book concludes: "We are all beasts—you and me."

After listening to the story or stories and before discussion, have students write briefly in their journals about the wild thing or beast within each of them. Each of us can remember some time when we felt like we were being a "beast." When have they been a "wild thing"? When can they remember becoming a "beast"? Sharing and discussion of these entries can follow. Students' responses might range from times they were mean to a younger sibling to situations in which they had fights with friends, rebelled against authority, or destroyed property. The focus of discussion might be the basic question of whether all of us have times when we do or say things that are destructive.

3. Developing Semantic Maps. Class discussion might continue by developing a semantic map about the word "bully." Begin by putting the word "bully" on the blackboard and circling it. Next, have students think of the associations they have for that word, and draw lines connecting appropriate relationships. Again, students might write in their journals on some of the following prompts:

     * What ideas come to mind when thinking of the term bully?
     * Can they remember a time when they were bullied? Was there a bully in their neighborhood? Were they ever a bully?
     * What family issues come to mind? Are there sibling relationships in which one child felt like he or she was being bullied or was being a bully?
     * What is the role of the adult when a young person is being a bully?

The idea is to have students make connections with their own experiences.

4. Creating Role-Plays. Have small groups role play a situation in which most of the students are part of the "in-group" (they wear buttons that say "cool" or wear special hats) and one or two students are part of the "out-group." As we well know, middle and high school students are often organized in cliques or groups. The role play should involve some aspect of school life today. For example,.the "in-group" tries to convince the others to do something that is not acceptable according to the standard rules (i.e., cheating, wearing particular clothes, shunning a particular student, drinking alcohol, smoking, etc.). Discussion should follow on questions like the following:

    *   What makes a group "in"? What makes a group "out"? How does the "in-group" in a school identify itself? Who identifies the "out-group"?
    *   How does the "in-group" keep their power? What tools do they use to convince others to follow them?
    *   Are "in-groups" good or bad for a school?
    *   What are the "in-groups" at your school? What are the "out-groups" at your school? How can they each be identified?

5. Using Short Stories as Parallels. Students might also want to read and discuss the short story "Priscilla and the Wimps" by Richard Peck in Don Gallo's *Sixteen*. Gallo (p. 169) raises some interesting and relevant points in the questions at the end of the collection of short stories: "Why do people like Monk think they are so special?" (Later students might think about how Monk is like Archie or Jack). "What do you think eventually happened to Monk?" (This same question might be asked about the bullies in the two novels. What do you think eventually happened to Archie, Brother Leon, Jack, Roger?) Discussions like these are best handled in small groups where everyone has the opportunity to respond.

Shirley Jackson's famous short story "The Lottery" also presents opportunities for an interesting parallel discussion. The box from which Archie chooses his white or black marble is reminiscent of the lottery box from which the villagers annually select their victim. Students can examine the dynamics of group behavior in this story as compared to the situations in the two novels. Why is it that the villagers continue to hold the lottery, in spite of the fact that other towns have already abolished it?

6. Using Poetry as Parallels. Just as short stories clarify and expand some of the themes, so, too, does poetry. A poem by Don Welch "We Used to Play" is about a fat kid named Fred Tooley:

Tooley would sit in Math IV
eating dirt stewed with asthma.
Miss Johnson said his system was lacking
(this was always after she'd spanked his hands),
but his brain wasn't. (Janesco, p.32).

A discussion comparing Tooley to Piggy helps students focus on some of their character traits.

Another poem in Janesco's collection, *Poetspeak*, is based on a fight between two teens which reflects the tension between two peer groups in a Midwest town and the violence of contemporary city life. The poem, "Fist Fight" by Doug Cockrell (p.36) suggests the lawlessness of today's society, a theme in both *The Chocolate War* and *Lord of the Flies*. Students' discussions might relate the events of the poem to similar conflicts in their own communities, as well as to the conflicts described in both novels.

7. Investigating *Coral Island*. Some students might want to investigate the connection between *Lord of the Flies* and Robert Michael Ballantyne's 1858 novel *Coral Island* which parallels Golding's book and is mentioned in two places. When the British officer discovers the boys on the island and saves Ralph from sure death at the hands of Jack and the hunters, he says ironically, "I know. Jolly good show. Like the Coral Island."

The two main characters in both books are named Ralph and Jack. The boys in Coral Island encounter cannibals and fear for their lives. They hunt pigs and set up a social organization. Golding himself said,

What I'm saying to myself is, 'Don't be such a fool, you remember when you were a boy, a small boy, how you lived on that island with Ralph and Jack and Peterkin . . . Now you are grown up . . . [Y]ou can see people are not like that; they would not behave like that if they were God-fearing English gentlemen, and they went to an island like that.'. . . [T]he devil would rise out of the intellectual complications of the three white men on the island. (Johnston, 1980, p.9)

Although not many students will want to read this 19th century adventure story, one or two serious readers might enjoy the opportunity to make the comparison between the ideas and styles of the two novels.

Responses to Reading

Activities While Reading the Two Core Novels

1. Keeping Double-Entry Journals. While reading *The Chocolate War* and *Lord of the Flies* have students keep a double-entry journal. Students draw a line

down the middle of the page. On the left side, they note particular passages in the text—by page number or by writing the phrase or key words—and then on the other side of the page they note how the passage makes them feel. Jotting down ideas as they read or noting passages that evoke particular responses will help them to frame their thinking in later discussion and writings. These entries should provide the specific examples and material to support their points of view in later, longer and more formal writings.

Since many of the comparisons in the two books will be with regard to characters, suggest that students keep a page for each of the characters: Jack, Ralph, Piggy, Roger, Jerry, Brother Leon, Archie, Ralph, Goober, and Emile. The class might be divided into groups with each group identifying passages describing particular characters. Later examination and discussion of those characters can be drawn from notations made about each character during the reading. Students will have prepared examples and phrases to support points they want to make about each character.

In keeping with a response-centered classroom, other areas for discussion should come from the questions and issues raised by the students themselves in their regular journal notations. Students might assemble in small groups for discussion on a regular basis while they are reading each of the two titles.

2. Examining Setting. Discussions and activities during the reading of each of the core novels include some of the following issues and questions related to setting:

* How does the setting of each book contribute to the reader's understanding of the themes in the book?
* Why did Golding choose to isolate a group of British boys on an idyllic remote island during a war as the framework for a story about the inherent evil in human beings? What is the effect of the juxtaposition of the beauty of the island and the events that happen there?
*What other setting could have been used?

The same questions could be asked of Cormier's decision to set *Chocolate War* in a Jesuit High School:

*In what ways does the religious setting contribute to emphasizing the power of the evil events that occur there?
* Would the book have a different impact and message if the story had been set in a public school instead of a parochial school?
*What other environment could have been used?

3. Examining Imagery. Tied to the issue of setting in the two books is the authors' use of imagery. Discuss the imagery in each of the books. *The Chocolate War* is filled with religious imagery. Identify some of this imagery from the first line, "They murdered him." which introduces the idea of Jerry as a Christ figure

to the fight at the end when the crowd is shouting for Jerry's defeat, "Kill him, kill him." Is there any similar religious imagery in *Lord of the Flies*? What is the significance of the "Lord" in the title? Consider Simon's conversation with the pig's head "Lord of the Flies" in Chapter Eight. Simon recognizes most clearly that the "beast" is really within the boys themselves: "I'm part of you" (p. 177). How is Simon different from the other boys on the island? Why is Simon killed? Compare Simon's death with Jerry's fight at the end of *The Chocolate War*. How are Simon and Jerry alike?

4. Exploring Setting and Imagery Through Art and Music. Students might choose to respond to the issues of setting and imagery with a variety of art projects. Because of the visual imagery in both books, they provide useful subjects for the more artistic student to adapt a visual form of response. Ranging from drawings or paintings of sets for stage or movie presentations, to illustrations of scenes in the novels, to abstract representations of each of the characters, to stained glass representations or collages, these novels offer a variety of possibilities for students' projects.

Another way to encourage students' understanding of setting and mood is to have them compare the mood established in a painting of a paradise island setting or a serene parochial school setting like those in the novels. Sharing slides of these paintings and engaging in discussion of the imagery is another way to connect art with a response to literature. For example, paintings like "In a Florida Jungle" (Cooper, p.156) and "In the Jungle,Florida" (Cooper, p.232), by Winslow Homer, both convey visually the luxuriant character of a tropical forest. Yet the two paintings have a different mood. Studying the second painting, students understand how the serpentine forms of the vines and the dense undergrowth broken by pools of water could arouse fear among young children as the light dims in the evenings. The first painting, showing palm trees swaying in the sea breezes with the white sand of the beach in the foreground has less of the feeling of foreboding and possible danger. The jungle looks beautiful and inviting.

Another painting by Winslow Homer, "Three Boys on the Shore" (Cooper, p.25), evokes a strong contrast with the mood of *Lord of the Flies*. This painting establishes a nostalgic image of the innocence and lazy pleasure of three boys sitting on the shore watching sailboats on the horizon. Students interested in art might want to research art books to find other paintings or photographs that are related to their response to the reading or might be used to illustrate one of the books read.

Just as art provides an outlet for response, so, too, can music. Some students might want to write ballads, raps, songs, or other musical representations of these novels. Students might be encouraged to try to compose music to fit the moods and feelings expressed or to find music that could be used for a background to a multi-media type of final project. Songs like Whitney Houston's

"The Greatest Love of All" might be introduced as an example of a popular song whose message is related to ideas in these books. Students could bring to class examples of other popular songs with messages about peer pressure, being an individual, participating in a group, etc.

5. Studying Characters' Names. Have students discuss the choices of names of the characters. The names in *Lord of the Flies* seem to be borrowed from *Coral Island* except for the fact that the character of Peterkin in *Coral Island* is Simon in *Lord of the Flies*. Explain why Golding might have made this change. What is the significance of names in *Chocolate War*? Names like Archie, the Vigils, and Trinity High School all suggest religious contexts. Why did Cormier select these names and others in the novel? Students should become aware of the fact that novelists make decisions about the names of their characters and often convey information about the characters in the names they choose.

6. Discussing the Concept of Friendship. Friendship is an interesting concept to examine in relation to the two core novels. What is the meaning of friendship in the context of these novels? Is Goober a friend of Jerry's? Consider Chapter 23 in particular. If you had been Goober, would you have responded to the events at Trinity in the same or a different way? Why? Is Jerry a good friend to Goober? What does Jerry mean at the end when he says, "Don't disturb the universe, Goober, no matter what the posters say." Is Piggy Ralph's friend? Why or why not? In the last few lines of the book, Ralph cries for "the fall through the air of the true, wise friend called Piggy" (p. 248). How does Piggy help Ralph to be a leader? Why does Ralph tell the others to call him Piggy?

The issue of friendship with members of the same sex is an important developmental task for young adults. Each of these novels forces serious consideration of what it means to be a real friend. Students might consider if there are any characters in these books that they would want to have as a friend.

7. Going Against the Grain. Do you know of any situations in your school or community in which someone went against the general opinion or rules of the larger group? What happened to that person? Do you know of any girls, for example, who tried to play sports on a boys team? How were they treated? Has someone in your school dressed differently or worn his or her hair differently than the usual styles? There has been at least one court decision in which a girl sued a California school for a couples-only prom rule. Are there laws to support the individual against the larger group in some situations? Why?

Students might also want to research some historical and political situations in which an individual or a small group acted against the general opinion. Cormier makes the connection between *The Chocolate War* and the Holocaust when Brother Leon tells the boys that they are like Nazi Germany in their silence. Golding's book was written right after World War II. What can we infer from those connections?

John F. Kennedy's book *Profiles in Courage* outlines some situations in American political history when an individual member of Congress took a position that was unpopular but important for society. The movie "JFK", although not historically accurate, introduces Jim Garrison, whose strident campaign for further investigation of Kennedy's assassination has not been a popular one. A study of the Civil Rights Movement in the United States presents a number of leaders who were not afraid to stand up for a position they believed in. Some students may research heroes and martyrs in the battle to end aparteid in South Africa or the struggles for democracy and a free economy in previously Communist countries today. Biographies of individuals in each of these historical situations might provide interesting and significant parallels to Jerry's and Ralph's struggles for their values.

8. Exploring the Concept of Hero. Is Ralph a hero? Why or why not? What about Piggy? Simon? Is Jerry a hero? What makes someone a hero? Students might discuss or write about the people they consider heroes today.

9. Questioning the Censors. Both *The Chocolate War* and *Lord of the Flies* have been attacked by critics and censors for their bleak and depressing view of human nature. Students should confront this issue by considering, if, indeed, the messages in both books are as hopeless as some have indicated. In an article in *Top of the News*, Betty Carter and Karen Harris(1980) argue that the message in *The Chocolate War* is particularly valuable for teens:

> The reason Jerry was not saved was because he stood alone. But he need not have been alone, as Cormier states clearly . . . Robert Cormier does not leave his readers without hope, but he does deliver a warning: they may not plead innocence, ignorance, or prior commitments when the threat of tyranny confronts them. He does not imply that resistance is easy, but he insists it is mandatory. (p. 283)

In discussions and in writing, students might compare and contrast the two books' messages.

Post Reading Activities for the Two Core Novels
When all students have finished reading both *The Chocolate War* and *Lord of the Flies*, discussion, writing, and activities should center on consideration of the common elements and issues in the two novels. In addition, responses to the novels using the arts, creative dramatics, music, and art should be encouraged as students begin to think about individual and group behaviors in the contexts of two books. A list of possible post-reading projects follows. This list is only a beginning of the kinds of possibilities that exist for students' responses. Perhaps the best kind of response is that which students themselves develop as a natural outgrowth of the their reading and thinking about the subject. The following list is presented as only a beginning of suggestions:

1. Media Presentations. Develop a newspaper or a "60 Minutes" type news broadcast using events and characters from the two books as the material for news stories, human interest stories, editorials, cartoons, book reviews, and advertisements. Reporters might interview Ralph and/or Jack about their survival on the island. An obituary might be written for Piggy or Simon. A news report might focus on the fight at Trinity High School in which one student was seriously injured or on the outstanding success of the chocolate sale at Trinity this year. An editorial might focus on violence among young people today and use evidence from the two books to support its argument. An assignment of this kind not only forces consideration about commonalities in the books, it also requires an understanding of the various elements of newspaper writing.

2. Famous Quotations. Individuals or groups might discuss and/or write about Churchill's phrase "The only thing we have to fear is fear itself." as it relates to both *Lord of the Flies* and *The Chocolate War*. Others might consider the poem "The Love Song of J. Alfred Prufrock" from which the words on the poster in Jerry's locker comes "Do I dare disturb the universe?" Both of these quotations lend themselves to serious examination in extended pieces of writing.

3. Charts or Venn Diagrams. Charts or Venn diagrams can be developed to help students compare and contrast the characters in the two novels. A Venn diagram is a graphic device that helps students visualize similarities and differences among characters. Two overlapping circles (or squares or triangles) divide the issues that are particular to each character and the chracteristics or situations that overlap. For example, a student's Venn diagram comparing Ralph in *Lord of the Flies* and Jerry in *The Chocolate War* might look like Figure 12.1.

A whole class discussion using students' journal notes would help students to make the connections between the protagonists, Jerry and Ralph; the antagonists, Brother Leon, Archie, and Emile Janza and Jack and Roger. Which of these characters is more evil and why? They might consider where Sam n' Eric, Piggy, Simon, and Goober, fit in this schema.

4. Character Comparisons. Comparisons between characters in the two books suggests another way to tie another form of writing instruction and practice to this unit. Taking on different roles, students might try some cross novel letter writing. For example, Jerry writes a letter to Ralph about the importance of standing up for your beliefs. Archie writes to Jack about how to maintain control of his group of hunters.

5. Leadership as an Issue. Discuss the issue of leadership. What does it take to be a leader in a group? Which of the boys in the two books demonstrates

leadership skills? How? Is Ralph a good leader? Is Jack? Piggy? Compare their styles of leadership.

Is Archie a good leader? Jerry? Brother Leon? What is Cormier saying about the nature of leadership? Do characters in either book abuse the power of leadership? How? Students then might consider the characteristics of leaders in their own groups, schools, or communities.

Figure 12.1

Archie	Same	Jack
Leader of Vigils	No conscience	Responsible for
Meets with adult leader		murders of Simon
	Manipulates others	and Piggy
(Brother Leon)		Leads boys away
Imposes "assignments	Others do his	from rules and
	dirty work	order
Responsible for Janza's		Demands all boys
fight with Jerry	Establishes	chant
	new	No adult present
School gang leader	rules	Hunter

6. The Problem of Evil. Discuss the problem of evil in the two books. Who is more evil, Jack or Roger, Brother Leon, Archie, or Emile Janza? Students might compare the evil characters in the two books and write about the nature of evil in human beings. Are these authors suggesting that there is no hope in the world because of these evil characters?

7. Human Defects. Golding and Cormier both suggest that defects in human nature cause societal problems. Do you agree? Based on these two books, what are the specific defects these authors see? Are there other defects that might be addressed in other novels? Students might write a paper discussing this point, then share their ideas in small groups before revising their writing into a final organized paper.

8. The Role of Ritual. What is the role of ritual in group behavior? Students might compare the rituals in the two books: Archie's box with the white and black marbles, the calling of names and numbers of boxes of chocolates sold, the assignments and the use of the conch, the hunters' dances, the masks and face paint, leaving a portion of the kill for the beast, the "Lord of the Flies."

9. Readers' Theater. Readers' theater presentations might be planned in which students select sections from each book that are parallel and work well together as a presentation. For example, one presentation might include a scene in which Archie uses the box and the black marble routine along with a scene involving ritual in *Lord of the Flies* such as a discussion of the use of the conch. Planning these groupings will involve students in making decisions about the parallel elements in the novels. Having selected appropriate scenes, scripts have to be developed and the performances rehearsed.

10. The Movie Versions. Both *Lord of the Flies* and *The Chocolate War* have been made into movies. Show the movies and reflect on the use of a visual medium to present the novels they have read. Why did the director or producer of *Lord of the Flies* choose to film it in black and white? What is different about the beginning and ending of the movie and the book? How is the visualized setting in the movie different from the setting they imagined when reading the book? What can a book do better than a movie? What can a movie do better than a book? What role does music play in the movie?

11. Games. Develop a board game based on the events of the two books. One such game, called Abuse of Power, might involve individuals assuming leadership, taking risks, and being rewarded or penalized for their decisions.

Additional Reading for the Unit

Using Adolescent Literature with the Two Core Novels

A variety of young adult novels explore some of the same issues as *Lord of the Flies* and *The Chocolate War*. Each of the following works touches, in some way, on the concepts of individual and group behavior explored in the two core books. To deepen students' understanding of the concepts, have them read at least one of the following books or play after they study the two core novels. Students might be assigned to groups based on their chosen book or play for discussions that focus on the ways in which this third work compares and contrasts with the first two.

1. *Killing Mr. Griffin* by Lois Duncan. This novel focuses on the evil control of a group in a different way than either of the core novels. With the force of his charismatic personality, Mark leads a small group of his friends in a mean,

practical joke on their English teacher. When Mr. Griffin dies as a result of the episode, Mark exacts promises from all the participants to maintain absolute secrecy about their involvement. Mark continues to perpetuate additional lawlessness in an effort to hide the murder. An evil individual, Mark can easily be compared to the evil characters in the other novels, Archie and Jack in particular from the core novels, but also Troy in *Downriver* and Angel and Indian in *Scorpions*. Students might want to continue their chart on which they identified the key characteristics of these evil people as a prewriting tool for a piece of writing on the nature of evil in human beings.

2. *Downriver* by Will Hobbs. A group of problem teens have been enrolled by their parents in a program designed to build self-discipline, confidence, and strong bodies by engaging in a variety of outdoor adventure experiences. The four boys and four girls, disgusted with the control exerted by the adult leader of their group, steal the van and rafting equipment and decide to run the Colorado River through the Grand Canyon on their own. One boy gains leadership and pushes the group towards dangerous limits in his attempts to maintain power.

Like *Lord of the Flies*, this is a kind of survival story as the young people dare to attack the rapids of the Grand Canyon with very little training and almost no information. Students might compare the organizational decisions of this group with those of the young people in the two core books. Peer pressure becomes a problem for Jessie, the protagonist of this novel. She is alternatively drawn to Troy and repelled by him. Students also should compare Troy, the power-hungry self-appointed leader of the group, with Ralph and Jack.

3. *Bless the Beasts & Children* by Glendon Swarthout. Like *Downriver*, this novel is about a group of misfits sent away to a camp by their parents. This group of Bedwetters, as they are called by the other campers, never wins the the various competitions that earn privileges. They can do nothing right, until Cotton, a camper who makes himself the leader of the group, helps them to begin to believe in themselves. In a last desperate action, they sneak out of camp to save a herd of buffalo who are about to be killed, at the same time saving themselves from their own lives of total defeat.

In addition to the concerns about group behavior and use of power, the allegorical and symbolic levels in this novel make it an interesting comparison to *Lord of the Flies* and to *The Chocolate War*. The evil in this book is in the form of a society that allows children (and buffaloes) to be throw-aways and misfits, unwanted and unloved. Like Jerry and Ralph who oppose the evil around them, Cotton stands up to the hierarchy at the camp that continuously identifies these children as losers.

Issues of leadership provide interesting material for written and oral discussion in this book as well. Like the martyrs in the two core books—Simon,

Piggy, and Jerry—Cotton, who leads the group with his own strong belief in their ability to accomplish what they set their minds to, is killed in the end.

4. *Scorpions* by Walter Dean Myers. In the urban world of gangs, drugs, and violence, twelve-year-old Jamal Hicks feels small, weak, and defenseless. "Lots of things made him feel the same way, small inside, and weak" (p. 22). His brother's gun, in his keeping while his brother serves a prison sentence for killing a grocer during a robbery, makes him feel tough. But just having a gun doesn't help him be the leader of the Scorpions and isn't enough protection when bigger and older kids provoke him and try to involve him in a criminal drug-running activity.

He is always getting into trouble, but Jamal doesn't want to become involved in illegal activity nor does he want to get into fights in school. He and his best friend, Tito, try to think of ways they can keep out of trouble. Like Jerry in *The Chocolate War*, he really tries to say no. But having a gun is tempting when he is taunted and teased by one of the bullies at his school. Students might analyze the similarities and differences in Jamal's situation and Jerry's. A Venn diagram might help them to visualize the ways in which these characters are alike and different and allow them to generalize about the dangers of peer pressure and longing for power.

5. *Alive* by Piers Paul Read. Introducing another concept in the exploration of issues of group behavior and leadership is this non-fiction account of the survival of a team of rugby players from Uruguay after a plane crash in the Andes. Sixteen of the 32 individuals who survived the original crash in 1972 were finally rescued after spending over a month in the bitter frozen wasteland of the Andes mountains. The issues involved in their survival, including the group's decision of cannibalism of the frozen bodies of their friends, raise fascinating questions for discussion and writing.

Because the survival story in this book is a real one, it offers interesting opportunities for comparison with *Lord of the Flies*. Students might consider questions of leadership, organization, and power. How did a group of young men who were actually stranded make decisions? What part of their energy was given to their rescue? What factors made individuals leaders in this situation? How was power exerted in this situation? Other questions might involve those who refused to eat the bodies of their fellow passengers. Was peer pressure put on those people to conform to the group? Although none of the young men in this book seem evil, they do have feelings of jealousy, greed, and frustration with the group.

6. "War of the Words" by Robin Brancato. This one act play in Donald Gallo's *Center Stage* involves a gang war between the the "Notes" and the "Grunts." These groups are divided by their "irreconcilable differences in

communication." The "Notes" are romantic and pedantic poetic types while the "Grunts" are punky and cool. Rather than solving their problems with a fight, the two gangs agree to enter a poetry writing contest. Designed for audience participation, the ending of the play suggests that the class be divided into two or more groups, each writing a poem for the competition. Another group then votes by applause on the winning poem. The play makes the point that rather than vicious fighting between groups, words can serve an important function in deciding leadership.

7. Additional Readings. The topic of using and abusing power provides endless possibilities of additional readings for creative students and enthusiastic teachers. The entire unit might be an extension of class study of Shakespeare's *Julius Caesar*. Other related play readings could include *A Man for All Seasons* by Robert Bolt, *The Children's Hour* by Lillian Hellman, and *The Crucible* by Arthur Miller. Additional novels such as *The Caine Mutiny* by Herman Wouk, *Animal Farm* or *1984* by George Orwell, *The Wave* by Morton Rhue, *Chernowitz* by Fran Arric, *Through the Hidden Door* by Rosemary Wells, or the trilogies by John Christopher that start with *The White Mountains* or *The Prince in Waiting* might also be read and discussed. Biographies of Henry VIII, Hitler, Mussolini, Stalin, and other historical figures who used and misused power would be valuable additions to this unit of study.

Culminating Projects Involving All Reading

By this time in the unit on the nature of evil, power, and control in individuals and groups, students have grappled with a series of significant questions in at least three works. Each book and play forces the reader to consider the nature of the forces that control our existence as human beings. Are humans inherently wicked, power-hungry, needing to push around those who are weak and powerless? How do leaders abuse their power? Is psychological manipulation a daily factor of the interaction of all the groups within which we operate? Is it possible for compassionate, caring, good individuals to become leaders in this world? What are the qualities we should look for in our leaders? Questions like these ultimately lead to consideration of current events in our schools, our local communities, and the world at large. It is important that after reading these depressing books about unscrupulous, ruthless people, students be helped to look towards the future in a positive way. They should be encouraged to think about the fact that it takes individuals like Ralph, Jerry, and Cotton to make positive change happen.

Students should be encouraged to make this leap of thought. Invite students to work in small groups to pull together the ideas they have considered while reading these books. Each group should prepare a project that in some way recognizes the connection between current societal problems and the books they have read. The possibilities for projects are endless, and the goal of the assignment is for students to creatively solve this problem on their own by exploring a number of topics and approaches.

Some groups could make movies, multi-media productions, slide shows, or plays. Others might make collages, paintings, murals, or collections of photographs. Music lovers might be inspired to write an opera, a musical, or songs. Another group might write a fairy tale or a modern fantasy or science fiction story in which a power-hungry individual is overcome by individuals who dare to challenge that power. (Students might read Madeleine L'Engle's *Wrinkle in Time* as an example). Specific examples might take on the characterisitics of any one of the following:

1. One group could prepare a slide show accompanied by music on the topic of standing up for what you believe in and saying no to drugs.

2. Students might be inspired to put on a play based on stories of individuals during World War II who dared to hide Jews from Hitler's forces.

3. Another group could prepare a debate based on a the current prosecution of men who were East German border guards who followed orders and shot people trying to escape to West Germany.

4. A group might research old newspaper files and collect copies of images of despots in recent history like Hitler and Saddam Hussein as well as pictures from events like the Tienamen Square Massacre, the recent civil war in Ethiopia, and South African battles to overthrow aparteid. Putting these together in a collage, they could write an essay about abuses of power.

5. Similar to the gangs' poetry contest in "War of the Words," students could write their versions between opposing forces of good and evil.

Imagine the excitement in a class with these kinds of activities!

Conclusion

Literature and the arts provide opportunities for our students to use their imaginations, stimulate deep thinking, and express their emotions. We need to provide them with outlets to express these responses in a wide variety of formats and to encourage their exploration of whole new boundaries of learning. They should write, draw, make music, films, perform plays, and talk.

William Golding and Robert Cormier as well as the authors of the supplementary books in this unit raise these issues of individual and group behaviors because they are serious concerns of our society. Purves, Rogers, and Soter (1990) suggest that "Without freedom of the imagination and personal order there can come a repressive or a revolutionary society" (p.175).

A unit of this kind offers a variety of different ways to look at how power is abused and leadership grabbed by unscrupulous power-hungry individuals, while offering some examples of people who dared to fight back. The reading, thinking, discussing, and other activities will help students to consider the factors that lead to repressive, dictatorial societies. They will better understand the needs and responsibilities of a true democracy and will move a step closer to being productive citizens of a free and democratic society.

References

Arrick, F. (1981). *Chernowitz*. New York: The New American Library.

Baker, K. (1990). *Where's the beast*. New York: Harcourt, Brace, & Jovanovich.

Ballantyne, R.M. (1957). *Coral island*. New York: E.P. Dutton. (originally published 1858).

Bolt, R. (1960). *A man for all seasons*. New York: Vintage Books.

Brancato, R. (1990). War of the words. In D. R. Gallo (Ed.), *Center Stage*. New York: Harper & Row.

Carter, B. & Harris, K. (1980). Realism in adolescent fiction: In defense of *The Chocolate War*. *Top of the news*.

Christopher, J. (1970). *The prince in waiting*. New York: Macmillan.

Christopher, J. (1967). *The white mountain*. New York: Macmillan.

Cockrell, D. (1983). Fist fight. In P. Janesco (Ed.), *Poetspeak*. New York: Bradbury Press.

Cormier, R. (1974). *The chocolate war*. New York: Pantheon (Dell).

Defoe, D. (1961). *Robinson Crusoe*. New York: E.P. Dutton.

Duncan, L. (1985). *Killing Mr. Griffin*. Boston: Little, Brown, & Company.

Garrison, J. (1991). *J.F.K.: On the trail of the assassins*. New York: Warner Books.

Giannelli, G. (1983). The chocolate war. *Connecticut English Journal, 15* (1).

Golding, W. (1954). *Lord of the flies*. New York: G.P. Putnam's Sons.

Hellman, L. (1934). *The children's hour*. New York: Random House.

Hobbs, W. (1991). *Downriver*. New York: Atheneum.

Homer, W. (1986). In a Florida jungle. In H.A. Cooper, *Winslow Homer Watercolors*. New Haven and London: National Gallery of Art and Yale University Press.

Homer, W. (1986). In the jungle, Florida. In H.A. Cooper, *Winslow Homer Watercolors*. New Haven and London: National Gallery of Art and Yale University Press.

Homer, W. (1986). Three boys on the shore. In H.A. Cooper, *Winslow Homer Watercolors*. New Haven and London: National Gallery of Art and Yale University Press.

Houston, W. (1985). The greatest love of all. *Whitney Houston*. New York: Arista Records, Incorporated.

Jackson, S. (1943). The lottery. *The lottery*. Cambridge: Robert Bentley.

Johnston, A. (1980). *Of earth and darkness: The novels of William Golding*. Columbia and London: University of Missouri Press.

Kennedy, J.F. (1956). *Profiles in courage*. New York: Harper & Row.

L'Engle, M. (1962). *Wrinkle in time*. New York: Ariel Books.

Miller, S. (1952). *The crucible*. New York: Penguin Books.

Myers, W.D. (1988). *Scorpions*. New York: Harper & Row.

Orwell, G. (1949). *1984*. New York: Harcourt, Brace, & Jovanovich.

Orwell, G. (1945). *Animal farm*. New York: The New American Library.

Peck, R. (1984). Priscilla and the wimps. In D.R. Gallo (Ed.), *Sixteen*. New York: Dell.

Purves, A.O., Rogers, T. & Soter, A. (1990). *How porcupines make love II*. New York: Longman.

Read, P.P. (1974). *Alive*. New York: Avon.

Rhue, M. (1981). *The wave*. New York: Dell Laurel-Leaf.

Sendak, M. (1963). *Where the wild things are*. New York: Harper & Row.

Swarthout, G. (1970). *Bless the beasts and children*. New York: Simon & Schuster.

Welch, D. (1983). We used to play. In P. Janesco (ed.), *Poetspeak*. New York: Bradbury Press.

Wells, R. *Through the hidden door*. New York: Scholastic.

Wouk, H. (1951). *The caine mutiny*. New York: Doubleday.

Wyss, J. (1949). *The Swiss family Robinson*. New York: Grossett & Dunlop.

Chapter 13

Dealing with the Abuse of Power in *1984* and *The Chocolate War*

KAY PARKS BUSHMAN AND JOHN H. BUSHMAN

Introduction

Despite the recent breakdown of Communism and its many totalitarian governments, history teaches us that the probability of power struggles and successful secessions of abusive dictators will remain prevalent. As a warning of the consequences of such autocratic governments, George Orwell wrote *1984* depicting a society representing the opposite of the ideal. Used in the high school classroom, this novel can be quite successful in promoting advanced thinking skills and language analysis. However, because the novel focuses primarily on adults in an environment detached from the world of today's teenager, bridging that gap with an effective young adult novel would provide a chance for greater success. Like *1984*, Robert Cormier's novel *The Chocolate War* depicts teenagers undergoing similar struggles of dealing with abusive authority. Using the two novels together could bring deeper meaning to them both.

Orwell's *1984* portrays a world gone wrong under the strictest government control. Citizens' jobs, food, clothing, living standards, daily routines, conversations, recreation, and relationships are all closely monitored and controlled by Big Brother in a world where, although no laws exist, overstepping the bounds of authority is punishable by death. In a world where no privacy exists, the only thing an individual can call his or her own is his or her mind; even so, the government is scientifically working on the means to decipher thoughts as well. When protagonist Winston Smith dares to pursue his individuality by seeking a means to undermine the state, he is totally crushed in this futile effort.

Similarly, Cormier's *The Chocolate War* portrays a school gone wrong under the control of Brother Leon, headmaster of Trinity School; Archie Costello, leader of the Vigils; and general peer pressure of the student body. Students are pressured by Archie to carry out "assignments" that are ignored by Brother Leon in order to keep peace with the Vigils. When Jerry Renault, assigned to refuse to sell chocolates in the school's major fund-raising campaign, continues to refuse to sell chocolates even after his assignment time is completed, Jerry, like Winston Smith in *1984*, experiences the crushing of his drive for individuality as he dares to "disturb the universe."

Parallels Between *1984* and *The Chocolate War*

Many parallels can be made between these two novels. Jerry and Winston both suffer from abusive authority—Jerry from Brother Leon who knowingly "looks the other way" as Jerry is ignored, threatened, and beaten in a campaign led by Archie and his Vigils; and Winston from Big Brother and inner party member O'Brien who oversees Winston's attempts to undermine the state and then imprison and torture him. Both protagonists are stripped of their most precious possessions—their drives to be individuals. In coping with their restrictions, both Jerry and Winston suffer feelings of alienation and isolation going through stages of distrust, needing to keep their emotions and fears to themselves for fear of further rejection and punishment. It is only when co-party member Julia proves to Winston that she loves him that he risks sharing his thoughts and dreams for a better life. Jerry, however, keeps his thoughts private until the end when, after being beaten severely by bully Emile Janza in front of the entire student body, Jerry shares with Goober, an earlier victim of the Vigils, never "to disturb the universe . . . [or] they murder you" (p. 187).

Another parallel between the two novels exists in the deception of appearance versus reality. In *The Chocolate War*, Trinity School is a prep school headed by a Catholic headmaster. Its main fund-raiser is for the students to sell boxes of chocolates. However, Brother Leon, distressed with financial struggles puts extra pressure on the students to meet higher quotas during this school year by selling old chocolates on which he got a good deal. In his desperation, he even manipulates Archie Costello to get the Vigils behind the campaign and ignores their misbehavior as a trade-off.

In *1984*, propaganda campaigns manipulate the citizens to believe that they live in a society that is highly productive and working for its citizens, providing standards of living which are at the highest levels in years. In reality, however, the purpose of the society of Oceania is to continually lower the standard of living, thus, keeping its citizens in a constant state of need and dependence.

To maintain the goals projected by the authority figures in both novels, language manipulation plays a large part. In *The Chocolate War*, persuasive, manipulative language is prevalent in dialogues between Archie and fellow-Vigil Obie, Archie and Brother Leon, and Brother Leon and his students. Likewise, language manipulation is prevalent in *1984* through linguist Syme's work in creating a new edition of the *Newspeak Dictionary*, and through doublespeak used in the "Two-Minutes Hate" and the interrogations of Winston by O'Brien in the "Ministry of Love." The entire concept of doublethink as a propaganda technique is an extreme example of language and thought manipulation. In both novels, the use of such language devices serves to keep the power figures in power.

Besides theme, other common literary techniques and elements are comparable in both novels. Both works make use of symbolism, effective points of view, flashback, and strong settings. These elements, along with others, can be explored through the following activities that suggest a step-by-step process to connect these two novels in one unit.

Pre-Reading Activities for *The Chocolate War*

Through discussion and/or writing have students explore the following topics:

1. Tell of an incident in which you were forced by an authority figure to do something that you didn't want to do.

2. Relay an incident in which you spoke out or acted out against a rule or a law.

3. Tell of a time in which you were pressured by peers to do something.

4. Tell of an incident in which you were bullied into doing something that you didn't want to do.

5. Tell of a situation when you felt too restricted to act in a way that you really wanted to.

6. What is something that you would be willing to fight for and why?

Reading *The Chocolate War*

While students are reading *The Chocolate War*, have them write response journals. Suggested questions to which they respond are the following:

1. What is your first reaction to the novel?

2. What feelings/emotions does the novel evoke in you?

3. What character(s) do you particularly like? Explain.

4. What character(s) do you particularly dislike? Explain.

5. Do any characters remind you of people whom you know? Explain.

6. Are you like any character in the novel? Explain.

7. What fears and/or concerns do you have for the characters? Explain.

8. What advice do you have for the characters?

9. What memory does the novel help you to recall?

10. How does Trinity compare with your school?

11. Comment on the title of the novel?

12. Would you change the ending of the novel? If so, how?

13. What questions and/or confusions do you have about the novel?

14. What do you consider to be the most important word, phrase, or quote in the novel? Explain.

15. What is the major point of the novel? Explain.

Post-Reading Activities for *The Chocolate War*

Provide students a chance to respond openly to the novel by asking each student to choose one journal entry to read aloud to the class. After each reading, allow students through class discussion to explore the ideas, concerns, and interpretations presented by their peers. Afterwards, put students into small groups to complete one of the following writing activities:

1. Have students give examples of how they feel unfairly restricted in school through school rules, school expectations, and/or relationships with teachers and/or peers.

2. Have students write a script for a role-play, improvisation, and/or skit in which they realistically have to deal with abusive authority.

These creative drama activities should include some means of resolution that deal with realistic consequences.

3. Have students choose one topic suggested by their response journals or by the discussion to focus on in a formal essay.

By completing this assignment, students experience the entire writing process by pre-writing, drafting, peer conferencing, revising, and editing.

Pre-Reading Activities for *1984*

To connect the two novels, have students brainstorm examples of abusive authority that exist in the society and government in which they live. Discuss how citizens cope and deal with such abuse and the consequences that might prevail.

Be sure to introduce the students to the word *totalitarianism*, and encourage them to point out totalitarian governments that still exist today. Explain that the novel *1984* depicts an example of a society under the control of a severe totalitarian government and that George Orwell wrote this novel as a warning of the consequences that could occur if citizens allow for the creation of such a government.

Reading *1984*

Due to the difficulty of this novel, teachers may opt to divide the reading into thirds; the breaks being the three sections in which the novel is written. While students are reading, assign them to write in their response journals. Suggested questions to which they respond are the following:

1. What is your first reaction to the novel?

2. What feelings/emotions does the novel evoke?

3. What characters remind you of people whom you know or have read about? Explain.

4. What situations in the novel remind you of situations in your life?

5. What advice would you give any of the characters?

6. What fears and/or concerns do you have for the characters? Explain.

7. Would you change the ending of the novel? If so, how?

8. What questions and/or confusions do you have about the novel?

9. What do you consider to be the most important word, phrase, or quote in the novel? Explain.

10. What is the major point of the novel? Explain.

Post-Reading Activities for *1984*

Provide students with a chance to respond openly to the novel by sharing journal entries aloud. Have these readings serve as the basis for class discussion. Finally, have students list any elements of the *1984* society that exist in their lives today.

Connecting Activities for *The Chocolate War* and *1984*

Literary Skills

1. Have students discuss how the following themes are addressed in both novels: dehumanization, appearance versus reality, alienation and isolation, suffering and violence.

2. Compare and contrast the characters of Jerry Renault and Winston Smith in terms of how they are abused, how they cope with the abuse, their motivations, and their changes.

3. Compare and contrast the settings of each novel and the effect they play on the entire work.

4. Discuss the symbolism used by Cormier and Orwell. The discussion might include the religious symbols and the names in *The Chocolate War* and Big Brother, the ministries, names, and the title in *1984*.

5. Compare and contrast the different points of view used by Cormier and Orwell. How might the novels have had a different effect if different points of views were used?

6. Discuss the flashbacks used in each of the novels and the effects of each.

Language Skills

1. Discuss the language manipulation used in each of the novels. The discussion might include dialogues between Archie and Obie, Archie and Brother Leon, Archie and Emile Janza, and Brother Leon and his students; propaganda in the "Two-Minutes Hate"; the interrogations of Winston by O'Brien; and the effects of Newspeak and Doublethink. The discussion should include the motivations of the abusive language as well as its effects.

2. Students identify examples of language abuse in their lives including advertisements, newspapers and magazine articles, political campaigns, instructions and explanations by authority figures.

Composition Skills:

1. As both books have seemingly open endings, have students write the next chapter of one of the novels.

2. Have students write the copy for a newspaper front page that is devoted entirely to one of the novels. The articles on the front page should be based on events and characters in the book.

3. Have students write formal essays concentrating on one of the themes linking the two novels by comparing and contrasting how that theme is presented in both books.

4. Concentrating on the three slogans, "War is Peace," "Freedom is Slavery," "Ignorance is Strength," have students choose one and, in a formal essay, explain how it relates to *The Chocolate War*.

5. In *1984*, citizens are divided into three groups—Inner Party, Outer Party, and Proles. Have students name, characterize, and describe the various groups found in *The Chocolate War* in a formal essay.

6. Since both novels have been attacked by censors throughout the United States, have students write a rationale against censoring one or both novels.

Speech/Creative Drama Skills:

1. As extensions to the novels, have students role-play situations in which they choose to "disturb the universe." Situations should be realistic in nature, consequence, and resolution.

2. Have students develop a "Meet the Character" spot for a talk show in which characters such as Jerry Renault, Archie Costello, Brother Leon, Winston Smith, Julia, and O'Brien are interviewed. Questions should relate to their feelings, motivations, lessons learned, etc.

3. Students select characters from the novels whom they would bring to trial for crimes they have committed. Students play the parts of the characters on trial, the prosecuting and defense attorneys, and the jury.

Conclusion

Orwell's *1984* has much to offer high school students. However, teachers must remember that the intended audience for this and most classics is adults. As a result, it is imperative to help students to read, understand, and make connections with the novel. Many times that extra help can be given by having students first read a young adult novel that parallels the classic in terms of a major theme. For *1984*, Robert Cormier's *The Chocolate War* can do just that.

References

Cormier, R. (1974). *The chocolate war*. New York: Dell Laurel-Leaf.
Orwell, G. (1949). *1984*. New York: Harcourt, Brace, & Jovanovich.

Chapter 14

Poetic Voices for Young Adult Readers

ROBERT C. SMALL, JR.

Let me tell you about John.

John once was a high school student, and a teacher like you and me taught John. John was a good student but in trouble a good deal. John started his life in a home with a father who was something like the manager of a garage. His father died when John was eight. Shortly after his father died, John's mother remarried. She left her children, then returned. She died six-years later when John was 14 years old.

John left school before he was 18 and took a job as a hospital orderly. At 21, he was licensed as a pharmacist. When John was 23, he spent his days taking care of his brother Thomas, but Tom died that year. By the time he was 23, John had also contacted an incurable illness.

He died when he was 26.

Could this be one of your students? Has John sat in your class or my class?

Let me tell you more about John.

At 19, John wrote a poem that his friends and teachers thought was so good that they sent it off to a publisher; and it was published. Teachers and friends celebrated. That same year, he had a second poem published, and it too was a great success.

A couple of years later, now 23, he had a collection of his poems published. The collection wasn't a great success. About that same time, he was diagnosed as fatally ill. Still, he pulled together poems he had written over the years and sent them off to a publisher who was a friend of a friend.

John died at 26, but his poems were sent out to the world.

John who?

John Keats.

John Keats the Poet

At 20, John wrote "On First Looking into Chapman's Homer."

At 21, he wrote "O Solitude."

At 23, he wrote *Endymion*.

At 23, he published "The Eve of St. Agnes," "The Eve of St. Mark," "Ode to Psyche," "La Belle Dame Sans Merci," "Ode to a Nightingale," "Ode on a Grecian Urn," "Ode on Melancholy," "Ode on Indolence," and "To Autumn."

A mere kid, John Keats wrote many of the most perfect and highly esteemed poems in the English language.

John was the age of many of our high-school students, or, at most, only a few, very few years older than they, when he wrote his poems, poems that we read with our students, poems that we praise, poems that we analyze for our students.

Can he speak to them? After all, he is their age. Shouldn't he be able to touch their problems and concerns?

At first glance, though, his style may be discouraging to both teacher and student.

In 1881, when he was 23, John wrote "When I Have Fears":

> When I have fears that I may cease to be
>   Before my pen has glean'd my teeming brain,
> Before high-piled books, in charact'ry,
>   Hold like rich garners the full ripen'd grain;
> When I behold, upon the night's starr'd face,
>   Huge cloudy symbols of a high romance,
> And think that I may never live to trace
>   Their shadows, with the magic hand of chance;
> And when I feel, fair creature of an hour,
>   That I shall never look upon thee more,
> Never have relish in the faery power
>   Of unreflecting love; — then on the shore
> Of the wide world I stand alone, and think
> Till love and fame to nothingness do sink. (Abrams, p. 356)

In *How Does a Poem Mean?* John Ciardi says of this poem,

> Above all else, poetry is a performance. Keats' overt subject in his sonnet was his own approaching death. But note this about poetry: Keats took the same *self-delighting pains* in writing about his death as he took in poems on overtly happy subjects, such as "On First Looking into Chapman's Homer" or the "Ode to a Nightingale." (p. 668)

Ciardi goes on to ask these questions of the poem and the poet:

> Why did Keats spend so much care on symmetry? What has symmetry to do with "the vanity of earthly wishes"? Why, too, did Keats bother to compare his mind to a field of grain, and the books he felt himself able to write, to storage bins? An elaborate figure. Why did Keats bother to construct it? Why did he search out such

striking phrases as "the magic hand of chance"? If Keats were really convinced that all human wishes are vain, why did he wish to phrase his idea with such earthly care? If *nothingness* is all, why bother to make *the something* a poem is? (Ciardi, p. 668)

Ciardi answers his own questions this way:

> [N]o matter how serious the overt message of a poem, the unparaphraseable and undiminishable life of the poem lies in the way it performs itself through the difficulties it imposes upon itself. The way *in which* it means is *what* it means. (Ciardi, p. 669-670)

But think who John Keats was. Not much older than our students when he wrote his first poems, here is how *The Norton Anthology of English Literature* describes John Keats:

> No major poet has had a less propitious origin. Keats's father was head ostler at a London livery stable; he married his employer's daughter and inherited the business. Mrs. Keats, by all reports, was a strongly sensuous woman, and a rather casual but affectionate mother to her four children—John (the first born), his two brothers, and a sister. Keats was sent to the Reverend John Clark's private school at Enfield, where he was a noisy, high-spirited boy; despite his small physique (when full-grown, he was barely over five-feet in height), he distinguished himself in skylarking and fist-fights. (Abrams, p. 343)

Sound familiar? Put in today's terms, we have dozens of kids like John in our classes. But somehow, John changed from a boy who, when he was 19, wrote poetry that Aileen Ward, in her National Book Award winning biography of him, describes as follows: "In style and sentiment, these poems are atrocious; yet they show Keats following the worst poetic fashions of his day" (p. 44). Ward describes the young adult Keats struggling with the change from youth to adulthood:

> The transition from boyhood to manhood is especially uncomfortable for a young man convinced that he has great ambitions but aware that the world is not convinced of them. Bernard Shaw described his own uneasy sense at this age of living under false pretences till at last he began to realize his potentialities and forced the world to acknowledge them. Till then, he noted, young men of talent are 'tormented by a shortcoming in themselves; yet they irritate others by a continual overweening.' (Ward, p. 58)

Twenty-years-old, Keats

> at dawn ... took a piece of paper, marked lines down the right-hand margin to guide him in his rhymes, and wrote out the poem

that had been taking shape in his head. When it was done, he made a copy and sent it off by messenger to Clarke, who found it on his breakfast table when he came down that morning. (Ward, p. 75)

That poem was "On First Looking into Chapman's Homer." Ward comments:

[I]t is not hard to imagine Clarke's amazement as he read the sonnet over. The poem was a miracle; not simply because of its mastery of form, or because Keats was only twenty when he wrote it in the space of an hour or two after a night without sleep. Rather because nothing in his earlier poetry gave any promise of this achievement: the gap between this poem and his summer work could only be leaped by genius . . . [T]he unity of form and feeling that begins in the first line and swells in one crescendo of excitement to the final crashing silence was instantaneous and unimprovable. After the reverberation of that ending has died away, something new appears to our eyes. The sonnet, we realize, is not about Chapman, or Homer, or even Keats's reading of Chapman's translation. It is about something much larger, more universal, the rapture of discovery itself . . . Keats felt the horizons of his world expanding beyond all expectation. It was the limitless possibilities of his own future that he saw spread out before him that morning, shining with the promise of El Dorado. (Ward, pp. 75-76)

John Keats was a teenager or not much more when he wrote the poems quoted above. Given his background, his education, his life, his death, he could be now in our English classes in the eighth, the tenth, the twelfth grades. He could be a GED student we teach one night a week. Are they thinking about the "limitless possibilities" of their own futures as Keats was that night? Do they see those possibilities "spread out" before them as Ward says that Keats did?

We hope so.

Poetic Language

But how do we bridge the gap in language between our students and the language of Keats? What do they know of Darien? Of Homer? Of gleaners? Of sonnets?

Clearly the bridge is not easy to build.

But our students do know about discovery. And of death. Of aspiration. And of failure. Of a song that says what they want to say, what they want to sing. And of love that is important, but, as Keats wrote,

> And when I feel, fair creature of an hour,
> That I shall never look upon thee more,
> Never have relish in the faery power

Of unreflecting love; — then on the shore
Of the wide world I stand alone, and think
Till love and fame to nothingness do sink. (Abrams, p. 365)

Surely our students, like the young man that Keats was when he wrote this poem about love, think of love, of whether love is worth giving up everything in their lives for. Keats did at 20. Our students do at 15, at 18, at 20. In fact, we probably do, too.

But the language that Keats, this boy poet, used stands between him and our students. Bridging that gap is his own youth: He wrote of the joys of discovery and the fears of death, exactly the feelings that our own students have, though they would, of course, use different language to express those joys and fears.

The Speakers in the Poems of Mel Glenn

And this is where I think Mel Glenn and his spectacular collections of poetry—*Class Dismissed!*, *Class Dismissed II*, *Back to Class*, and *My Friend's Got this Problem, Mr. Chandler*—can help us both to draw our students into poetry and also bridge the gap between the language of the young John Keats and the language of our young high school students in the last decade of the 20th century.

In his four collections of poetry, Glenn has given voice to the teenagers of our time. Luanne Sheridan, in *Back To Class* starts her poem,

How can I write a composition
About my future
When I don't even know about my past?
How can I make sense of
What will be
When I don't know what was? (Glenn, 1988, p. 4)

Winston Himes, in the same collection, says

Measuring my life in points-pre-game average
I felt I was a shoo-in for the
Best player on the team.
When I saw there were other guys better than me
I felt I was a shoo-in for the starting five.
When I saw there were *still* guys better than me
I felt I was a shoo-in for the team.
When I was cut, Mr. Worthington, out of pity,
Appointed me the team manager. (Glenn, 1988, p. 36)

As manager, Winston goes on to describe his life this way:
Now I stand on the sidelines,

> Basking in the glow of winning seasons and
> Measuring my life in wet towels and
> Ace bandages. (Glenn, 1988, p. 36)

And he ends his look at his life with the line
> All my dreams have dribbled away. (Glenn, 1988, p. 36)

Poems like these speak to today's teenagers. But they also give a voice to the pain of being young, the pain of being young and fearing that life will give them nothing that they hoped for: "When I have fears that I may cease to be." Winston Himes has already understood that he may cease to be by a death as great as the one Keats faced, a death in life, a death from dreams that have "dribbled away." Here is what Terrance Kane says about love:
> She comes to me the other day and says,
> 'Terry, you're not going to like this,
> But I think we should see other people.'

But Terry isn't ready:
> 'I only want to see you,' I say.

Cindy, however, has made up her mind:
> 'No good,' she says. 'I'm going away to
> school soon
> And I want to feel free, so here's your
> ring back.'

And Terry asks the question that John Keats asked:
> When does the pain go away . . .
> When does it go away? (Glenn, 1991, p. 17)

In "Chapman's Homer," Keats wrote
> Much have I travell'd in the realms of gold,
> And many goodly states and kingdoms seen;
> Round many western islands have been
> Which bards in fealty to Apollo hold.
> Oft of one wide expanse had I been told
> That deep-brow'd Homer ruled as his demesne. (Abrams, p. 356)

But listen to Andy Fierstein in *Back to Class*:
> In this library
> I've been to London and Tara
> And the Great Sarah.
> Palm trees in Bali,

Oases in Mali, Ruins in Greece,
Beaches in Nice,
Yellowstone Park,
Rome after dark . . . (Glenn, 1988, p. 64)

Realms of gold? Goodly states and kingdoms? Western islands? Fierstein ends his poem with this line:
'Depends on what's in the catalogue file.' (Glenn, 1988, p. 64)

The Bridge Between Keats and Glenn

The first-person student poems of Mel Glenn, with their contemporary language, speak directly to most of our students. Reading them is easy; identifying other students who are like the speakers is easy and ironically satisfying; identifying *with* at least some of them is easy, if painful.

Writing a poem or two in the style of Glenn's speakers is, though not nearly as easy as it looks, within the grasp of most of our students—and, of course, at least a few students may surprise us with the expressiveness hidden within them.

But then, if we share with them the poems of a young man who died only a few years after he left high school, a man who worked in a hospital, who came from a broken home, a young man much like many of them, though they may ask why he chose to be so hard to understand, they will give him the chance that Keats needs to say to them, "Here is how I felt. You know that feeling well. So I wrote in the way that I did. Give me a chance to speak to you—though almost two centuries stand between us—because I'd like to speak to you." That bridge of youth and joy and much pain is a mighty bridge.

References

Abrams, M.H. (Ed.). (1962). *The Norton anthology of English literature*, 2. New York: W.W. Norton and Company.

Cerf, B. & Klopper, D.S. (1932). *John Keats and Percy Bysshe Shelley: Complete poems*. New York: The Modern Library.

Ciardi, J. (1959). *How does a poem mean?* Boston: Houghton Mifflin.

Glenn, M. (1988). *Back to class*. New York: Clarion Books.

Glenn, M. (1991). *My friend's got this problem, Mr. Chandler*. New York: Clarion Books.

Keats, J. (1818). When I have fears. In M.H. Abrams (Ed.), (1962). *The Norton anthology of English literature*, 2. New York: W.W. Norton and Company.

Ward, A. (1963). *John Keats: The making of a poet: A biography*. New York: The Viking Press.

References

Abrams, M.H. (Ed.). (1962). *The Norton anthology of English literature, 2.* New York: W.W. Norton and Company.

Armour, R. (1960). *The classics reclassified.* New York: McGraw-Hill.

Baker, K. (1990). *Where's the beast.* San Diego: Harcourt, Brace, & Jovanovich.

Bernstein, L., Laurents, A. & Sondheim, S. (1958). *West side story.* New York: Random House.

Bloom, B. (Ed.). (1956). *Taxonomy of educational objectives: Handbook I: The cognitive domain.* New York: David McKay.

Bloom, H. (Ed.). (1988). *Arthur Miller's Death of a Salesman: Modern critical interpretations.* New York: Chelsea House.

Carlsen, G.R. (1967). *Books and the teenage reader.* New York: Bantam Books.

Carroll, P.S. (1990). Southern literature for young adults: The novels of Sue Ellen Bridgers. *The ALAN Review. 18* (1).

Carter, B. & Harris, K. (1980). Realism in adolescent fiction: In defense of *The Chocolate War. Top of the news.*

Cerf, B. & Klopper, D.S. (1932). *John Keats and Percy Bysshe Shelley: Complete poems.* New York: The Modern Library.

Ciardi, J. (1959). *How does a poem mean?* Boston: Houghton Mifflin Company.

Cline, R.K.J. (1990). *Focus on families: A reference handbook.* Santa Barbara: ABC-CLIO.

Deal, B. (1961). "Antaeus." In J.S. Simmons and M. Stern (Eds.), *The short story and you: An introduction to understanding and appreciation.* Lincolnwood, Illinois: National Textbook Company.

Donelson, K. and Nilsen, A.P. (1989). *Literature for today's young adults, 3rd ed.* Glenview, Illinois: Scott, Foresman.

Engel, E. (1986). *The genius of Mark Twain.* Raleigh, North Carolina: Dickens Fellowship.

Gallo, D.R., Chair and the Committee on the Senior High School Booklist. (1985). *Books for you: A booklist for senior high students.* Urbana, Illinois: National Council of Teachers of English.

Garrison, J. (1991). *J.F.K.: On the trail of the assassins.* New York: Warner Books.

Gates, H.L., Jr.. (1990). Zora Neale Hurston: A negro way of saying. Afterword in Z.N. Hurston, *Their eyes were watching God.* New York: Perennial Library of Harper & Row.

Gauch, P.L. (1984). Good stuff in adolescent fiction. *Top of the News. 40* (winter).

Giannelli, G. (1983). The chocolate war. *Connecticut English Journal, 15* (1).

Gordon, K. (Dir.). (1988). *The chocolate war.* Forum Home Video, VHS, 95 min.

Hermence, B. (1990). *Before freedom: 48 oral histories of former North and South Carolina slaves.* New York: Penguin Books.

Homer, W. (1986). In a Florida jungle. In H.A. Cooper, *Winslow Homer Watercolors.* New Haven and London: National Gallery of Art and Yale University Press.

Homer, W. (1986). In the jungle, Florida. In H.A. Cooper, *Winslow Homer Watercolors.* New Haven and London: National Gallery of Art and Yale University Press.

Homer, W. (1986). Three boys on the shore. In H.A. Cooper, *Winslow Homer Watercolors.* New Haven and London: National Gallery of Art and Yale University Press.

Johnson, J.W. (1985). The creation. In J.E. Miller, Jr., C.C. de Dwyer, and K.M. Wood (Eds.), *The United States in literature, 7th ed.* Glenview, Illinois: Scott, Foresman. (originally published in 1927)

Johnston, A. (1980). *Of earth and darkness: The novels of William Golding.* Columbia and London: University of Missouri Press.

Kennedy, J.F. (1956). *Profiles in courage.* New York: Harper.

Kirby, D. and Liner, T. (1988). *Inside out: Developmental strategies for teaching writing, 2nd ed.* Portsmouth, New Hampshire: Boynton/Cook Publishers.

Koon, H.W. (Ed.). (1983). *Twentieth century interpretations of Death of a Salesman.* New York: Prentice-Hall.

Krathwhol, D., Bloom, B., and Masia, B.B. (Eds.). (1964). *Taxonomy of educational objectives: Handbook II: The affective domain.* New York: David McKay.

Matthews, D., Chair and the Committee to Revise *High Interest—Easy Reading.* (1988). *High interest—easy reading for junior and senior high school students.* 5th ed. Urbana, Illinois: National Council of Teachers of English.

Neill, D. (1964). *A short history of the English novel.* New York: Macmillan.

Nilsen, A.P. (Ed.), and the Committee on the Junior High and Middle School Booklist. (1991). *Your reading: A booklist for junior high and middle school students.* 8th ed. Urbana, Illinois: National Council of Teachers of English.

Poe, E.A. (1992). Intensifying transactions through multiple text explorations. In Nicholas J. Karolides (Ed.), *Reader response in the classroom: Evoking and interpreting meaning in literature.* White Plains, New York: Longman.

Poe, E.A. (1991). A teacher's guide to the Signet Classic Edition of Nathaniel Hawthorne's *The Scarlet Letter.* New York: Penguin USA.

Probst, R. (1988). *Response and analysis: Teaching literature in junior and senior high school.* Portsmouth, New Hampshire: Boynton/Cook.

Purves, A.O., Rogers, T. & Soter, A. (1990). *How porcupines make love II.* New York: Longman.

Reed, A.J.S. (1987). *A teacher's guide to the signet classic edition of William*

Shakespear's Romeo and Juliet. New York: The New American Library.

Register, C. (1975). American feminist literary criticism: A bibliographic introduction. In J. Donovan (Ed.), *Feminist literary criticism.* Kentucky: The
University Press of Kentucky.

Rosenblatt, L.M.. (1989). The transactional theory of the literary: Implications
for research. In C.R. Cooper (Ed.), *Researching response to literature and the
teaching of literature: Points of departure.* Norwood, New Jersey: Ablex.

Rudman, M. & Rosenberg's, S.P. (summer, 1991). Confronting history: Holocaust books for children. *The New Advocate, 4* (3).

Rygiel, M.A. (1992). *Shakespeare among schoolchildren: Approaches for the
secondary classroom.* Urbana, Illinois: The National Council of Teachers of
English.

Terkel, S. (1970). *Hard times: An oral history of the Great Depression in America.*
New York: Pantheon.

Totten S. (1980). Person to person: An oral history project. In C. Carter and Z.
Rashkis (Eds.), *Ideas for teaching English in the junior high and middle
school.* Urbana, Illinois: National Council of Teachers of English.

Ward, A. (1963). *John Keats: The making of a poet: A biography.* The Viking
Press.

Yetman, N.R. (Ed.). (1970). *Life under the peculiar institution: Selections from
the slave narrative collection.* New York: Holt, Rinehart, & Winston.

Classics Bibliography

Angelou, M. (1990). *I know why the caged bird sings*. New York: Bantam Books.

Angelou, M. (1990). *I shall not be moved*. New York: Random House.

Angelou, M. (1978). *And still I rise*. New York: Random House.

Ballantyne, R.M. (1957). *Coral island*. New York: E.P. Dutton. (originally published 1858).

Bolt, R. (1960). *A man for all seasons*. New York: Vintage books.

Defoe, D. (1961). *Robinson Crusoe*. New York: E.P. Dutton.

Dickens, C. (1962). *Great expectations*. New York: Macmillan, . (originally published 1861).

Dickinson, E. (1938). Much madness. In M. Bianchi and A.L. Hampson (Eds.), *The Poems of Emily Dickinson*. Boston: Little, Brown, & Company.

Douglass, F. (1989). *Narrative of the life of Frederick Douglass*. New York: Anchor. (originally published in 1845).

Ellison, R. (1947). *Invisible man*. New York: Random House.

Fitzgerald, F.S. (1925). *The great gatsby*. New York: Charles Scribner's Sons.

Frank, A. (1972). *Anne Frank: The diary of a young girl*. New York: Simon & Schuster, Inc. (originally published 1952).

Gilman, C.P. (1973). *The yellow wallpaper*. New York: Feminist Press.

Golding, W. (1954). *Lord of the flies*. New York: G.P. Putnam's Sons.

Hansberry, L. (1969). *To be young, gifted, and black*. New York: Signet.

Hawthorne, N. (1983). *The scarlet letter*. New York: Penguin USA (Signet).

Hellman, L. (1934). *The children's hour*. New York: Random House.

Hurston, Z.N. (1990). *Their eyes were watching God*. New York: Harper & Row. (originally published 1937).

Hurston, Z.N. (1942). *Dust tracks on a road*. Philadelphia: J.B. Lippincott.

Ibsen, H. (1965). A doll house. *Four major plays, 1*. New York: Signet.

Jackson, S. (1943). The lottery. *The lottery*. Cambridge: Robert Bentley.

Keats, J. (1818). When I have fears. In M.H. Abrams (Ed.), (1962). *The Norton anthology of English literature, 2*. New York: W.W. Norton & Company.

King, M.L., Jr. (1992). I have a dream. *African-American literature: Voices in a tradition*. Austin: Holt, Rinehart, & Winston.

Lee, H. (1960). *To kill a mockingbird*. New York: Warner Books.

Lester, J. (1991). Black folktales. In R.W. Baron, O.L. Logan, and K. Clark. (Eds.), *Motherwit: An Alabama midwife's story*. New York: Plume.

Logan, O.L. and Clark, C. (Eds.). (1991). *Motherwit: An Alabama midwife's story*. New York: Plume.

Miller, S. (1952). *The crucible*. New York: Penguin Books.

Miller, A. (1949). *Death of a salesman*. New York: Penguin Books.

Orwell, G. (1949). *1984*. New York: Harcourt, Brace, & Jovanovich.

Orwell, G. (1945). *Animal farm*. New York: The New American Library.

Salinger, J.D. (1964). *The catcher in the rye*. New York: Bantam Books.

Shakespeare, W. (1942). *Romeo and Juliet*. In W.A. Neilson and C.J. Hill (Eds.), *The Complete Plays and Poems of William Shakespeare*. Cambridge: Houghton Mifflin. (originally published 1609).

Twain, M. (1940). *The adventures of Huckleberry Finn*. New York: Heritage Press.

Walker, A. (1982). *The color purple*. New York: Harcourt, Brace, & Jovanovich.

Walker, A. (1972). My sister Molly who in the Fifties. In *Revolutionary Petunias and Other Poems*. New York: Harcourt, Brace, & Jovanovich.

Walker, M. (1967). *Jubilee*. Boston: Houghton Mifflin.

Wouk, H. (1951). *The caine mutiny*. New York: Doubleday.

Wright, R. (1940). *Native son*. New York: Harper & Row.

Wright, R. (1937). *Black boy*. New York: Harper & Row.

Wyss, J. (1949). *The Swiss family Robinson*. New York: Grossett & Dunlop.

Zeffirelli, F. (1968). *Romeo and Juliet*. Paramount Home Video, VHS, 138 mins.

Young Adult Bibliography

Aaron, C. (1982). *Gideon*. Philadelphia: J.B. Lippincott Company.

Aaron, C. (1972). *Better than laughter*. New York: Harcourt, Brace, & Jovanovich.

Abells, C. (1986). *The children we remember*. New York: Greenwillow Books.

Adler, D.A. (1989). *We remember the Holocaust*. New York: Henry Holt & Company.

Angier, B. & Corcoran, B. (1977). *Ask for love and they give you rice pudding*. New York: Bantam Books.

Appleman-Jurman, A. (1990). *Alicia: My story*. New York: Bantam Books.

Armstrong, W.H. (1969). *Sounder*. New York: Scholastic.

Arnold, C. & Silverstein, H. (1985). *Anti-Semitism: A modern perspective*. New York: Julian Messner.

Arrick, F. (1981). *Chernowitz*. New York: The New American Library.

Asher, S. (1987). *Everything is not enough*. New York: Delacorte Press.

Avi. (1992). *Blue heron*. New York: Bradbury Press.

Avi. (1990). *The true confessions of Charlotte Doyle*. New York: Orchard.

Baklanov, G. (1989). *Forever nineteen*. Translated from Russian by Antonina W. Bouis. Philadelphia: J.B. Lippincott Company.

Baylor, B. (1991). *Yes is better than no*. Tucson, Arizona: Treasure Chest.

Benjamin, C.L. (1984). *Nobody's baby now*. New York: Macmillan.

Betancourt, J. (1990). *More than meets the eye*. New York: Bantam Books.

Blume, J. (1981). *Tiger eyes*. New York: Dell Laurel-Leaf.

Blume, J. (1975). *Forever*. New York: Bradbury Press.

Blume, J. (1974). *Blubber*. New York: Dell Laurel-Leaf.

Blume, J. (1973). *Deenie*. New York: Dell Laurel-Leaf.

Blume, J. (1970). *Iggie's house*. New York: Bradbury Press.

Blume, J. (1970). *Are you there, God? It's me Margaret*. New York: Dell Laurel-Leaf.

Bonham, F. (1970). *Viva Chicano*. New York: E.P. Dutton.

Borland, H. (1984). *When the legends die*. New York: Bantam Books.

Brancato, R. (1990). War of the words. In D. R. Gallo (Ed.), *Center Stage*. New York: Harper & Row.

Brancato, R. (1978). *Blinded by the light*. New York: Alfred A. Knopf.

Brancato, R. (1978). *Winning*. New York: Bantam Books.

Branscum, R. (1976). *Toby, Granny and George*. New York: Doubleday.

Bridgers, S.E. (1987). *Permanent connections*. New York: Harper & Row.

Bridgers, S.E. (1982). *Notes for another life*. New York: Bantam Books.

Bridgers, S.E. (1979). *All together now*. New York: Bantam Books.

Bridgers, S.E. (1977). *Home before dark*. New York: Bantam Books.

Brigg, E. (1972). *Stand up and fight: The story of Emil Brigg*. London: George G. Harrap & Company.

Brooks, B. (1986). *Midnight hour encore*. New York: Harper Trophy.

Brooks, B. (1984). *The moves make the man*. New York: Harper & Row.

Butterworth, W. (1980). *Leroy and the old man*. New York: Four Winds Press.

Buzz, F and Cubias, D. (1991). *Journey of the sparrows*. New York: E.P. Dutton.

Calvert, P. (1987). *Stranger, you and I*. New York: Charles Scribner's Sons.

Carter, F. (1986). *The education of Little Tree*. Albuquerque: University of New Mexico Press.

Castaneda, O. (1991). *Among the volcanoes*. New York: Lodestar Books.

Chopin, K. (1988). A pair of silk stockings. *The awakening and selected short stories*. New York: Bantam Books.

Christopher, J. (1970). *The prince in waiting*. New York: Macmillan.

Christopher, J. (1967). *The white mountain*. New York: Macmillan.

Cockrell, D. (1983). Fist fight. In P. Janesco (Ed.), *Poetspeak*. New York: Bradbury Press.

Cohen, B. (1987). *People like us*. New York: Bantam Books.

Collier, J.L. (1987) *Outside looking in*. New York: Macmillan.

Collier, J.L. (1986) *When the stars begin to fall*. New York: Dell Laurel-Leaf.

Corcoran, B. (1986). *I am the universe*. New York: Atheneum.

Cormier, R. (1992). *Tunes for bears to dance to*. New York: Delacorte Press.

Cormier, R. (1990). *Other bells for us to ring*. New York: Delacorte Press.

Cormier, R. (1977). *I am the cheese*. New York: Pantheon (Dell).

Cormier, R. (1974). *The chocolate war*. New York: Pantheon (Dell).

Cossi, O. (1990). *The magic box*. Gretna: Pelican Publishing Company.

Crew, L. (1991). *Nekomah creek*. New York: Delacorte Press.

Crutcher, C. (1990). *Running loose*. New York: Dell Laurel-Leaf.

Crutcher, C. (1989). *Chinese handcuffs*. New York: Greenwillow Books.

Crutcher, C. (1987). *The crazy horse electric game*. New York: Greenwillow Books.

Crutcher, C. (1986). *Stotan!* New York: Dell Laurel-Leaf.

Daly, M. (1986). *Acts of love*. New York: Scholastic.

Danziger, P. (1991). *Earth to Matthew*. New York: Delacorte Press.

de Jenkins, L.B. (1988). *The honorable prison*. New York: Lodestar Books.

Delton, J. (1981). *Two blocks down*. New York: Harper & Row.

Duncan, L. (1985). *Killing Mr. Griffin*. Boston: Little, Brown, & Company.

Erickson, J. (1984). *Joni*. New York: Bantam Books.

Fair, R.L. (1966). *Cornbread, Earl, and me*. New York: Bantam Books.

Fluek, T.K. (1990). *Memories of my life in a Polish village: 1930-1949*. New York: Alfred A. Knopf.

Forman, J. (1968). *The traitors*. New York: Farrar, Straus, & Giroux.

Frank, A. (1972). *Anne Frank: The diary of a young girl*. New York: Pocket Books.

Friedman, I.R. (1990). *The other victims: First person stories of non-Jews persecuted by the Nazis*. Boston: Houghton Mifflin.

Gaines, E.J. (1971). *The autobiography of Miss Jane Pittman*. New York: Bantam Books.

Garland, S. (1992). *Song of the buffalo boy*. New York: Harcourt, Brace, & Jovanovich.

George, J.C. (1972). *Julie of the wolves*. New York: Harper & Row.

Gilman, D. (1984). *Girl in buckskin*. New York: Fawcett Juniper

Glass, F. (1977). *Marvin and Tige*. New York: St. Martin's Press.

Glenn, M. (1988). *Back to class*. New York: Clarion Books.

Glenn, M. (1991). *My friend's got this problem, Mr. Chandler*. New York: Clarion Books.

Godden, R. (1990). *Thursday's children*. New York: Dell Laurel-Leaf.

Green, C.J. (1989). *The war at home*. New York: Macmillan/McElderry Books.

Greenberg, J. (1964). *I never promised you a rose garden*. New York: The New American Library.

Greene, B. (1973). *Summer of my German soldier*. New York: Dial Press.

Griffin, J.H. (1961). *Black like me*. Boston: Houghton Mifflin.

Guest, J. (1977). *Ordinary people*. New York: Ballantine Books.

Guy, R. (1985). *My love, my love, or, the peasant girl*. New York: Henry Holt & Company.

Guy, R. (1973). *The friends*. New York: Henry Holt & Company.

Hall, L. (1972). *Sticks and stones*. New York: Follet (Dell).

Hamilton, V. (1984). *A little love*. New York: Philomel.

Hanlon, E. (1981). *It's too late for sorry*. New York: Dell Laurel-Leaf.

Hartman, E. (1982). *War without friends*. Translated by Patricia Crampton. New York: Crown.

Haskins, J. (1976). *The story of Stevie Wonder*. New York: Lothrop, Lee, & Shepard.

Hautzig, E. (1987). *The endless steppe*. New York: Harper Keypoint.

Hersey, J. (1946). *Hiroshima*. New York: Alfred A. Knopf.

Hinton, S.E. (1967). *The outsiders*. New York: Dell Laurel-Leaf.

Hobbs, W. (1991). *Downriver*. New York: Atheneum.

Hobbs, W. (1989). *Bearstone*. New York: Atheneum.

Hobbs, W. (1988). *Changes in latitudes*. London: Pan Horizons Publishers.

Hoffman, A. (1988). *At risk*. New York: Berkley Books.

Holland, I. (1972). *The man without a face*. Philadelphia: J.B. Lippincott Company.

Houston, J.W. & Houston, J.D. (1990). *Farewell to Manzanar*. New York: Bantam Books.

Houston, W. (1985). The greatest love of all. *Whitney Houston*. New York: Arista Records, Incorporated.

Howe, N. (1986). *In with the out crowd*. Boston: Houghton Mifflin.

Irwin, Hadley. (1990). *Can't hear you listening*. New York: Collier Macmillan.

Irwin, Hadley. (1988). *So long at the fair*. New York: McElderry.

Irwin, Hadley. (1987). *Kim / Kimi*. New York: Macmillan.

Jaspersohn, W. (1990). *Grounded*. New York: Bantam Books.

Kellogg, M. (1984). *Tell me that you love me, Junie Moon*. New York: Farrar, Straus, & Giroux.

Kerr, M.E. (1987). *Night kites*. New York: Harper & Row.

Kerr, M.E. (1982). *Little Little*. New York: Harper & Row.

Kerr, M.E. (1978). *Gentlehands*. New York: Bantam Books.

Kerr, M.E. (1972). *Dinky Hocker shoots smack*. New York: Dell Laurel-Leaf.

Klein, N. (1989). *Now that I know*. New York: Bantam Books.

Klein, N. (1986). *Going backwards*. New York: Scholastic.

Kornfeld, A. (1975). *In a bluebird's eye*. New York: Holt, Rinehart, & Winston.

Kosinsky, J. (1972). *The painted bird*. New York: Bantam Books.

Kuchler-Silberman, L. (1990). *My hundred children*. New York: Dell Laurel-Leaf.

Laird, C. (1990). *Shadow of the wall*. New York: Greenwillow Books.

Laird, E. (1992). *Kiss the dust*. New York: E.P. Dutton.

Lampman, E.S. (1972). *Go up the road*. New York: Atheneum.

Lasky, K. (1986). *Beyond the divide*. New York: Dell Laurel-Leaf.

Lasky, K. (1986). *Pageant*. New York: Four Winds Press.

Lee, M. (1980). *The people therein*. Boston: Houghton Mifflin.

Leitner, I. & Leitner, I.A. (1990). *Fragments of Isabella*. New York: Dell Laurel-Leaf.

L'Engle, M. (1979). *A wind in the door*. New York: Fararr, Straus, & Giroux.

L'Engle, M. (1978). *A swiftly tilting planet*. New York: Farrar, Straus, & Giroux.

L'Engle, M. (1981). *The ring of endless light*. New York: Dell Laurel-Leaf.

L'Engle, M. (1962). *Wrinkle in time*. New York: Ariel Books.

L'Engle, M. (1974). *The summer of the great grandfather*. New York: Farrar, Straus, & Giroux

Levitin, S. (1970). *Journey to America*. New York: Macmillan.

Levoy, M. (1977). *Alan and Naomi*. New York: Harper & Row.

Levy, M. (1990). *No way home*. New York: Dell Laurel-Leaf.

Lingard, J. (1990). *Tug of war*. New York: Lodestar Books.

Lingard, J. (1973). *Across the barricades*. New York: Grosset & Dunlap.

Lipsyte, R. (1991). *The brave*. New York: Harper Collins.

Lipsyte, R. (1977). *One fat summer*. New York: Harper & Row.

Lipsyte, R. (1967). *The contender*. New York: Harper & Row.

Lowry, L. (1989). *Number the stars*. New York: Dell-Yearling.

Lyle, K.L. (1974). *Fair day, and another step begun*. Philadelphia: J.B. Lippincott Company.

MacKinnon, B. (1984). *The meantime*. Boston: Houghton Mifflin.

Magorian, M. (1981). *Good night, Mr. Tom*. New York: Harper & Row.

Mahy, M. (1985). *Catalogue of the universe*. New York: Antheneum.

Marino, J. (1990). *The day that Elvis came to town*. Boston: Little, Brown, & Company.

Maruki, T. (1980). *Hiroshima no pika*. New York: Lothrop, Lee, & Shepard.

Mazer, H. (1990). *The last mission*. New York: Dell Laurel-Leaf.

Mazer, H. (1990). *The war on Villa Street*. New York: Dell Laurel-Leaf.

Mazer, N.F. (1990). *D . . . My name is Danita*. New York: Scholastic.

Mazer, N.F. (1988). *After the rain*. New York: William Morrow.

Mazer, N.F. (1983). *Someone to love*. New York: Dell Laurel-Leaf.

Mazer, N.F. (1982). *When we first met*. New York: Macmillan.

McCartney, P. (1990). Ebony and ivory. *Tripping the Live Fantastic*. Hollywood: Capitol Records.

McDermott, A. (1987). *That night*. New York: Farrar, Straus, & Giroux.

McGuire, J. (1990). *Crossing over*. New York: Ivy Books.

McKinley, R. (1984). *Hero and the crown*. New York: Greenwillow Books.

Melton, D. (1986). *A boy called hopeless*. Kansas, MO: Landmark.

Meltzer, M. (1988). *Rescue: The story of how Gentiles saved Jews in the Holocaust*. New York: Harper & Row.

Meyer, C. (1990). *Because of Lissa*. New York: Bantam Books

Miklowitz, G.D. (1990). *The war between the classes*. New York: Dell Laurel-Leaf.

Miklowitz, G.D. (1987). *Good-bye tomorrow*. New York: Delacorte (Dell).

Morrison, T. (1987). *Beloved*. New York: Alfred A. Knopf.

Morrison, T. (1974). *Sula*. New York: Alfred A. Knopf.

Moskin, M.D. (1990). *I am Rosemarie*. New York: Dell Laurel-Leaf.

Mowat, F. (1990). *And no birds sang*. New York: Bantam/Seal Paperback.

Myers, W.D. (1992). *Somewhere in the darkness*. New York: Scholastic.

Myers, W.D.. (1990). *Hoops*. New York: Dell Laurel-Leaf.

Myers, W.D. (1988). *Scorpions*. New York: Harper & Row.

Neimark, A.E. (1986). *One man's valor: Leo Baeck and the Holocaust*. New York: Lodestar Books.

O'Brien, R.C. (1974). *Z for Zachariah*. New York: Dell Laurel-Leaf.

O'Dell, S. (1977). *Carlota*. Boston: Houghton Mifflin.

Okimoto, J.D. (1990). *Molly by any other name*. New York: Scholastic.

Olsen, T. (1956). I stand here ironing. *Tell me a riddle*. New York: Delacorte Press.

Ossowski, L. (1985). *Star without a sky*. Translated by Ruth Crowley. Minneapolis: Lerner.

Paterson, K. (1991). *Lyddie*. New York: E.P. Dutton.

Paterson, K. (1980). *Jacob have I loved*. New York: Harper & Row.

Paterson, K. (1977). *Bridge to Terabithia*. New York: Thomas Y. Crowell.

Paulsen, G. (1991). *The monument*. New York: Dell Laurel-Leaf.

Paulsen, G. (1990). *Canyons*. New York: Bantam Books.

Paulsen, G. (1990). *The crossing*. New York: Dell Laurel-Leaf.

Paulsen, G. (1985). *Dogsong*. New York: Bradbury Press.

Peck, R. (1991). *Unfinished portrait of Jessica*. New York: Delacorte Press.

Peck, R. (1986). *Remembering the good times*. New York: Dell Laurel-Leaf.

Peck, R. (1984). Priscilla and the wimps. In D.R. Gallo (Ed.), *Sixteen*. New York: Dell Laurel-Leaf.

Pevsner, S. (1989). *How could you do it, Diane?* New York: Clarion Books.

Pfeffer, S.B. (1991). *Most precious blood*. New York: Bantam Books.

Pfeffer, S.B. (1990). *About David*. New York: Dell Laurel-Leaf.

Piercy, M. (1973). A work of artifice. *To be of use*. New York: Doubleday.

Pinkwater, D. (1982). *The snarkout boys and the avocado of death*. New York: Lothrop, Lee, & Shepard.

Potok, C. (1991). *My name is Asher Lev*. New York: Fawcett Crest.

Potok, C. (1967). *The chosen*. New York: Fawcett Crest.

Qualey, M. (1991). *Everybody's daughter*. Boston: Houghton Mifflin.

Read, P.P. (1974). *Alive*. New York: Avon.

Reiss, J. (1972). *The upstairs room*. New York: Harper & Row.

Reiss, J. (1987). *The journey back*. New York: Harper & Row.

Rhue, M. (1981). *The wave*. New York: Dell Laurel-Leaf.

Richmond, S. (1985). *Wheels for walking*. Boston: Atlantic Monthly Press.

Richter, H.P. (1987). *Friedrich*. Translated by Edite Kroll. New York: Viking Penguin/Puffin Books.

Richter, H.P. (1987). *I was there*. Translated by Edite Kroll. New York: Viking Penguin/Puffin Books.

Riddell, R. (1992). *Ice warrior*. New York: Atheneum.

Rittner, C. (Ed.). (1986). *The courage to care*. New York: University Press.

Roth-Hano, R. (1988). *Touch wood: A girlhood in occupied France*. New York: Four Winds Press.

Rubenstein, R. (1975). *The cunning of history: The Holocaust and the American future*. New York: Harper & Row.

Ruckman, I. (1989). *Who invited the undertaker?* New York: Thomas Y. Crowell.

Rylant, C. (1986). *A fine white dust*. New York: Bradbury Press.

Salisbury, G. (1992). *Blue skin of the sea*. New York: Delacorte Press.

Sallis, S. (1980). *Only love*. New York: Harper & Row.

Santiago, D. (1984). *Famous all over town*. New York: E.P. Dutton.

Sauer, J. (1990). *Hank*. New York: Delacorte Press.

Scoppettone, S. (1991). *Happy endings are all alike*. Boston: Alyson Publications.

Scoppettone, S. (1981). *Trying hard to hear you*. New York: Bantam Books.

Sebestyen, O. (1979). *Words by heart*. Boston: Little, Brown, & Company.

Sendak, M. (1963). *Where the wild things are*. New York: Harper & Row.

Sender, R.M. (1990). *The cage*. New York: Bantam Books.

Serraillier, I. (1974). *Escape from Warsaw*. New York: Scholastic.

Shreve, S. (1980). *The masquerade*. New York: Alfred A. Knopf.

Siegal, A. (1985). *Grace in the wilderness: After the liberation 1945-1948*. New

York: Farrar, Straus, & Giroux.

Siegal, A. (1981). *Upon the head of the goat: A childhood in Hungary 1939-1944*. New York: Farrar, Straus, & Giroux.

Smith, K. (1989). *Skeeter*. Boston: Houghton Mifflin.

Speare, E. (1961). *The witch of blackbird pond*. Boston: Houghton Mifflin.

Spinelli, J. (1990). *Maniac Magee*. Boston: Little, Brown, & Company.

Spinelli, J. (1984). *Who put that hair in my toothbrush?* Boston: Little, Brown, & Company.

Staples, S.F. (1989). *Shabanu: Daughter of the wind*. New York: Alfred A. Knopf.

Swarthout, G. (1970). *Bless the beasts and children*. New York: Simon & Schuster.

Tate, E.E. (1990). *Thank you, Dr. Martin Luther King, Jr*. New York: Bantam Skylark Books.

Tate, E.E. (1987). *The secret of Gumbo grove*. New York: Bantam Books.

Taylor, M.D. (1990). *On the road to Memphis*. New York: Dial Press.

Taylor, M.D. (1987). *The gold cadillac*. New York: Dial Press.

Taylor, M.D. (1981). *Let the circle be unbroken*. New York: Puffin Books.

Taylor, M.D. (1976). *Roll of thunder, hear my cry*. New York: Bantam Books.

Telemaque, E. (1978). *It's crazy to stay Chinese in Minnesota*. Nashville: T. Nelson.

ten Boom, C., Sherrill, J. & Sherrill, E. (1990). *The hiding place*. New York: Bantam Books.

Terris, S. (1987). *Nell's quilt*. New York: Farrar, Straus, & Giroux.

Thesman, J. (1991). *The rain catchers*. Boston: Houghton Mifflin.

Thomas, M. (Ed.). (1987). *Free to be . . . a family: A book about all kinds of belonging*. New York: Bantam Books.

Townsend, S. (1986). *The Adrian Mole diaries*. Grove Press.

Uchida, Y. (1977). *Journey to Topaz*. New York: Charles Scribner's Sons.

Voigt, C. (1986). *Come a stranger*. New York: Atheneum.

Voigt, C. (1986). *Izzy, willy-nilly*. New York: Atheneum.

Voigt, C. (1985). *The runner*. New York: Ballantine (Fawcett Juniper).

Voigt, C. (1985). *Jackaroo*. New York: Fawcett Juniper.

Voigt, C. (1983). *A solitary blue*. New York: Atheneum.

Voigt, C. (1981). *Homecoming*. New York: Atheneum.

Volavkova, H. (Ed.). (1971). *I never saw another butterfly*. 2nd ed. New York: McGraw Hill.

Welch, D. (1983). We used to play. In P. Janesco (ed.), *Poetspeak*. New York: Bradbury Press.

Wells, R. *Through the hidden door*. New York: Scholastic.

White, R. (1992). *Weeping willow*. New York: Farrar, Straus, & Giroux.

Wiesel, E. (1990). *Night*. Translated by Stella Rodway. New York: Bantam Books.

Wiesel, E. (1982). *Dawn*. New York: Bantam Books.

Wilkinson, B. (1987). *Not separate, but equal*. New York: Harper & Row.

Zamoyska-Panek, C. & Holmberg, F.B. (1990). *Have you forgotten: A memoir of Poland 1939-1945*. New York: Doubleday.

Zieman, J. (1977). *The cigarette sellers of Three Crosses Square*. New York: Avon.

Zindel, P. (1990). *I never loved your mind*. New York: Bantam Books.

Zindel, P. (1987). *The amazing and death-defying diary of Eugene Dingman*. New York: Bantam Books.

Zindel, P. (1968). *The pigman*. New York: Harper & Row.

Index

Contributors

Joan F. Kaywell is an Assistant Professor of English Education at the University of South Florida where she teaches English methods and adolescent literature classes. She received her Ph.D. from the University of Florida. She has published articles in *English Journal, High School Journal, Middle School Journal,* and the *Florida English Journal.*

John H. Bushman is currently Professor of Curriculum and Instruction (English Education) at the University of Kansas, Lawrence. He is co-editor of the Books for the Teen Age Reader Column for *English Journal* and director of The Writing Conference, Inc. and the Jayhawk Writing Project. He has written numerous articles and books on the teaching of English and is coauthor of *Using Adult Literature in the English Classroom.*

Kay Parks Bushman, currently the president of ALAN, is the language arts department chair at Ottawa High School, Kansas and teaches young adult literature classes at the University of Kansas, Lawrence. She is co-editor of the Books for the Teen Age Reader Column for *English Journal* and coauthor of *Using Young Adult Literature in the English Classroom.*

Pamela "Sissi" Carroll is an assistant professor of English Education at Florida State University, Tallahassee and is also the director of the North Florida Writing Project. She is particularly interested in multiethnic/multicultural issues in literature, as well as Southern literature for young adults.

Leila Christenbury, a former high school English teacher, is associate professor of English Education at Virginia Commonwealth University, Richmond. She is co-editor of *The ALAN Review* and director of the Capital Writing Project. Her primary work is directed toward preservice teachers entering the classroom.

Ruth Cline, a past president of NCTE, retired in May 1992 from her position as professor of English Education at the University of Colorado, Boulder. Still active on a number of committees, she is coauthor of a regular column in *The ALAN Review* and is co-author of *A Guide to Young Adult Literature*.

Bonnie O. Ericson is an associate professor of English Education at California State University, Northbridge, where she teaches secondary English methods and reading and writing across the curriculum classes. An active member of NCTE, she has served the organization in a number of capacities.

Joan Fowinkle teaches sophomore advanced and regular English in an inner-city school in San Diego, California. She hold a B.S. in English/Speech Education from the University of South Florida

Jo Higgins is a third year teacher at Kathleen High School, Lakeland, Florida, where she teaches junior English, creative writing, and journalism. She is pursuing her master's degree in English Education at the University of South Florida.

Ted Hipple is professor of English Education at the University of Tennessee, where he formerly headed the Department of Curriculum and Instruction. One of the founders of ALAN, he is currently its Executive Secretary. He has written and spoken widely about adolescent literature and includes among his publications the critical biography *Presenting Sue Ellen Bridgers*.

Patricia P. Kelly, associate professor of English Education at Virginia Tech in Blacksburg, is editor of *SIGNAL,* IRA's special interest group journal on adolescent literature. A past president of ALAN, she is also co-editor of *Virginia English Bulletin* and co-director of the Southwest Virginia Writing Project.

Diana Mitchell teaches at Sexton High School in Lansing, Michigan. She is a co-author on the third edition of *Explorations in the Teaching of English*, and speaks frequently on how to most effectively use young adult literature in the classroom.

Elizabeth Poe taught high school English for 13 years, and is now an assistant professor of English education at the University of Wisconsin-Eau Claire. Immediate past president of ALAN, she is also author of *Focus on Sexuality: A Reference Handbook* and the Penguin USA teacher's guides for *The Scarlet Letter* and *Beloved*.

Arthea "Charlie" Reed is currently professor of education and chair of the Education Department at the University of North Carolina at Asheville. She is author of *Reaching Adolescents: A Parents' Guide to Books for Teens and Preteens,* and *In the Classroom: An Introduction to Education*. She is also a co-editor of the Signet Classic Teachers' Guide Series.

Barbara G. Samuels, is currently assistant professor of Language Arts and Reading at the University of Houston-Clear Lake, where she teaches courses in children's literature, young adult literature, and language arts. Co-director of the Greater Houston Area Writing Project, she received her Ph.D. from the University of Houston. A former president of ALAN, she has written extensively about reading responses of young adults in *The ALAN Review, English Journal,* and *Journal of Reading*.

Robert Small, currently Dean of the College of Education and Human Development at Ranford University, Virginia, is co-editor of *The ALAN Review* and chairs the NCTE/IRA Joint Task Force on Intellectual Freedom and SIGNAL.